RAIL ATLAS
OF
BRITAIN
AND
IRELAND

Compiled by **S. K. Baker**

Oxford Publishing Company

Fourth Edition
Copyright© 1984 Oxford Publishing Co.

ISBN 0-86093-281-8

Printed in Great Britain by:
Butler & Tanner Ltd., Frome, Somerset.

Published by:
Oxford Publishing Co.
Link House
West Street
POOLE, Dorset

PREFACE TO FIRST EDITION

The inspiration for this atlas was two-fold; firstly a feeling of total bewilderment by 'Llans' and 'Abers' on first visiting South Wales four years ago, and secondly a wall railway map drawn by a friend, Martin Bairstow. Since then, at university, there has been steady progress in drawing the rail network throughout Great Britain. The author feels sure that this atlas as it has finally evolved will be useful to all with an interest in railways, whether professional or enthusiast. The emphasis is on the current network since it is felt that this information is not published elsewhere.

Throughout, the main aim has been to show clearly, using expanded sheets where necessary, the railways of this country, including the whole of London Transport and light railways. Passenger lines are distinguished by colour according to operating company and all freight-only lines are depicted in red. The criterion for a British Rail passenger line has been taken as at least one advertised passenger train per day in each direction. On passenger routes, to assist the traveller, single and multiple track sections, with crossing loops on single lines have been shown. Symbols are used to identify both major centres of rail freight, such as colliers and power stations, and railway installations such as locomotive depots and works. Secondary information, for example junction names and tunnels over 100 yards long, with lengths if over one mile has been shown.

The author would like to express his thanks to members of the Oxford University Railway Society and to Nigel Bird, Chris Hammond and Richard Warson in particular for help in compiling and correcting the maps. His cousin, Dr Tony McCann deserves special thanks for removing much of the tedium by computer sorting the index, as do Oxford City Libraries for providing excellent reference facilities.

June 1977

PREFACE TO FOURTH EDITION

This fully revised fourth edition of the Rail Atlas has been updated to show the numerous changes in the rail system since the third edition. The coverage of the maps has been extended to include the whole of Ireland, with five insets of the major Irish towns. Eleven additional insets enable parts of Britain to be shown more clearly. To reflect the increasing importance of counties for rail support, county boundaries have also been added.

The author would like to thank those friends who have helped him to collect material for this new edition and also everyone who has written to him, expressing their appreciation of the Atlas and supplying much useful information.

Stuart K. Baker
Preston, Lancashire
July 1984

CONTENTS

	Page
Preface to 1st and 4th Editions	(i)
Key to symbols and codes used on maps	(ii)
Glossary of Abbreviations	(ii)
Diagram showing incidence of maps	(iii)
Maps	1–88
Index to Passenger Stations	89–107
Index to B.R.E.L. Works	107
Index to Minor Railways	107
Index to B.R. Depots and Stabling Points	108
Index to Freight Terminals and Yards	109–115

Publisher's Note

Although situations are constantly changing on the railways of Britain every effort has been made by the author to ensure complete accuracy of the maps in the book at the time of going to press.

KEY TO ATLAS

		Surface	Tunnel	Tube
British Rail — Passenger *Also Irish and Isle of Man Railways*	Multiple Track	———	→– –←	--------
	Single Track	+++++++	+)+ + +(+	+++++++
London Transport *(Line indicated by code)* **Also Greater Glasgow and Tyne & Wear**	Multiple Track	C ————	C →– –←	C -------
	Single Track	C +++++	C +)+ + +(+	C +++++++
Preserved & Minor Passenger Railways	Multiple Track	▬·▬·▬	→)–··–(←
	Single Track	—·–·—·–	→)·–·(←
Freight only lines — *(British Rail & Others)*	No Single/ Multiple Distinction	————	→– –←

Advertised Passenger Station:	Saltburn ———●———
Crossing Loop at Passenger Station:	Newtown +++++✳+++++
Crossing Loop on Single Line:	*Murthly* +++++✕+++++
Unadvertised/Excursion Station:	Melton* ———●———

Major Power Signalboxes	<u>PRESTON</u>	B.R. Region Breaks	LM ER ——│——
Carriage Sidings	—┤ C.S.	Colliery *(including opencast site)*	———▲
Freight/Marshalling Yard	TINSLEY	Power Station	———△
Freightliner Terminal	—┤FLT	Oil Refinery	———●
National Carriers Depot	——┤NCL	Oil or Bitumen Terminal	———○
Locomotive Depot/Stabling Point	■ BS	Cement Works or Terminal	———■
British Rail Engineering Ltd.	▨BREL	Quarry	———□
Junction Names	——✕——	Other Freight Terminal	———┤
	Haughley Junc.		
Country Border	▨▨▨▨	County Boundary	∿∿

GLOSSARY OF ABBREVIATIONS

ABM	Associated British Maltsters	GPO	General Post Office
ABP	Associated British Ports	ICI	Imperial Chemical Industries
ARC	Amey Roadstone Corporation	LIFT	London International Freight Terminal
ASW	Allied Steel & Wire	MDHC	Mersey Docks & Harbour Company
B & I	British & Irish Line	MIFT	Manchester International Freight Terminal
BICC	British Insulated Callenders Cables	MOD	Ministry of Defence
BIS	British Industrial Sand	MSC	Manchester Ship Canal
BL	British Leyland	NCB	National Coal Board
BOC	British Oxygen Company	NCL	National Carriers Limited
BP	British Petroleum	NEGB	North Eastern Gas Board
BSC	British Steel Corporation	NWGB	North Western Gas Board
C. & W.	Carriage and Wagon	OLE	Overhead Line Equipment
Cal-Mac	Caledonian MacBrayne	P.S.	Power Station
CCE	Chief Civil Engineer	PTE	Passenger Transport Executive
CEGB	Central Electricity Generating Board	P.W.	Permanent Way
CM & EE	Chief Mechanical & Electrical Engineer	RHM	Rank Hovis McDougall
C.S.	Carriage Sidings	RMC	Ready Mix Concrete
CS&TE	Chief Signal & Telegraph Engineer	RPSI	Railway Preservation Society of Ireland
ECLP	English Clays Lovering & Pochin	S. & T.	Signal & Telegraph
EMU	Electric Multiple Unit	SAI	Scottish Agricultural Industries
FLT	Freightliner Terminal	SGD	Scottish Grain Distillers
GEC	General Electric Company	SMD	Scottish Malt Distillers
GLC	Greater London Council	UKAEA	United Kingdom Atomic Energy Authority
GMC	Greater Manchester Council	UKF	United Kingdom Fertilisers
		WMGB	West Midlands Gas Board

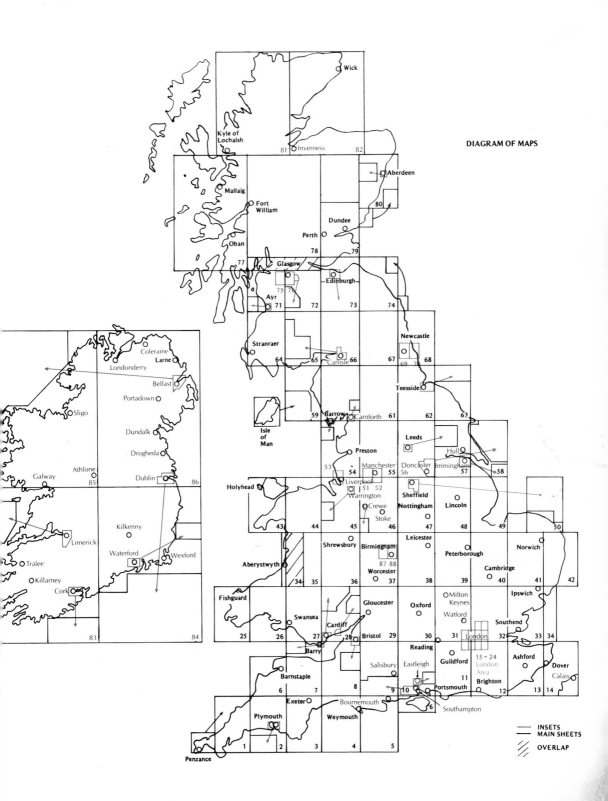

DIAGRAM OF MAPS

INSETS
MAIN SHEETS
OVERLAP

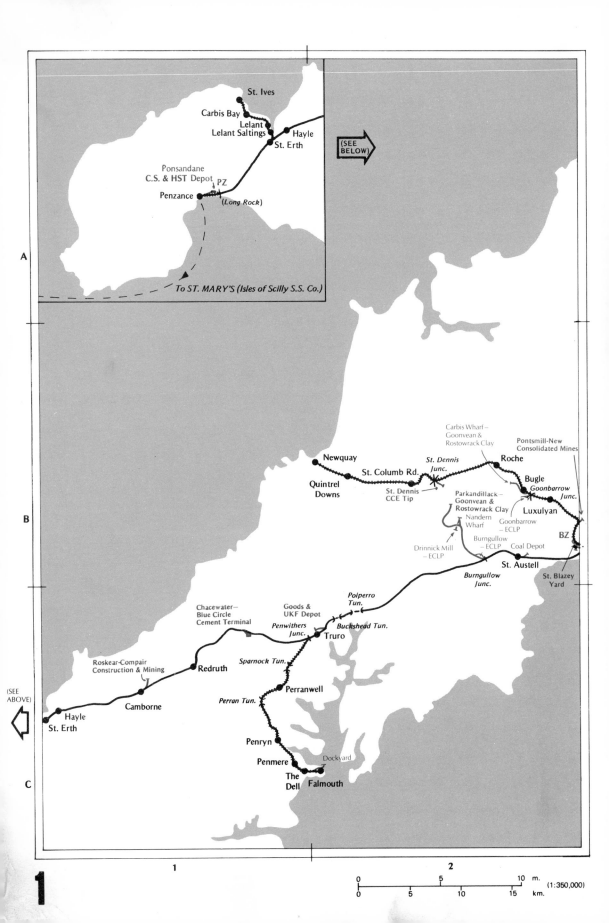

St. Ives
Carbis Bay
Lelant
Lelant Saltings
St. Erth
Hayle

Ponsandane
C.S. & HST Depot
PZ
Penzance
(Long Rock)

(SEE BELOW)

A

To ST. MARY'S (Isles of Scilly S.S. Co.)

Carbis Wharf –
Goonvean &
Rostowrack Clay

Pontsmill–New
Consolidated Mines

Newquay
St. Dennis
Junc.
Roche

St. Columb Rd.
Bugle
Goonbarrow
Junc.

Quintrel
Downs
St. Dennis
CCE Tip
Parkandillack–
Goonvean &
Rostowrack Clay
Goonbarrow
– ECLP
Luxulyan

B
Nandern
Wharf
BZ
Drinnick Mill
– ECLP
Burngullow
– ECLP
Coal Depot

St. Austell
St. Blazey
Yard

Burngullow
Junc.

Chacewater–
Blue Circle
Cement Terminal
Goods &
UKF Depot
Polperro
Tun.

Penwithers
Junc.
Buckshead Tun.

Roskear-Compair
Construction & Mining
Sparnock Tun.
Truro

Redruth

(SEE
ABOVE)
Perranwell

Perran Tun.
Camborne

Hayle
St. Erth
Penryn

Penmere
Dockyard
The
Dell
Falmouth

C

1   2

0   5   10 m.

0   5   10   15 km.   (1:350,000)

1

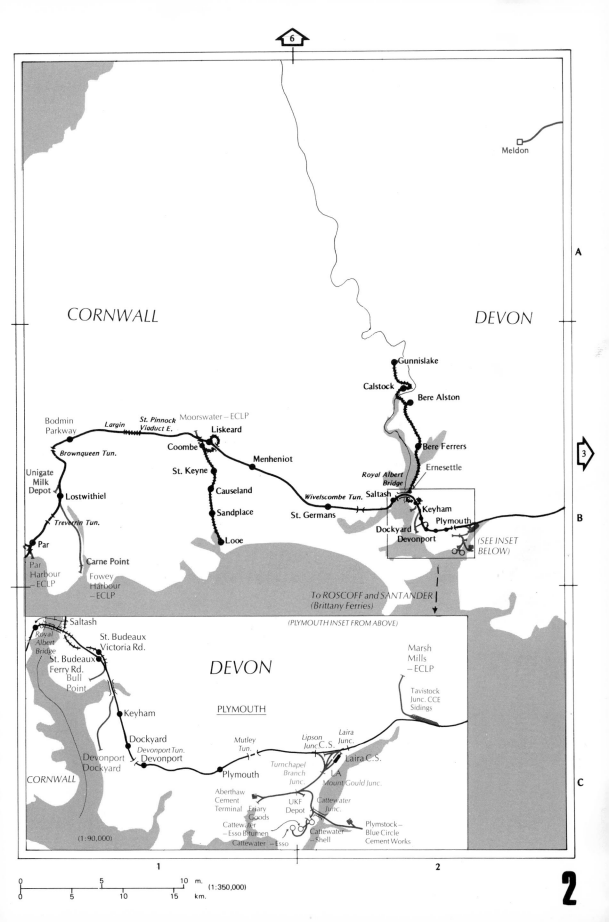

Meldon

CORNWALL

DEVON

A

Gunnislake

Calstock

Bere Alston

3

Bodmin
Parkway

Largin

*St. Pinnock
Viaduct E.*

Moorswater – ECLP

Liskeard

Bere Ferrers

Brownqueen Tun.

Coombe

Menheniot

Bere Ferrers

Unigate
Milk
Depot

St. Keyne

*Royal Albert
Bridge*

Ernesettle

Lostwithiel

Causeland

Wivelscombe Tun.

Saltash

Keyham

B

Treverrin Tun.

Sandplace

St. Germans

Plymouth

Par

Looe

Dockyard

Devonport

*(SEE INSET
BELOW)*

Par
Harbour
– ECLP

Carne Point

Fowey
Harbour
– ECLP

To ROSCOFF and SANTANDER
(Brittany Ferries)

(PLYMOUTH INSET FROM ABOVE)

Saltash

*Royal
Albert
Bridge*

St. Budeaux
Victoria Rd.

Marsh
Mills
– ECLP

St. Budeaux
Ferry Rd.

DEVON

Bull
Point

Keyham

PLYMOUTH

Tavistock
Junc. CCE
Sidings

Dockyard

Devonport Tun.

*Mutley
Tun.*

*Lipson
Junc.* C.S.

*Laira
Junc.*

Devonport
Dockyard

Devonport

Laira C.S.

CORNWALL

Plymouth

*Turnchapel
Branch
Junc.*

LA

Mount Gould Junc.

C

Aberthaw
Cement
Terminal

Friary
Goods

UKF
Depot

*Cattewater
Junc.*

Cattewater
– Esso Bitumen

Cattewater
– Shell

Plymstock –
Blue Circle
Cement Works

Cattewater – Esso

(1:90,000)

0   5   10 m.
0   5   10   15 km.

(1:350,000)

1

2

2

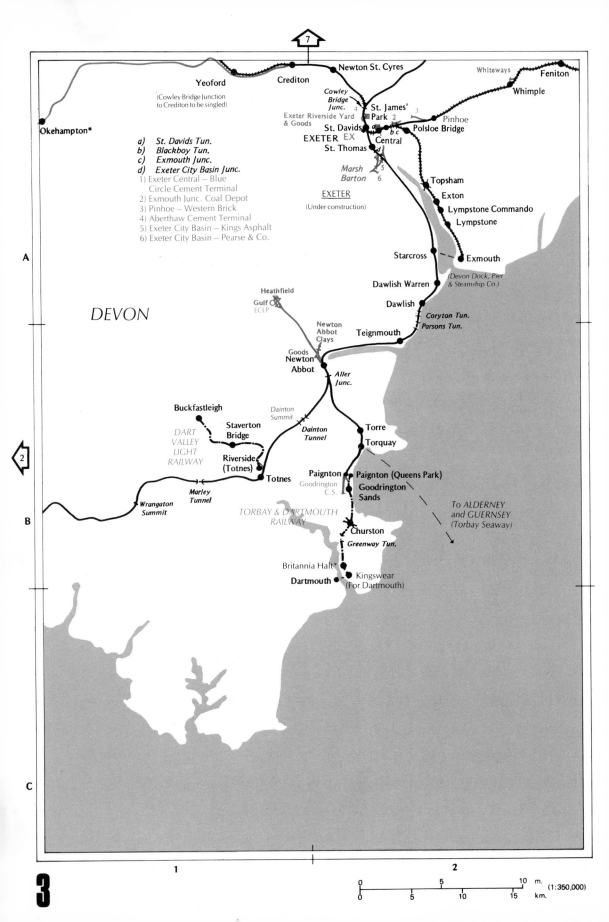

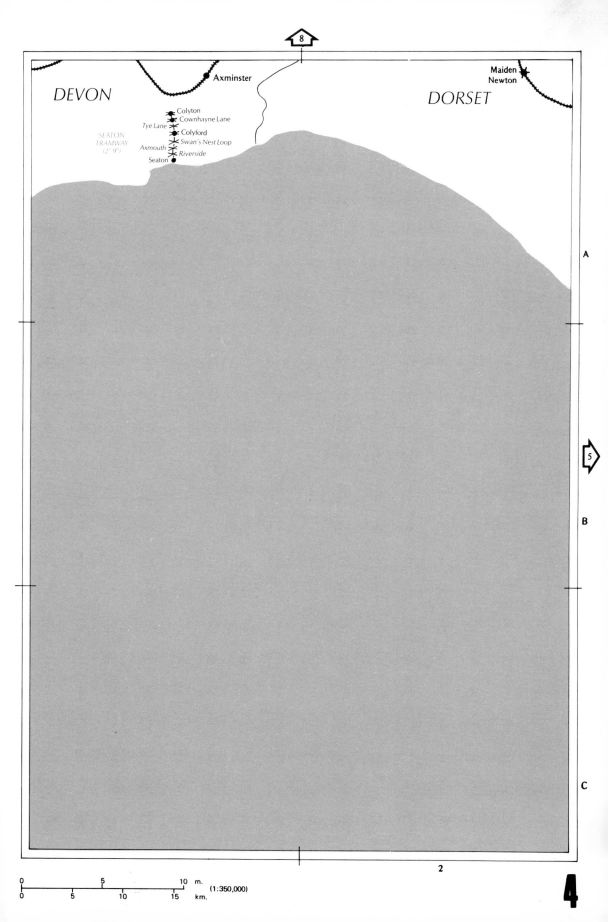

DEVON

DORSET

Axminster

Maiden
Newton

Colyton
Cownhayne Lane
Tye Lane
Colyford
*SEATON
TRAMWAY
(2' 9")*
Swan's Nest Loop
Axmouth
Riverside
Seaton

A

5

B

C

2

0   5   10   m.
0   5   10   15   km.   (1:350,000)

4

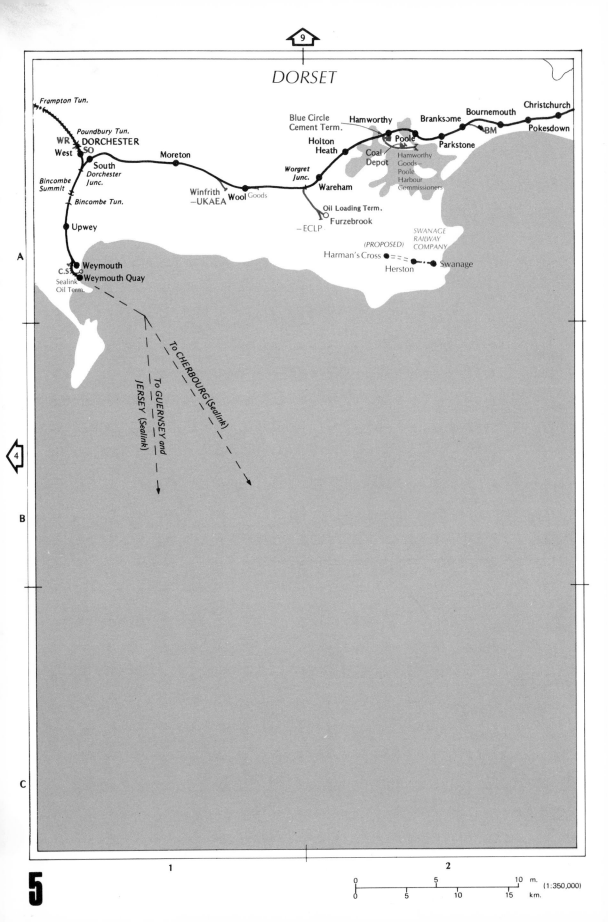

DORSET

Frampton Tun.

Poundbury Tun.
WR DORCHESTER
West SO
South
Dorchester
Junc.

Bincombe
Summit

Bincombe Tun.

Upwey

Moreton

Winfrith
—UKAEA Wool Goods

Worgret
Junc.

Wareham

Oil Loading Term.
—ECLP Furzebrook

Blue Circle
Cement Term. Hamworthy Branksome Bournemouth Christchurch
Holton Poole BM Pokesdown
Heath Parkstone
Coal Hamworthy
Depot Goods —
Poole
Harbour
Commissioners

SWANAGE
RAILWAY
COMPANY
(PROPOSED)
Harman's Cross Swanage
Herston

Weymouth
C.S. Weymouth Quay
Sealink
Oil Term.

To CHERBOURG (Sealink)

To GUERNSEY and
JERSEY (Sealink)

A

4

B

C

1 2

0 5 10 m.
(1:350,000)
0 5 10 15 km.

5

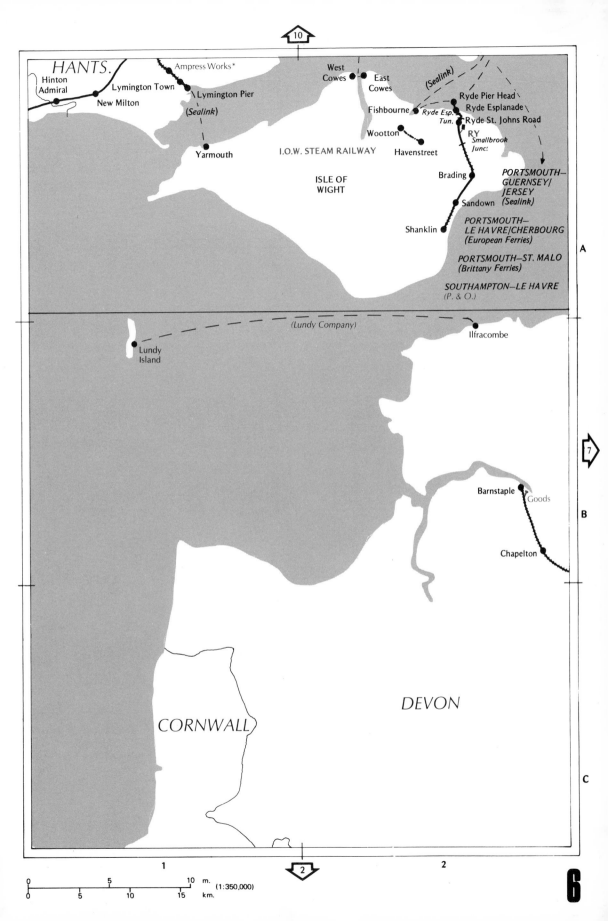

HANTS.

Hinton
Admiral

Ampress Works*

Lymington Town

New Milton

Lymington Pier

(Sealink)

West
Cowes

East
Cowes

Ryde Pier Head

Ryde Esplanade

Fishbourne

*Ryde Esp.
Tun.*

Ryde St. Johns Road

Yarmouth

Wootton

I.O.W. STEAM RAILWAY

Havenstreet

RY *Smallbrook
Junc:*

ISLE OF
WIGHT

Brading

*PORTSMOUTH–
GUERNSEY/
JERSEY*

Sandown

(Sealink)

Shanklin

*PORTSMOUTH–
LE HAVRE/CHERBOURG*
(European Ferries)

A

PORTSMOUTH–ST. MALO
(Brittany Ferries)

SOUTHAMPTON–LE HAVRE
(P. & O.)

(Lundy Company)

Ilfracombe

Lundy
Island

7

Barnstaple

Goods

B

Chapelton

DEVON

CORNWALL

C

1

2

2

0   5   10 m.   (1:350,000)

0   5   10   15 km.

6

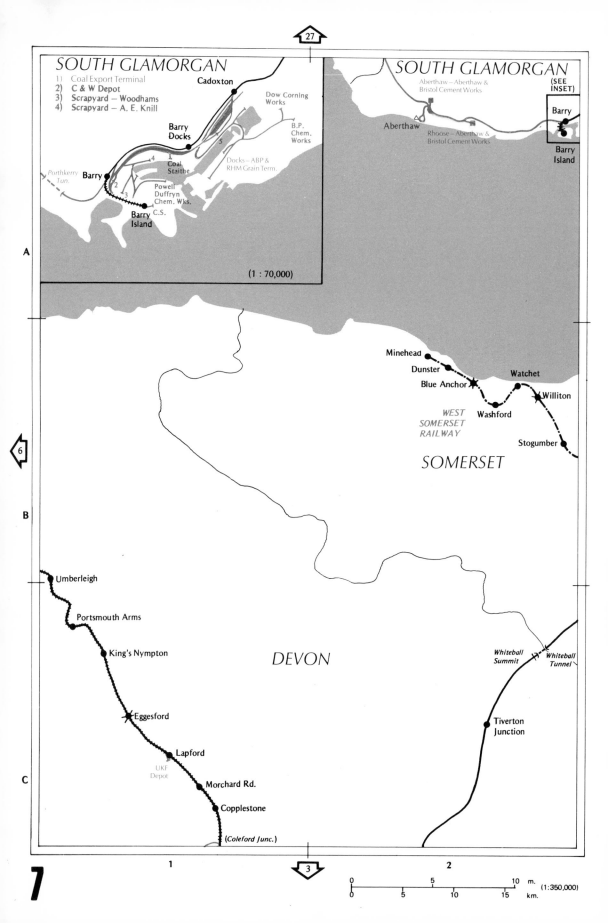

SOUTH GLAMORGAN

1) Coal Export Terminal
2) C & W Depot
3) Scrapyard — Woodhams
4) Scrapyard — A. E. Knill

Cadoxton

Dow Corning
Works

Barry
Docks

B.P.
Chem.
Works

5

Docks – ABP &
RHM Grain Term.

*Porthkerry
Tun.*

Barry

4

Coal
Staithe

2

3

Powell
Duffryn
Chem. Wks.

Barry
Island

C.S.

(1 : 70,000)

SOUTH GLAMORGAN

(SEE
INSET)

Aberthaw – Aberthaw &
Bristol Cement Works

Barry

Aberthaw

Rhoose – Aberthaw &
Bristol Cement Works

Barry
Island

A

Minehead

Dunster

Blue Anchor

Watchet

Williton

Washford

*WEST
SOMERSET
RAILWAY*

Stogumber

SOMERSET

6

B

Umberleigh

Portsmouth Arms

King's Nympton

DEVON

*Whiteball
Summit*

*Whiteball
Tunnel*

Eggesford

Lapford

Tiverton
Junction

UKF
Depot

Morchard Rd.

C

Copplestone

(Coleford Junc.)

7

1

3

2

0 ————— 5 ————— 10 m.

(1:350,000)

0 —— 5 —— 10 —— 15 km.

Cogan
Dinas
Powys
Dingle Rd.
Penarth
Cadoxton
Barry Docks
(SEE CARDIFF
INSET PAGE 28)
(SEE BARRY
INSET PAGE 7)

Bristol Temple Meads
Flax Bourton
Tun.
Parson St.
(SEE INSET BELOW)
St. Annes Park No. 2 Tun.
St. Annes Park No. 3 Tun.

Nailsea and
Backwell
Yatton

AVON

Weston
Milton
Worle Junc.
Weston-s-
Mare
Uphill
Junc.

A

Highbridge

Huntspill
(Puriton)

Clifton Down
Tunnel
Redland
Montpelier
Tun.
Montpelier
Narroways
Hill Junc.
Stapleton
Road
Eastern
Road
Junc.

Clifton Down

AVON

Aberthaw
Cem. Term.
Barton Hill
Wagon Shops
Lawrence
Hill
Avonside Wharf –
Blue
Circle
Cem. T.
Dr. Days
Junc.
East
Depot
CCE
Sidings
Avonside
Wharf – DCL
Wapping Wharf
– Western Fuel
Coal Depot
Sidings
Bristol
Temple
Meads
BR
PM
Marsh Pond –
Rugby
Cement
Terminal
Pylle Hill
Bristol
West Junc.
BRISTOL
Ashton
Gate
P.W.
sdgs.
Bedminster

Goods & UKF Depot
Bridgwater
British
Cellophane
Works
Sidings

Malago Vale (BJ)
C.S.
Parson St.
Junc.
Parson Street
FLT
West Depot C.S.

a) Bristol East Junc.
b) North Somerset Junc.
1) Kingsland Rd. Gds.

(1:70,000)

Castle Cary

9

Crowcombe

Bishops
Lydeard
Norton
Fitzwarren –
Taunton
Cider
WSR
Taunton
WK
CCE
Concrete
Works
Cogload Junc.
Somerton Tunnel

SOMERSET

Fairwater
CCE Depot
Silk
Mill
Crossing
Aberthaw
Cement Term.

B

Sherborne

Yeovil Pen Mill
CCE Sidings
Yeovil Junc.
WR

Thornford

Hewish
Summit
Crewkerne
Yetminster

DEVON

Crewkerne
Tun.
Chetnole

Chard Junc.
Milk Depot –
Unigate
DORSET
Evershot
Tun.
Evershot
Summit

C

Honiton
Summit
Honiton
Tunnel
Honiton
Goods

0   5   10   m.   (1:350,000)
0   5   10   15   km.

8

1

Keynsham

Saltford T'un.

Twerton Long Tun.

Oldfield Park

Bath Spa

Bathampton Junc.

Box Tunnel (1 m. 1452 yds.)

Middle Hill Tun.

Thingley Junc.

Melksham

Pewsey

AVON

Bradford-on-Avon

Freshford

Avoncliff

Bradford Tun.

Bradford Juncs.

N.
W.
S.

Trowbridge

WESTBURY

Hawkeridge Junc.

Blue Circle Cement Wks.

Westbury **WY**
Westbury Yard

Heywood Road Junc.

WILTSHIRE

Bedlam Tun.
Great Elm Tun.

Frome North Junc.

Fairwood Junc.

Dilton Marsh

Tarmac Stone Loading T.

ARC Whatley Quarry
(West Somerset)

Clink Road Junc.

Frome
Goods

Mobil

a) Fisherton Tunnel
b) Tunnel Junction
c) Laverstock North Junc.
d) Laverstock South Junc.

Cranmore — Anglo
American Asphalt

Merehead — Foster
Yeoman

Beechgrove

Warminster

WR

SO

(HEYTESBURY)

Blatchbridge Junc.

Mendip Vale

Cranmore **W**

E

EAST.
SOM.
RLY.

Merehead Quarry Loop Junctions

Witham East Somerset Junc.

SOMERSET

Bruton

ECC — Quidhampton Clay Term.

Chilmark

Dinton

Gds. *a*
b c
d

Wilton Junc.

Salisbury
Yd. *d*

B

Buckhorn Weston Tun.

UKF Depot

Tisbury

SALISBURY

Gillingham

Templecombe

HAMPSHIRE

St. Denys

Bevois Park
(Up Yard)

Bitterne

DORSET

Totton

Redbridge

Freightliner
Wagon Shops

Millbrook
FLT

Millbrook

Goods & Car Term.

Tunnel & Rugby
Cement Terms.

Northam Junc.

Scrapyard —
Pollock & Brown

Blue Circle
Cement Term.

Sidings

Redbridge
CCE Depot

Eling Wharf —
ARC Stone Term.

Maritime
FLT

Southampton

Western
Docks — ABP

GPO
Terminal

Southampton Tun.

Dibles
Wharf —
Powell
Duffryn
Fuels

Northam (Down
Yard) & Grain
Terminal

Woolston

Sholing

Marchwood — MOD

Town
Quay

Royal
Pier

Eastern
Docks — ABP
Southampton
Ocean Terminal*

C

Lyndhurst
Road

(SOUTHAMPTON INSET FROM MAP 10)   (1:90,000)

To HYTHE

To COWES

9

1

2

0 ___ 5 ___ 10 m.

0 ___ 5 ___ 10 ___ 15 km.

(1:350,000)

A

8

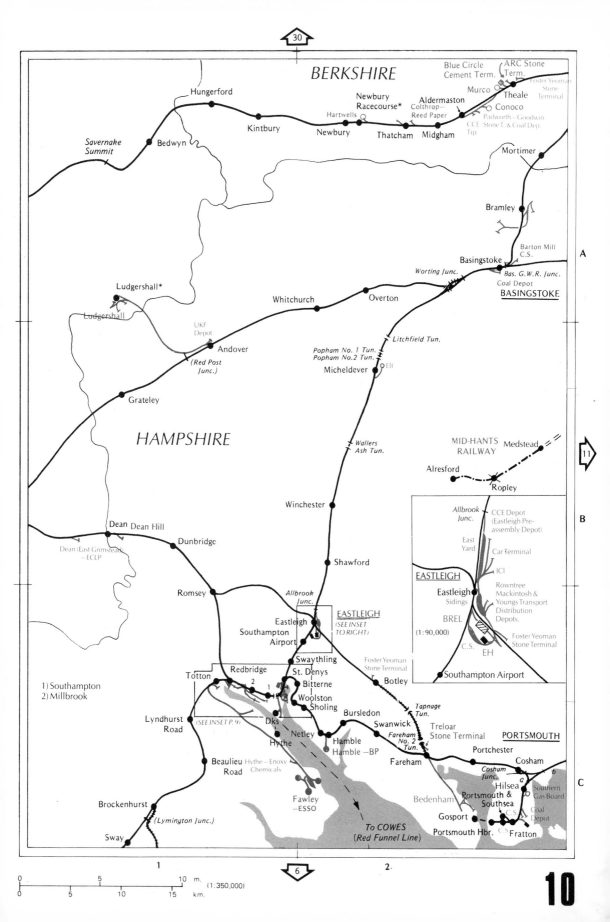

BERKSHIRE

Hungerford

Kintbury

Newbury Racecourse*

Hartwells

Newbury

Thatcham

Midgham

Aldermaston
Colthrop–
Reed Paper

Blue Circle
Cement Term.

Murco

Theale

ARC Stone
Term.

Foster Yeoman
Stone
Terminal

Conoco

Padworth – Goodwin
CCE Stone T. & Coal Dep.
Tip

Savernake
Summit

Bedwyn

Mortimer

Bramley

Barton Mill
C.S.

Basingstoke

Worting Junc.

Bas. G.W.R. Junc.
Coal Depot

BASINGSTOKE

A

Ludgershall*

Ludgershall

UKF
Depot

Andover

(Red Post
Junc.)

Whitchurch

Overton

Litchfield Tun.

Popham No. 1 Tun.
Popham No.2 Tun.

Eli

Micheldever

Grateley

HAMPSHIRE

Wallers
Ash Tun.

MID-HANTS
RAILWAY

Medstead

11

Alresford

Ropley

Winchester

Dean Dean Hill

Dunbridge

Dean (East Grimstead)
– ECLP

Allbrook
Junc.

CCE Depot
(Eastleigh Pre-
assembly Depot)

East
Yard

Car Terminal

ICI

EASTLEIGH

Eastleigh
Sidings

Rowntree
Mackintosh &
Youngs Transport
Distribution
Depots.

BREL

(1:90,000)

C.S.

EH

Foster Yeoman
Stone Terminal

Southampton Airport

B

Shawford

Romsey

Allbrook
Junc.

Eastleigh

EASTLEIGH
(SEE INSET
TO RIGHT)

Southampton
Airport

Swaythling

Botley

Foster Yeoman
Stone Terminal

Tapnage
Tun.

Totton

Redbridge

2   1

St. Denys

Bitterne

Woolston
Sholing

Bursledon

Swanwick

Treloar
Stone Terminal

PORTSMOUTH

1) Southampton
2) Millbrook

Lyndhurst
Road

(SEE INSET P. 9)

Dks

Netley

Hythe

Hamble
Hamble –BP

Fareham
No. 2
Tun.

Fareham

Portchester

Cosham

Cosham
Junc.

Hilsea

Southern
Gas Board

C

Beaulieu
Road

Hythe – Enoxy
Chemicals

Bedenham

Portsmouth &
Southsea

Coal
Depot

Brockenhurst

(Lymington Junc.)

Fawley
–ESSO

Gosport

Portsmouth Hbr.

C.S.

Fratton

Sway

To COWES
(Red Funnel Line)

0   5   10 m.

(1:350,000)

0   5   10   15 km.

1

2.

10

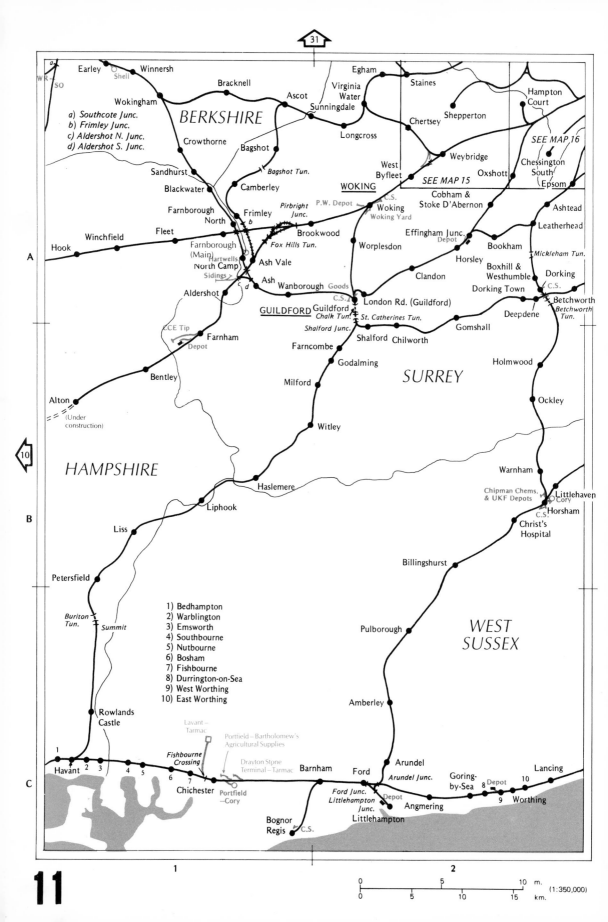

a) *Southcote Junc.*
b) *Frimley Junc.*
c) *Aldershot N. Junc.*
d) *Aldershot S. Junc.*

Earley
Winnersh
Bracknell
Wokingham

Egham
Staines
Hampton Court
Virginia Water
Sunningdale
Ascot
Shepperton
Chertsey

BERKSHIRE

Crowthorne
Longcross

Weybridge
SEE MAP 16

Sandhurst
Bagshot
West Byfleet
Oxshott
Chessington South
Epsom

Blackwater
Camberley
Bagshot Tun.
WOKING
SEE MAP 15

Farnborough North
Frimley
Pirbright Junc.
P.W. Depot
C.S.
Woking
Cobham & Stoke D'Abernon
Ashtead

Hook
Winchfield
Fleet
b
Woking Yard
Leatherhead

Fox Hills Tun.
Brookwood
Worplesdon
Effingham Junc.
Depot
Bookham
Mickleham Tun.

Farnborough (Main)
Hartwells
Ash Vale
Horsley
Boxhill & Westhumble

A
North Camp
Sidings
c d
Ash
Wanborough
Goods
Clandon
Dorking
Dorking Town

Aldershot
London Rd. (Guildford)
C.S.
Betchworth
Betchworth Tun.
Deepdene

CCE Tip
GUILDFORD
Guildford
Chalk Tun.
St. Catherines Tun.

Farnham
Depot
Shalford Junc.
Shalford
Chilworth
Gomshall

Farncombe
Godalming
Holmwood

Bentley
Milford
SURREY

Alton
(Under construction)
Witley
Ockley

10

HAMPSHIRE
Warnham

Haslemere
Chipman Chems. & UKF Depots
Littlehaven
Cory

Liphook
C.S.
Horsham

B
Liss
Christ's Hospital

Petersfield
Billingshurst

Buriton Tun.
Summit

1) Bedhampton
2) Warblington
3) Emsworth
4) Southbourne
5) Nutbourne
6) Bosham
7) Fishbourne
8) Durrington-on-Sea
9) West Worthing
10) East Worthing

Pulborough

WEST SUSSEX

Rowlands Castle

Lavant – Tarmac

Amberley

Portfield – Bartholomew's Agricultural Supplies

Fishbourne Crossing
Drayton Stone Terminal – Tarmac
Barnham
Ford
Arundel
Lancing

1
Havant
2
3
4
5
6
7
Chichester
Portfield – Cory
Arundel Junc.
Goring-by-Sea
Depot
8
10

C
Ford Junc.
Littlehampton Junc.
Depot
9
Worthing

Bognor Regis
C.S.
Littlehampton
Angmering

1
2

0   5   10 m.
(1:350,000)
0   5   10   15 km.

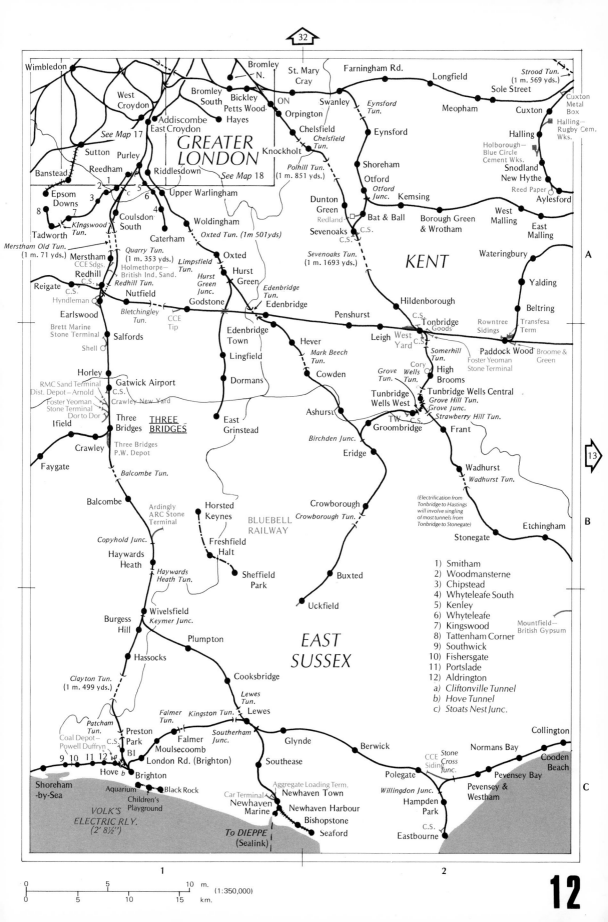

Wimbledon
Bromley N.
St. Mary Cray
Farningham Rd.
Longfield
Sole Street
Strood Tun.
(1 m. 569 yds.)
West Croydon
Bromley South
Bickley
Petts Wood
ON
Swanley
Meopham
Cuxton
Cuxton Metal Box
Addiscombe
East Croydon
Hayes
Orpington
Eynsford Tun.
Halling—Rugby Cem. Wks.
See Map 17
Chelsfield
Eynsford
Halling
Sutton
Purley
Chelsfield Tun.
Otford
Holborough—Blue Circle Cement Wks.
GREATER
Knockholt
Shoreham
Snodland
New Hythe
Banstead
Reedham
Riddlesdown
LONDON
Polhill Tun.
(1 m. 851 yds.)
Otford Junc.
Kemsing
Reed Paper
Epsom Downs
Upper Warlingham
See Map 18
Dunton Green
West Malling
Aylesford
Tadworth
Kingswood Tun.
Coulsdon South
Caterham
Woldingham
Redland
Bat & Ball
Borough Green & Wrotham
East Malling
Merstham Old Tun.
(1 m. 71 yds.)
Merstham
Oxted Tun. (1m 501yds)
Sevenoaks
C.S.
KENT
A
Wateringbury
Reigate
Redhill
CCE Sdgs.
C.S.
Quarry Tun.
(1 m. 353 yds.)
Holmethorpe—British Ind. Sand.
Oxted
Limpsfield Tun.
Sevenoaks Tun.
(1 m. 1693 yds.)
Yalding
Nutfield
Redhill Tun.
Hurst Green Junc.
Hurst Green
Edenbridge Tun.
Hildenborough
Beltring
Hyndleman
Bletchingley Tun.
CCE Tip
Godstone
Edenbridge
Penshurst
C.S.
Tonbridge Goods
Rowntree Sidings
Transfesa Term.
Earlswood
Brett Marine Stone Terminal
Salfords
Shell
Edenbridge Town
Hever
Mark Beech Tun.
Leigh
West Yard
C.S.
Paddock Wood
Broome & Green
Lingfield
Cowden
Somerhill Tun.
Foster Yeoman Stone Terminal
Horley
RMC Sand Terminal Dist. Depot — Arnold
Foster Yeoman Stone Terminal Dor to Dor
Gatwick Airport
C.S.
Crawley New Yard
Dormans
Grove Tun.
Cory Wells Tun.
High Brooms
Tunbridge Wells Central
Grove Hill Tun.
Ifield
THREE BRIDGES
East Grinstead
Ashurst
Tunbridge Wells West
Grove Junc.
Strawberry Hill Tun.
Three Bridges
Three Bridges P.W. Depot
Birchden Junc.
Groombridge
TW C.S.
Frant
Crawley
Faygate
Eridge
Wadhurst
Wadhurst Tun.
13
Balcombe Tun.
Crowborough
(Electrification from Tonbridge to Hastings will involve singling of most tunnels from Tonbridge to Stonegate)
B
Balcombe
Ardingly ARC Stone Terminal
Horsted Keynes
BLUEBELL RAILWAY
Crowborough Tun.
Stonegate
Etchingham
Copyhold Junc.
Freshfield Halt
Haywards Heath
Sheffield Park
Buxted
1) Smitham
2) Woodmansterne
3) Chipstead
4) Whyteleafe South
5) Kenley
6) Whyteleafe
7) Kingswood
8) Tattenham Corner
9) Southwick
10) Fishersgate
11) Portslade
12) Aldrington
a) Cliftonville Tunnel
b) Hove Tunnel
c) Stoats Nest Junc.
Haywards Heath Tun.
Uckfield
Burgess Hill
Wivelsfield
Keymer Junc.
Mountfield—British Gypsum
Plumpton
EAST SUSSEX
Hassocks
Cooksbridge
Clayton Tun.
(1 m. 499 yds.)
Lewes Tun.
Falmer Tun.
Kingston Tun.
Lewes
Collington
Patcham Tun.
Coal Depot—Powell Duffryn
C.S.
Preston Park
Falmer
Moulsecoomb
Southerham Junc.
Glynde
Berwick
Normans Bay
Cooden Beach
9 10 11 12 a
B1
London Rd. (Brighton)
Southease
CCE Siding
Stone Cross Junc.
Polegate
Pevensey Bay
Shoreham-by-Sea
Aquarium
Hove b
Brighton
Black Rock
Children's Playground
Car Terminal
Newhaven Town
Aggregate Loading Term.
Willingdon Junc.
Pevensey & Westham
C
VOLK'S ELECTRIC RLY.
(2' 8½")
Newhaven Marine
Newhaven Harbour
Bishopstone
Hampden Park
To DIEPPE
(Sealink)
Seaford
C.S.
Eastbourne

0 ————— 5 ————— 10 m.
0 —— 5 —— 10 —— 15 km.
(1:350,000)

12

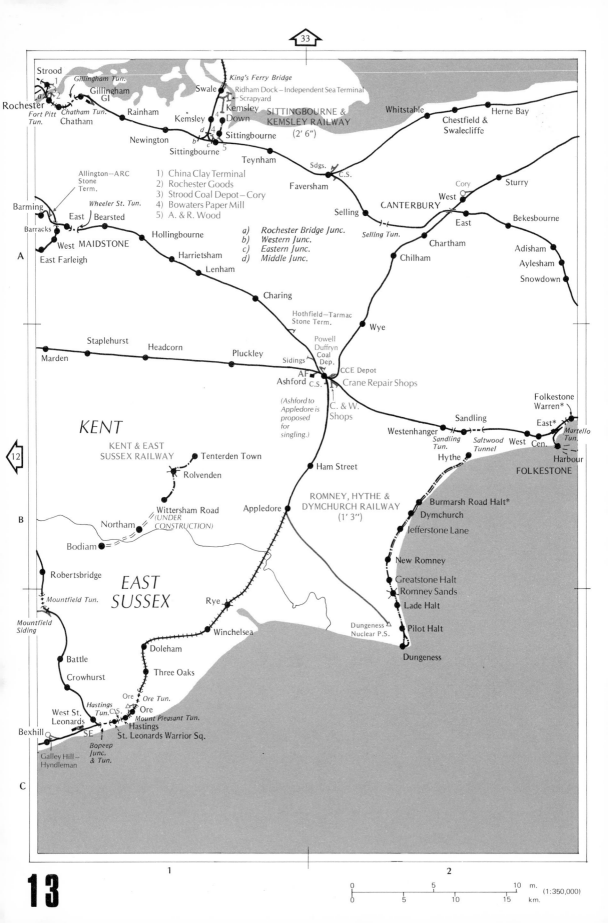

Strood

Rochester

Fort Pitt Tun.

Chatham Tun.

Chatham

Gillingham

Gillingham Tun.

Gl

Rainham

Newington

Kemsley

Sittingbourne

Sittingbourne

Swale

Kemsley Down

King's Ferry Bridge

Ridham Dock – Independent Sea Terminal

Scrapyard

SITTINGBOURNE & KEMSLEY RAILWAY (2' 6")

Teynham

Faversham

Sdgs.
C.S.

Whitstable

Chestfield & Swalecliffe

Herne Bay

Sturry

Cory

West

CANTERBURY

East

Bekesbourne

Adisham

Aylesham

Snowdown

Selling

Selling Tun.

Chartham

Chilham

1) China Clay Terminal
2) Rochester Goods
3) Strood Coal Depot – Cory
4) Bowaters Paper Mill
5) A. & R. Wood

a) *Rochester Bridge Junc.*
b) *Western Junc.*
c) *Eastern Junc.*
d) *Middle Junc.*

Allington–ARC Stone Term.

Wheeler St. Tun.

Barming

East

Barracks

West MAIDSTONE

East Farleigh

Bearsted

Hollingbourne

Harrietsham

Lenham

Charing

Hothfield–Tarmac Stone Term.

Wye

A

KENT

KENT & EAST SUSSEX RAILWAY

Tenterden Town

Rolvenden

Wittersham Road
(UNDER CONSTRUCTION)

Northam

Bodiam

Staplehurst

Marden

Headcorn

Pluckley

Sidings

AF
C.S.

Ashford

(Ashford to Appledore is proposed for singling.)

Powell Duffryn Coal Dep.

CCE Depot

Crane Repair Shops

C. & W. Shops

Ham Street

Appledore

ROMNEY, HYTHE & DYMCHURCH RAILWAY (1' 3")

Westenhanger

Sandling Tun.

Sandling

Saltwood Tunnel

West Cen.

Hythe

Folkestone Warren*

East*

Martello Tun.

Harbour

FOLKESTONE

Burmarsh Road Halt*

Dymchurch

Jefferstone Lane

New Romney

Greatstone Halt

Romney Sands

Lade Halt

Dungeness Nuclear P.S.

Pilot Halt

Dungeness

B

EAST SUSSEX

Robertsbridge

Mountfield Tun.

Mountfield Siding

Battle

Crowhurst

Rye

Winchelsea

Doleham

Three Oaks

Ore

Ore Tun.

Hastings Tun. C.S.

West St. Leonards

Bexhill

Galley Hill – Hyndleman

SE

Ore

Mount Pleasant Tun.

Hastings

St. Leonards Warrior Sq.

Bopeep Junc. & Tun.

C

1

2

13

0   5   10 m.
0   5   10   15 km.

(1:350,000)

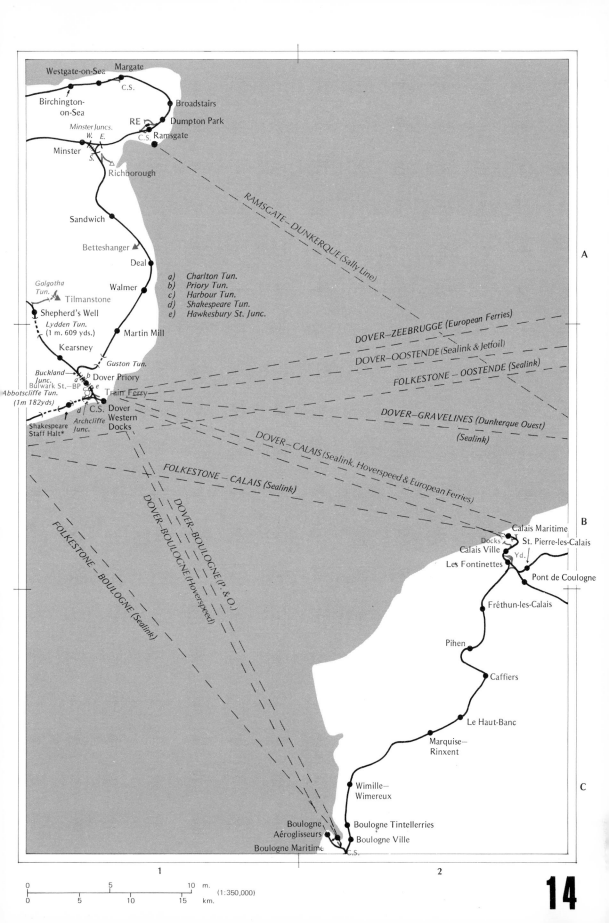

Westgate-on-Sea Margate
Birchington-on-Sea
C.S.
Broadstairs
RE Dumpton Park
Minster Juncs. C.S. Ramsgate
W. E.
Minster
S.
Richborough

Sandwich

Betteshanger

Deal

Walmer

a) Charlton Tun.
b) Priory Tun.
c) Harbour Tun.
d) Shakespeare Tun.
e) Hawkesbury St. Junc.

Golgotha
Tun.
Tilmanstone
Shepherd's Well
Lydden Tun.
(1 m. 609 yds.)
Kearsney
Martin Mill
Guston Tun.
Buckland
Junc. b Dover Priory
Bulwark St.–BP a e
Abbotscliffe Tun. c
(1m 182yds) Train Ferry
d C.S. Dover
Shakespeare Archcliffe Western
Staff Halt* Junc. Docks

RAMSGATE–DUNKERQUE (Sally Line)

DOVER–ZEEBRUGGE (European Ferries)

DOVER–OOSTENDE (Sealink & Jetfoil)

FOLKESTONE — OOSTENDE (Sealink)

DOVER–GRAVELINES (Dunkerque Ouest)
(Sealink)

DOVER–CALAIS (Sealink, Hoverspeed & European Ferries)

FOLKESTONE — CALAIS (Sealink)

DOVER–BOULOGNE (P. & O.)

DOVER–BOULOGNE (Hoverspeed)

FOLKESTONE — BOULOGNE (Sealink)

Calais Maritime
Docks St. Pierre-les-Calais
Calais Ville Yd.
Les Fontinettes
Pont de Coulogne

Fréthun-les-Calais

Pihen

Caffiers

Le Haut-Banc

Marquise–
Rinxent

Wimille–
Wimereux

Boulogne Boulogne Tintellerries
Aéroglisseurs Boulogne Ville
Boulogne Maritime C.S.

A

B

C

1 2

0 5 10 m.
0 5 10 15 km.
(1:350,000)

14

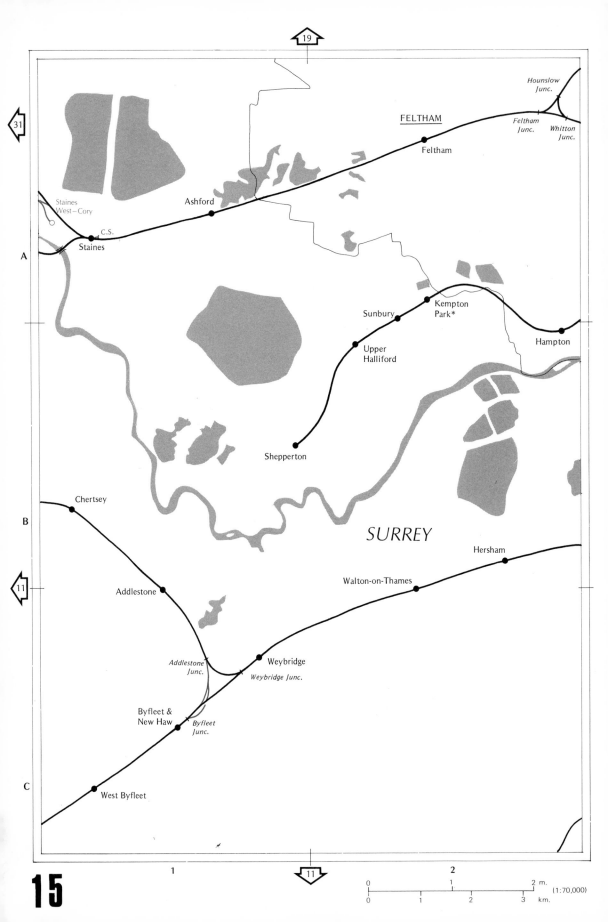

19

31

FELTHAM

Hounslow Junc.

Feltham Junc.

Whitton Junc.

Feltham

Staines West–Cory

Ashford

C.S.

Staines

A

Sunbury

Kempton Park*

Hampton

Upper Halliford

Shepperton

Chertsey

SURREY

B

Hersham

Walton-on-Thames

Addlestone

11

Weybridge

Addlestone Junc.

Weybridge Junc.

Byfleet & New Haw

Byfleet Junc.

C

West Byfleet

1

11

2

0   1   2 m.

0   1   2   3 km.

(1:70,000)

15

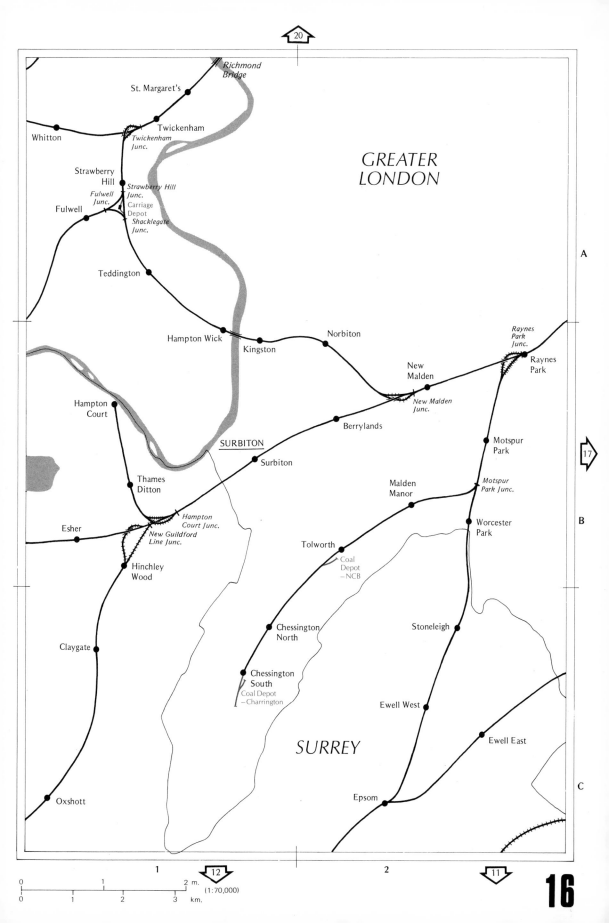

Richmond Bridge

St. Margaret's

Twickenham

Whitton

Twickenham Junc.

Strawberry Hill

Strawberry Hill Junc.

Fulwell Junc.

Fulwell

Carriage Depot

Shacklegate Junc.

GREATER LONDON

A

Teddington

Hampton Wick

Kingston

Norbiton

Raynes Park Junc.

Raynes Park

New Malden

New Malden Junc.

Hampton Court

Berrylands

SURBITON

Surbiton

Motspur Park

17

Thames Ditton

Hampton Court Junc.

New Guildford Line Junc.

Esher

Malden Manor

Motspur Park Junc.

Worcester Park

B

Tolworth

Coal Depot —NCB

Hinchley Wood

Claygate

Chessington North

Stoneleigh

Chessington South

Coal Depot —Charrington

Ewell West

Ewell East

C

SURREY

Oxshott

Epsom

0   1   2 m.
(1:70,000)

0   1   2   3 km.

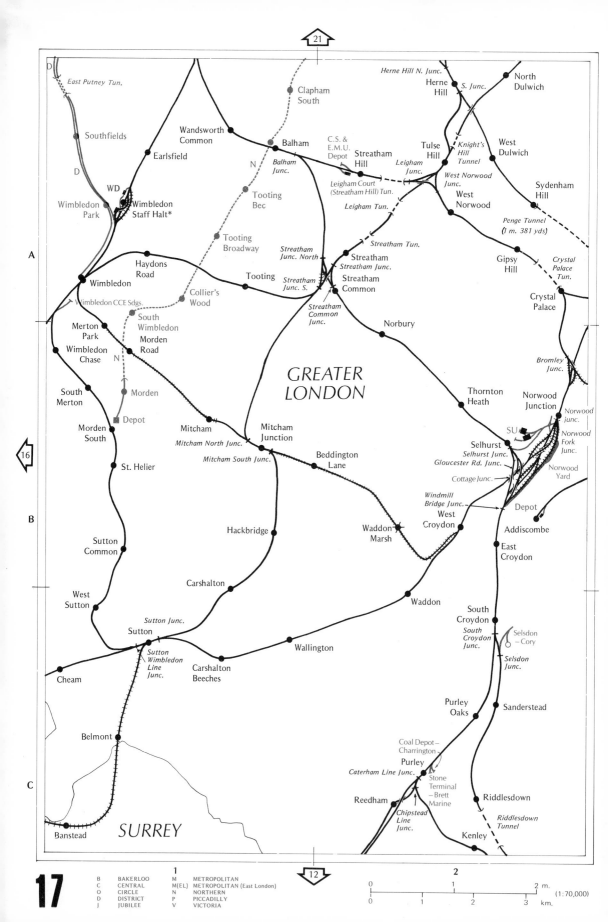

D   East Putney Tun.

Southfields

Earlsfield

Wandsworth Common

Balham

Clapham South

C.S. & E.M.U. Depot

Streatham Hill

Herne Hill N. Junc.

Herne Hill   S. Junc.

North Dulwich

Knight's Hill Tunnel

Tulse Hill

West Dulwich

West Norwood Junc.

West Norwood

Sydenham Hill

WD

Wimbledon Park   Wimbledon Staff Halt*

N

Balham Junc.

Tooting Bec

Leigham Junc.

Leigham Court (Streatham Hill) Tun.

Penge Tunnel (1 m. 381 yds)

Tooting Broadway

Haydons Road

Wimbledon

Tooting

Leigham Tun.

Streatham Junc. North

Streatham Tun.

Streatham Common

Gipsy Hill

Crystal Palace Tun.

A

Streatham Junc. S.

Streatham Junc.

Streatham Common Junc.

Crystal Palace

Wimbledon CCE Sdgs.

Merton Park

Collier's Wood

South Wimbledon

Norbury

Bromley Junc.

Wimbledon Chase

N

Morden Road

GREATER LONDON

Thornton Heath

Norwood Junction

Norwood junc.

South Merton

Morden

Depot

Norwood Fork Junc.

Morden South

Mitcham

Mitcham Junction

SU

Selhurst

Norwood Yard

St. Helier

Mitcham North Junc.

Mitcham South Junc.

Beddington Lane

Selhurst Junc.

Gloucester Rd. Junc.

Cottage Junc.

B

Hackbridge

Waddon Marsh

Windmill Bridge Junc.

West Croydon

Depot

Addiscombe

Sutton Common

East Croydon

West Sutton

Carshalton

Waddon

South Croydon

South Croydon Junc.

Selsdon – Cory

Sutton Junc.

Wallington

Sutton

Selsdon Junc.

Cheam

Sutton Wimbledon Line Junc.

Carshalton Beeches

Purley Oaks

Sanderstead

Belmont

Coal Depot – Charrington

Purley

Caterham Line Junc.

Stone Terminal – Brett Marine

Riddlesdown

C

Reedham

Chipstead Line Junc.

Riddlesdown Tunnel

SURREY

Banstead

Kenley

17

B	BAKERLOO	M	METROPOLITAN
C	CENTRAL	M(EL)	METROPOLITAN (East London)
C	CIRCLE	N	NORTHERN
D	DISTRICT	P	PICCADILLY
J	JUBILEE	V	VICTORIA

1   2

0   1   2 m.

0   1   2   3 km.

(1:70,000)

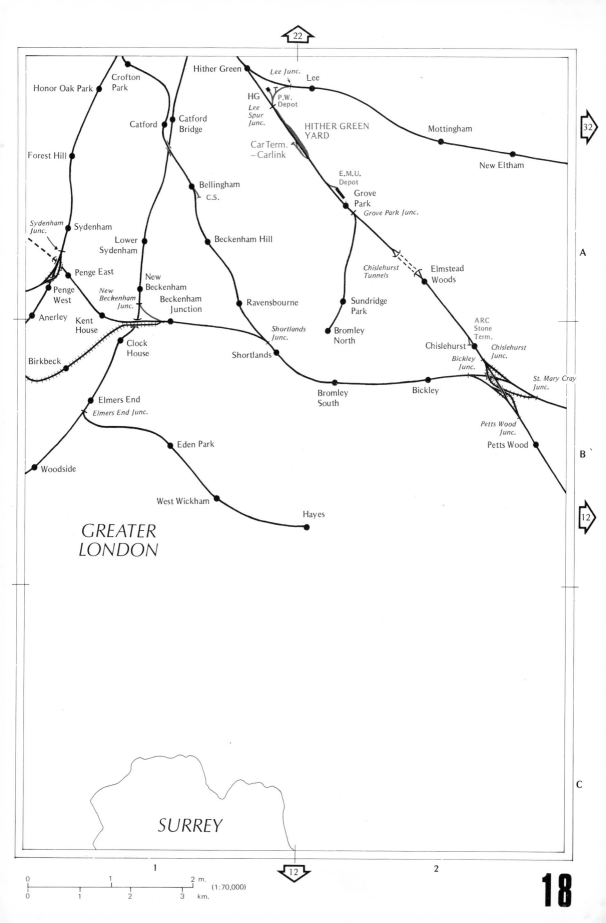

Honor Oak Park

Crofton Park

Hither Green

Lee Junc.

Lee

HG

P.W. Depot

Lee Spur Junc.

HITHER GREEN YARD

Mottingham

Catford

Catford Bridge

Car Term. —Carlink

New Eltham

Forest Hill

Bellingham

C.S.

E.M.U. Depot

Grove Park

Grove Park Junc.

Sydenham Junc.

Sydenham

Beckenham Hill

Lower Sydenham

Penge East

New Beckenham Junc.

New Beckenham

Beckenham Junction

Ravensbourne

Chislehurst Tunnels

Elmstead Woods

A

Penge West

Sundridge Park

Anerley

Kent House

Shortlands Junc.

Bromley North

ARC Stone Term.

Chislehurst

Chislehurst Junc.

Birkbeck

Clock House

Shortlands

Bickley Junc.

St. Mary Cray Junc.

Elmers End

Elmers End Junc.

Bromley South

Bickley

Petts Wood Junc.

B

Eden Park

Petts Wood

Woodside

West Wickham

Hayes

12

GREATER LONDON

SURREY

C

0   1   2 m.   (1:70,000)

0   1   2   3   km.

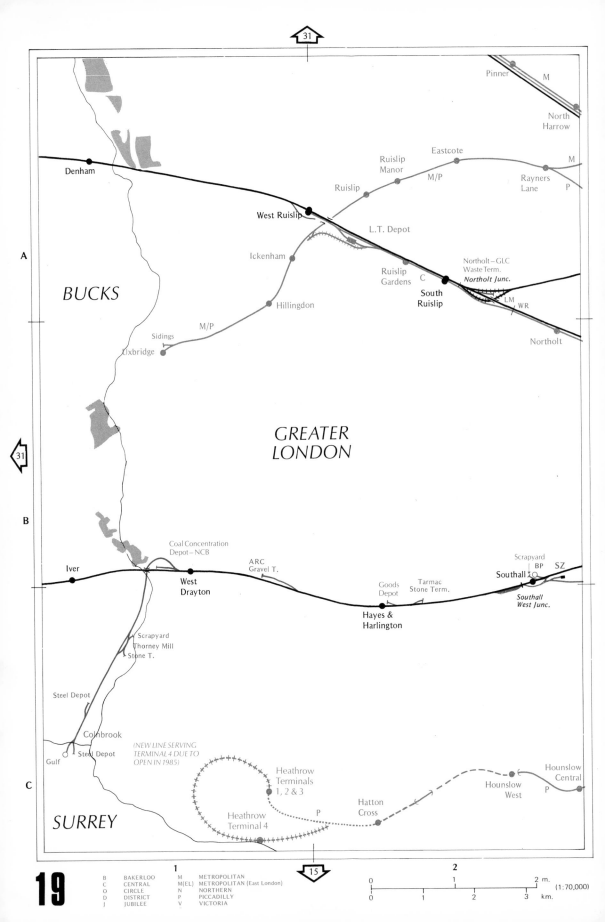

Pinner
M
North
Harrow
M
Eastcote
Ruislip
Manor
M/P
Rayners
Lane
P
Denham
Ruislip
West Ruislip
L.T. Depot
Northolt – GLC
Waste Term.
Northolt Junc.
Ickenham
Ruislip
Gardens
C
South
Ruislip
LM
WR
Hillingdon
Northolt

A

BUCKS

Sidings
M/P
Uxbridge

GREATER
LONDON

31

B

Coal Concentration
Depot – NCB
Scrapyard
BP
SZ
Iver
West
Drayton
ARC
Gravel T.
Goods
Depot
Tarmac
Stone Term.
Southall
Hayes &
Harlington
*Southall
West Junc.*

Scrapyard
Thorney Mill
Stone T.

Steel Depot

Colnbrook
Steel Depot
Gulf
*(NEW LINE SERVING
TERMINAL 4 DUE TO
OPEN IN 1985)*
Heathrow
Terminals
1, 2 & 3
Hatton
Cross
P
Hounslow
West
Hounslow
Central
P

C

SURREY

Heathrow
Terminal 4
P

1

19

B	BAKERLOO	M	METROPOLITAN
C	CENTRAL	M(EL)	METROPOLITAN (East London)
O	CIRCLE	N	NORTHERN
D	DISTRICT	P	PICCADILLY
J	JUBILEE	V	VICTORIA

2

0   1   2 m.
(1:70,000)
0   1   2   3   km.

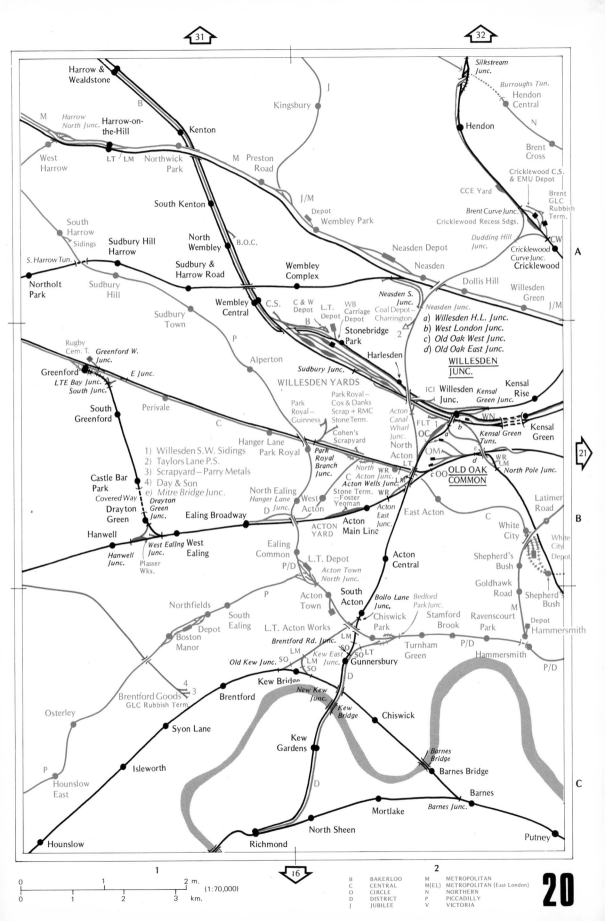

Harrow & Wealdstone

Harrow North Junc.

Harrow-on-the-Hill

Kenton

West Harrow

Preston Road

South Harrow Sidings

South Kenton

South Harrow

Northwick Park

Sudbury Hill Harrow

North Wembley

B.O.C.

Wembley Park

Depot

J/M

Kingsbury

J

Silkstream Junc.

Burroughs Tun.

Hendon Central

Hendon

Brent Cross

N

Cricklewood C.S. & EMU Depot

CCE Yard

Brent GLC Rubbish Term.

Brent Curve Junc.

Cricklewood Recess Sdgs.

Dudding Hill Junc.

Cricklewood Curve Junc.

CW

Cricklewood

A

S. Harrow Tun.

Northolt Park

Sudbury Hill

Sudbury Town

Sudbury & Harrow Road

Wembley Complex

Wembley Central

C.S.

C & W Depot

L.T. Depot

WB Carriage Depot

Stonebridge Park

B

Coal Depot – Charrington

Neasden S. Junc.

Neasden Depot

Neasden

Dollis Hill

Willesden Green

J/M

Neasden Junc.

a) Willesden H.L. Junc.
b) West London Junc.
c) Old Oak West Junc.
d) Old Oak East Junc.

WILLESDEN JUNC.

Alperton

P

Harlesden

2

Sudbury Junc.

WILLESDEN YARDS

Rugby Cem. T.

Greenford W. Junc.

Greenford

LTE Bay Junc.

South Junc.

E Junc.

Park Royal – Cox & Danks Scrap + RMC Stone Term.

Park Royal – Guinness

ICI

Willesden Junc.

Kensal Green Junc.

Kensal Rise

Kensal Green

WN

Acton Canal Wharf Junc.

FLT 1

OC

North Acton

OM

b

a

Kensal Green Tuns.

South Greenford

Perivale

C

Hanger Lane Park Royal

Cohen's Scrapyard

Park Royal Branch Junc.

1) Willesden S.W. Sidings
2) Taylors Lane P.S.
3) Scrapyard – Parry Metals
4) Day & Son
e) Mitre Bridge Junc.

Castle Bar Park

Covered Way

Drayton Green

Drayton Green Junc.

Hanwell

West Ealing Junc.

Plasser Wks.

West Ealing

Ealing Broadway

North Ealing Hanger Lane Junc.

West Acton

North Acton Junc.

Acton Wells Junc.

Stone Term. – Foster Yeoman

WR

C

Acton East Junc.

East Acton

LT

OO

OLD OAK COMMON

c

d

e

WR LM

North Pole Junc.

Latimer Road

C

White City

White City Depot

Hanwell Junc.

Acton Main Line

ACTON YARD

South Ealing

Northfields

Depot Boston Manor

Ealing Common

P/D

L.T. Depot

Acton Town North Junc.

Acton Town

Acton Central

South Acton

Bollo Lane Junc.

Bedford Park Junc.

Chiswick Park

Stamford Brook

Shepherd's Bush

Goldhawk Road

Ravenscourt Park

Shepherd's Bush

M

Depot Hammersmith

Osterley

Syon Lane

Isleworth

Hounslow East

P

Brentford Goods
GLC Rubbish Term.

4
3

Brentford

Kew Bridge

Old Kew Junc.

SO

Brentford Rd. Junc.

LM SO

LM

SO

LM

Kew East Junc.

Gunnersbury

L.T. Acton Works

New Kew Junc.

Kew Bridge

Turnham Green

SO

LT

Hammersmith

P/D

P/D

Kew Gardens

Chiswick

Barnes Bridge

Barnes Bridge

D

Hounslow

Richmond

North Sheen

Mortlake

Barnes Junc.

Barnes

Putney

C

21

B

0   1   2 m.

0   1   2   3 km.

(1:70,000)

1

2

B	BAKERLOO	M	METROPOLITAN
C	CENTRAL	M(EL)	METROPOLITAN (East London)
O	CIRCLE	N	NORTHERN
D	DISTRICT	P	PICCADILLY
J	JUBILEE	V	VICTORIA

20

a) *Belsize Fast Tun. (1m 11yd.)*
b) *Belsize Slow Tun. (1m 107yd.)*
c) *Smithfield Tun.*
d) *Engine Shed Junc.*
e) *Camden Rd. E. Junc.*
f) *S. Tottenham W. Junc.*
g) *S. Tottenham E. Junc.*
h) *Tottenham S. Junc.*
j) *Gasworks Tun.*
k) *Camden Rd. Junc.*

l) *Blackfriars Junc.*
m) *Metropolitan Junc.*
n) *Storey St. Junc.*
p) *Borough Market Junc.*
q) *Freight Terminal Junc.*
r) *Dock Junc.*
s) *Tottenham N. Cve. No. 1 Tun.*
t) *Tottenham N. Cve. No. 2 Tun.*
u) *Tottenham N. Cve. No. 3 Tun.*

GREATER LONDON

1) St. Paul's
2) Mansion House
3) Monument
4) Aldgate
5) Temple
6) Embankment
7) Piccadilly Circus
8) Warren Street
9) West Hampstead
10) Emu Depot
11) Stewarts Lane –
    RMC Stone Term.

(Broad St. is
proposed for
closure –
service to
be diverted
via new curve
at Hackney to
Liverpool St.)

(SEE INSET PAGE 22)

KING'S CROSS

LONDON BRIDGE

VICTORIA

EUSTON

WEST HAMPSTEAD

20
17

21

B	BAKERLOO	M	METROPOLITAN
C	CENTRAL	M(EL)	METROPOLITAN (East London)
O	CIRCLE	N	NORTHERN
D	DISTRICT	P	PICCADILLY
J	JUBILEE	V	VICTORIA

0 ___ 1 ___ 2 m.
0 ___ 1 ___ 2 ___ 3 km.

(1:70,000)

Blackhorse Rd.
Wood St.
Barkingside

St. James Street
Walthamstow Central
Walthamstow Queens Road

C

Snaresbrook
Newbury Park

V V

Copper Mill Junc.

(Copper Mill Junc. to Stratford is proposed for closure to passengers)

Leyton Midland Road

Wanstead
Redbridge
Gants Hill

C

Clapton Junc.

Lea Bridge

Leytonstone

Leytonstone High Rd.

IL

Clapton Tun.

Clapton

TEMPLE MILLS YARD

Leyton P.W. Yard

Leyton

Ilford

C.S.

Queens Road Tun.

BREL

Wanstead Park

Forest Gate Junc.

Manor Park

C.S.

A

Hackney Downs N. Junc.

Hackney Downs
Homerton (Proposed)

Hackney Wick

Stratford High Meads Junc.

SR

Loughton Branch Junc. Sth.

Coal Depot – Fraser

Woodgrange Park

Lea Junc.

SF

Forest Gate

Woodgrange Park Junc.

EM

Barking Stn. Junc.

Hackney Central (Proposed curve)

LIFT

g

T

C.S.

Maryland

East Ham

M/D

Barking

London Fields

h

a c d

Stratford

Upton Park

Barking C.S.

D

TF

b

& T Depot

Barking Tilbury Line Junc. West

Cambridge Heath

Thornton Fields C.S.

Stratford Market Goods

Plaistow

Barking Tilbury Line Junc. East

Rugby Cem. Term.

Carless

Bethnal Green

C

Mile End–Tarmac Stone Term.

Bow Goods

TO

Pudding Mill Lane

Steetley Chem. Wks.

West Ham

a) Carpenters Rd. N. Junc.
b) Carpenters Rd. S. Junc.
c) Stratford Western Junc.
d) Stratford Southern Junc.
e) Charlton Junc.
f) South Bermondsey Junc.
g) Channelsea S. Junc.
h) Channelsea N. Junc.

Bethnal Green E. Junc.

Bow Rd.

Bow Rd.

M/D

Bethnal Green

M/D

Mile End

Devons Road

Bromley-by-Bow

Abbey Mills Junc.

32

Stepney Green

Canning Town

Whitechapel

Fawe St.

West Ham –Cohens Scrapyard

M(EL)

Stepney East

Limehouse

East India Dock Road

Custom House Victoria Dock

B

Shadwell

West Ferry Road

North Quay

Poplar

Bow Creek (Thames Wharf) –Coutinho Steel Term.

Silvertown Tun.

Wapping

Canary Wharf

Silvertown

North Woolwich

Rotherhithe

South Quay

Glengall Grove

Scrapyard – Ward Ferrous Metals

M(EL)

Millwall Park

(Proposed L.T. Light Rapid Transit System)

Angerstein Wharf

Foster Yeoman Stone Term.

Dock St. St. Tun.

Coleman St. Tun.

(Woolwich Free Ferry)

Southwark Park Junc.

Surrey Docks

Island Gardens

Thames Metal (Scrapyard)

Marcon RMC Stone Term.

Mount St. Tun.

Calderwood St. Tun.
Cross St. Tun. Goods

Plumstead

Surrey Canal Junc.

North Kent East Junc.

Westcombe Park

Charlton

Woolwich Dockyard

George IV Tun.

Woolwich Arsenal

C.S.

South Bermondsey

L.T. Depot

Greenwich College Tun.

CCE Works

Charlton Tun.

Primrose Hill

Camden Road Junc.

New Cross Gate C.S.

St. James Sdgs.

Deptford

Maze Hill

Angerstein Junc.

e

Primrose Hill Tuns.

Camden Juncs.

N N

Camden Road

Queens Road (Peckham)

New Cross Gate

New Cross

Greenwich

Tanners Hill Junc.

Blackheath Tunnel

Camden Carriage Sidings

Up Empty Carriage Line Tun.

Camden Town

Morn. Cres.

Nunhead

Lewisham Vale Junc.

St. John's

Lewisham

Blackheath Junc.

Kidbrooke Tun.

Park St. Tuns.

Up Empty Carriage Shed

Nunhead Junc.

Brockley

Parks Bridge Junc.

Blackheath

Kidbrooke

(INSET FROM MAP 21)
(1:35,000)

Down Empty Carriage Shed

(TO EUSTON)

EN

Ladywell Junc.

Courthill Loop Junc. North

Courthill Loop Junc. South

(To be moved East)
Eltham Well Hall

Falconwood

C

Ladywell

Eltham Park (To close)

22

1

2

0   1   2 m.
(1:70,000)
0   1   2   3 km.

B   BAKERLOO   M   METROPOLITAN
C   CENTRAL   M(EL) METROPOLITAN (East London)
O   CIRCLE   N   NORTHERN
D   DISTRICT   P   PICCADILLY
J   JUBILEE   V   VICTORIA

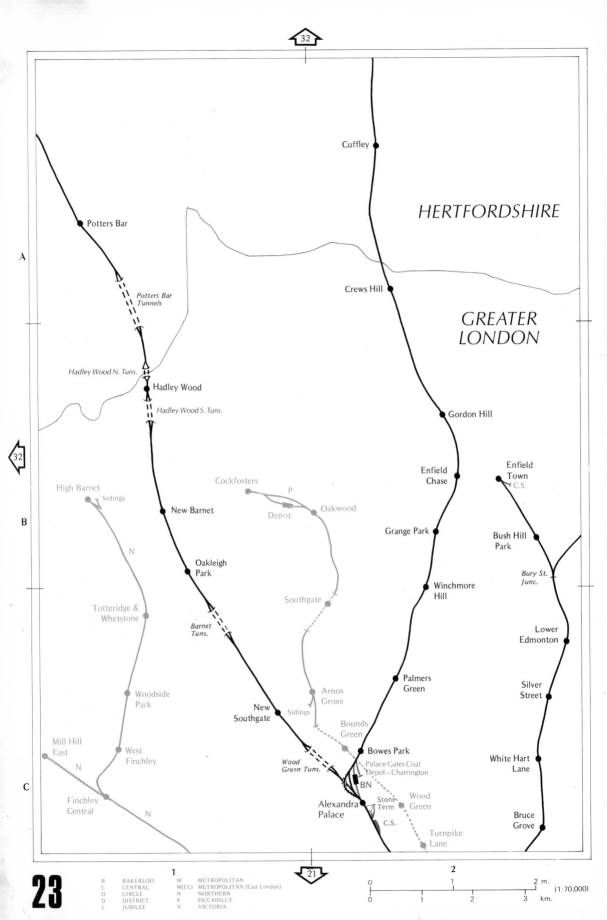

Cuffley

HERTFORDSHIRE

Potters Bar

A

Potters Bar Tunnels

Crews Hill

GREATER LONDON

Hadley Wood N. Tuns.

Hadley Wood

Hadley Wood S. Tuns.

Gordon Hill

Enfield Chase

Enfield Town
C.S.

Cockfosters

P

High Barnet

Sidings

Oakwood

New Barnet

Depot

Grange Park

Bush Hill Park

B

N

Bury St. Junc.

Oakleigh Park

Southgate

Winchmore Hill

Totteridge & Whetstone

Barnet Tuns.

Lower Edmonton

Woodside Park

Arnos Grove

Palmers Green

Silver Street

Mill Hill East

New Southgate

Sidings

Bounds Green

West Finchley

N

Wood Green Tuns.

Bowes Park

White Hart Lane

Palace Gates Coal Depot – Charrington

C

Finchley Central

N

BN

Stone Term

Wood Green

Alexandra Palace

C.S.

Bruce Grove

Turnpike Lane

23

B	BAKERLOO	M	METROPOLITAN
C	CENTRAL	M(EL)	METROPOLITAN (East London)
O	CIRCLE	N	NORTHERN
D	DISTRICT	P	PICCADILLY
J	JUBILEE	V	VICTORIA

1

2

0   1   2 m.
(1:70,000)
0   1   2   3 km.

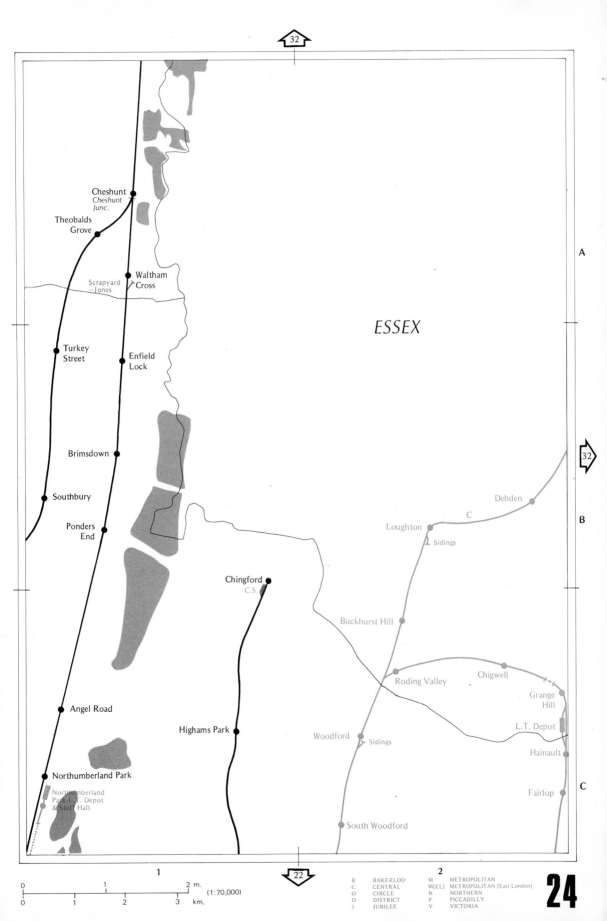

Cheshunt
Cheshunt Junc.

Theobalds
Grove

Scrapyard
—Jones

Waltham
Cross

ESSEX

A

Turkey
Street

Enfield
Lock

Brimsdown

Southbury

Ponders
End

Debden

C

Loughton

⊥ Sidings

B

32

Chingford
C.S.

Buckhurst Hill

Roding Valley

Chigwell

Grange
Hill

L.T. Depot

Angel Road

Highams Park

Woodford

⊥ Sidings

Hainault

C

Fairlop

Northumberland Park

Northumberland
Park L.T. Depot
& Staff Halt

South Woodford

2

B	BAKERLOO	M	METROPOLITAN
C	CENTRAL	M(EL)	METROPOLITAN (East London)
C	CIRCLE	N	NORTHERN
D	DISTRICT	P	PICCADILLY
J	JUBILEE	V	VICTORIA

0   1   2 m.
|___|___|___|___|___| (1:70,000)
0   1   2   3 km.

24

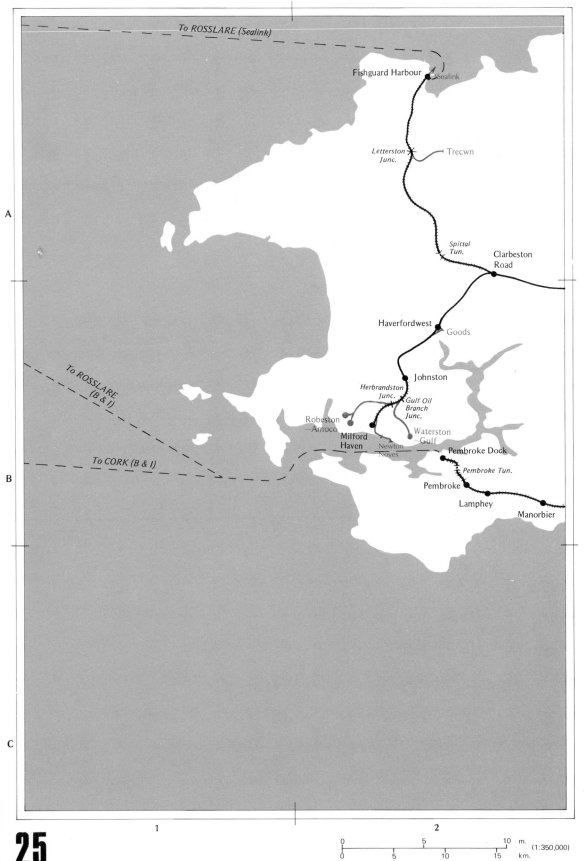

To ROSSLARE (Sealink)

Fishguard Harbour
Sealink

Letterston
Junc.
Trecwn

Spittal
Tun.
Clarbeston
Road

Haverfordwest
Goods

Johnston

Herbrandston
Junc.
Gulf Oil
Branch
Junc.

To ROSSLARE
(B & I)

Robeston
—Amoco
Waterston
—Gulf
Milford
Haven
Newton
Noyes
Pembroke Dock

To CORK (B & I)

Pembroke Tun.

Pembroke
Lamphey
Manorbier

25

0   5   10   m.
0   5   10   15   km.
(1:350,000)

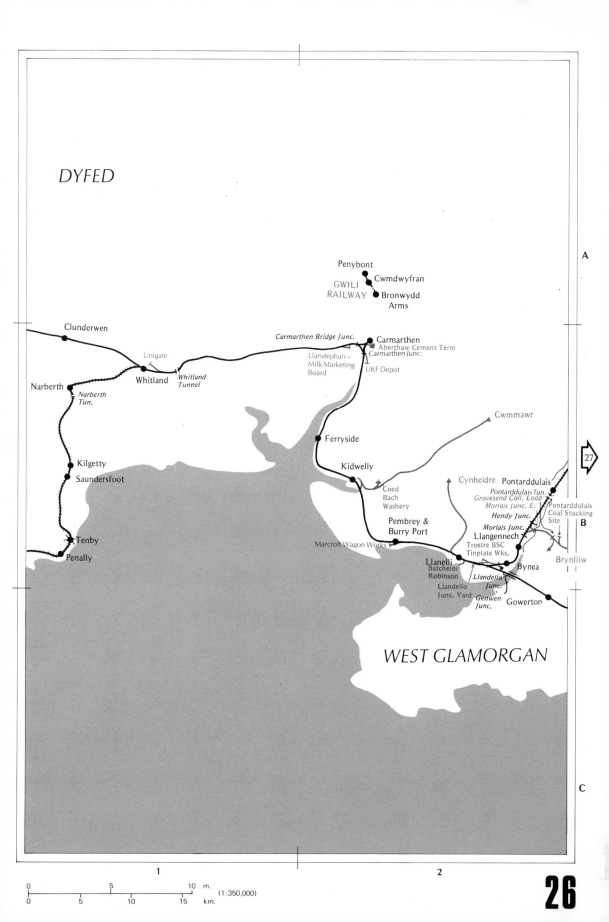

DYFED

Penybont
GWILI · Cwmdwyfran
RAILWAY ● Bronwydd
Arms

Clunderwen

Carmarthen Bridge Junc. Carmarthen
Aberthaw Cement Term
Unigate Llanstephan— *Carmarthen Junc.*
Milk Marketing
Whitland *Whitland* Board
Tunnel UKF Depot
Narberth
Narberth
Tun. Cwmmawr

Ferryside

Kilgetty Kidwelly
Saundersfoot Cynheidre Pontarddulais
Coed *Pontarddulais Tun.*
Bach *Grovesend Coll. Loop*
Washery *Morlais Junc. E.* Pontarddulais
Hendy Junc. Coal Stocking
Pembrey & Site
Burry Port *Morlais Junc.*
Tenby Llangennech
Penally Marcroft Wagon Works Trostre BSC
Tinplate Wks. Brynlliw
Bynea
Llanelli
Batchelor
Robinson *Llandeilo*
Llandeilo *Junc.*
Junc. Yard *Genwen* Gowerton
Junc.

WEST GLAMORGAN

27

A

B

C

1 2

0   5   10 m.
                        (1:350,000)
0   5   10   15 km.

26

DYFED

POWYS

Llangammarch

Llanwrtyd

Sugar Loaf Tun. (Summit)

Cynghordy

Llandovery

Llanwrda

Llangadog

A

1) Pontlottyn
2) Merthyr Vale
3) Quaker's Yard
4) Mountain Ash – NCB Workshops
5) Danygraig FLT
6) Port Tennant – Railcar Services
7) Swansea Burrows Sidings
8) Gower Chemicals
9) Penallta Junc. Tip – NCB
10) Coal Stocking Site
a) Jersey Marine North Junc.
b) Dynevor Junc.
c) Jersey Marine South Junc.

Llandeilo

Ffairfach

Llandybie

Ammanford

26

Betws Drift
Pantyffynnon
Wernos Washery

Gwaun-Cae-Gurwen

Cwmgorse Branch Junc.

Onllwyn

BRECON MOUNTAIN RAILWAY (2 ft. gauge)

Pontsticill

Penderyn – ARC

MID GLAMORGAN

Pant

Rhymney

1

Abernant

Aberpergwm

Hirwaun

Merthyr Tydfil

Cwm Bargoed Opencast

B

Penllergaer Tun.

Llangyfelach Tun. (1m 193yds.)

BSC Velindre Tinplate Works

Clydach on Tawe–Inco Nickel Works

Steel Supply – Coal Term.

Blaenant

WEST GLAMORGAN

Tower

Aberdare
Aberdare*

Pentre-bach

Troed-y-rhiw

Merthyr Vale

Taff Merthyr & Trelewis Drift Deep Navigation

Llangyfelach

Felin Fran Tip

Felin Fran

Landore Junc.

Lon Las Tun.

Neath & Brecon Junc.

Neath

Abercwmboi Phurnacite Plant

Treherbert

C.S.

Maerdy

Mountain Ash*

Black Lion

2

Nelson & Llancaiach

9

Cockett Tun.

Swansea Loop Juncs.

LE
WE

Llandarcy

C

a b

North British Maritime Shipping

Court Sart Junc.

Briton Ferry Yard

Treorchy

Ystrad Rhondda

Penrhiwceiber (Penrikyber)

4

3

C.S.

6 8–BP

7

5

Ford Wks.

Maesteg Washery

Garw Washery

Llynfi Junc.

Llwynypia

Tonypandy

Lady Windsor

Abercynon

Stormstown Junc.

10

Swansea

Swansea Eastern Coal Depot

Swansea Docks–ABP

Baglan Bay BP Chems.

St. Johns

Cwmdu

Dinas

Porth

Trehafod

BSC Ore Terminal
BSC – Abbey & Margam Wks.

MARGAM YARD

Port Talbot Coal Depot

PORT TALBOT

Ogmore Vale Washery

Pontypridd

Trefforest

NCB Coke Wks.

Nantgarw

NCB Coke Wks.

Margam Middle Junc.
Margam Moors Junc.
Mill Pit

Tondu Middle Junc.

Cwm

Trefforest Estate

MG

Water St. Junc.

Newlands Junc.

Bridgend Llynfi Junc.

Bridgend E. Junc.

Llanharan

Llantrisant

Llantrisant Ely Valley Junc.

Bridgend

Bridgend–Ford Works

C

SOUTH GLAMORGAN

1

0   5   10 m.
(1:350,000)
0   5   10   15 km.

2

27

SOUTH GLAMORGAN

HEREFORD & WORCESTER

GWENT

Llandaf

Gabalfa Coal Dep.
BR—Maindy Wagon Works
Powell Duffryn Maindy Wagon Wks.

CARDIFF
Cathays

Roath Goods

Pengam FLT

Scrap
Pengam

Works—Painter
Henry Wiggins
Shelwick Junc.
Colas Bitumen
Moorfields
Bulmers Works
Hereford HF

(Shelwick–Ledbury to be singled)

Leckwith Juncs.
Canton–Isis Link
CF
Cardiff Queen St.
Cardiff Central

ASW–Tremorfa

Kennis & Brown

NEWPORT

Maindee W. Junc.
Maindee N. Junc.
Maindee CCE Depot
Maindee E. Junc.

Ninian Park*
Radyr Branch Junc.
Penarth Curve N. Junc.
Penarth Curve South Junc.
(ASW=Allied Steel & Wire)
Grangetown

Tidal Yard
Long Dyke Junc.
ASW–Rod Mill
ASW–Castle
Roath Dock
Gulf
Queen Alex. Dock
Texaco

Cardiff Bute Rd.
Taff Wagon Repairs
Ferry Road–Howards Oil

Newport
Godfrey Rd. Sdgs.
Gwent Coal Depot
C & W

East Usk Yard
East Usk Junc.

Hillfield Tun.
Gaer Junc.
Maesglas CCE Tip
b
Park Junc.
Ebbw Junc.
BSC Whitehead
Dock St. Sdgs.

Braithwaites Steel
Monsanto Chem. Wks.

A

Cogan Junc.
Cogan
Cogan Tun.
Dingle Road
Penarth

Alexandra Dock Junc. Yards
Docks
Alphasteel Works

a) Alexandra Dock Junc
b) Waterloo Loop Junc.

Uskmouth

(1 : 90,000)

Abergavenny

BSC Ebbw Vale (Tinplate Wks.)
PONTYPOOL & BLAENAVON RAILWAY SOC.

Rose Heyworth
Marine

Glascoed
Little Mill Junc.

1) Birchgrove
2) Rhiwbina
3) Whitchurch (S. Glam.)
4) Coryton
5) Llandaf
6) Radyr Yard, P.W. Depot
7) Powell Duffryn Wagon Works
8) Shirehampton – Hallam Oil
9) Norsk Hydro Works
10) ISC Chemicals
11) Isis Link Depot
12) Stoke Gifford CCE Tip
13) Stoke Gifford Yard

GLOS.

B

Tir-phil
Aberbeeg
Oakdale

Pontypool

Lydney

Brithdir
Bargoed
Gilfach Fargoed
Pengam
Penalita
Hengoed
Penar Tun.
Newbridge Coal Depot
Celynen South

BSC - Panteg Wks.
Panteg–Fibreglass
Cwmbran (proposed)

Tidenham
Wye Valley Junc.
Chepstow
Fairfield–Mabey Engineering Wks.

Ystrad Mynach N. Junc.
Ystrad Mynach
S. Junc.
Lime Kiln Junc.

Llanbradach
Bedwas
Machen

Newport

GWENT

AVON

Bedwas Coke Wks.—British Benzole
Caerphilly

Aber

Caerphilly Tun.
(1 m. 173 yds.)
Cefn-onn
Llanishen

Iron Ore Term.
Coal Term.
BSC Llanwern

Caerwent
Severn Tunnel Junction
Car Term
Sudbrook
Caldicot
Ashton Paper Mill
ST SEVERN TUNNEL JUNCTION YARD

Severn Tunnel (4m 628yds.)
Pilning
Patchway Tunnels
Stoke Gifford Junc.

Taffs Well
Radyr
4 3 2 1
5
6
Heath High Level
Heath Low Level

(SEE INSET ABOVE RIGHT)

Severn Beach
Hallen Marsh Junc.
St. Andrew's Road
ICI Severnside
Charlton Tun.
Patchway
Bristol Parkway

C

CARDIFF Queen St. Cen.
Bute Rd.
Grangetown
(SEE INSET ABOVE LEFT)

Avonmouth
Rowntree Mackintosh
9
10
11
Shirehampton
Sea Mills
8
Clifton Down

N. Filton Plat.*
12 13
Filton
Coal Depot – Western Fuels
Stapleton Road

1

2

SEE INSET PAGE 8

28

0   5   10 m.
0   5   10   15 km.
(1:350,000)

29

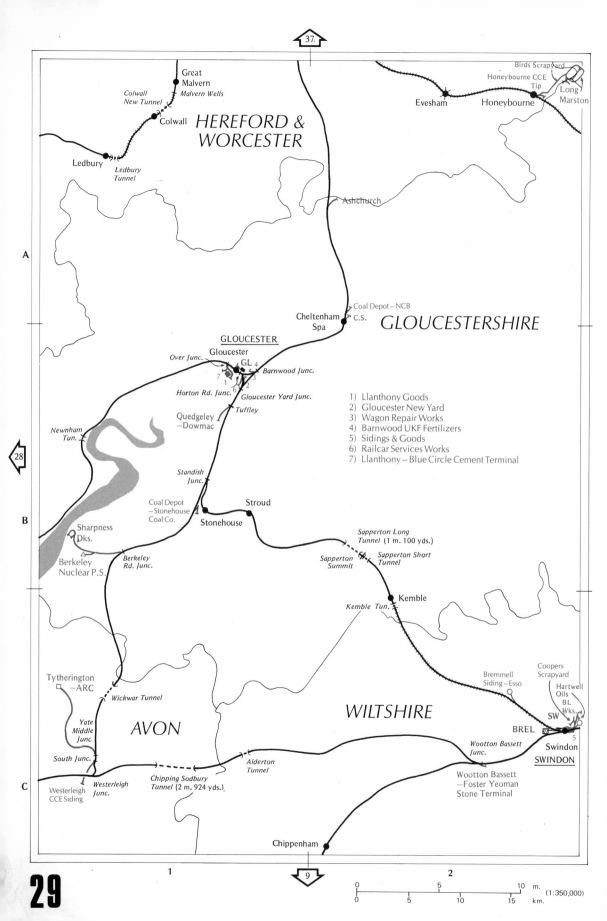

Birds Scrapyard
Honeybourne CCE Tip
Long Marston

Great Malvern
Malvern Wells
Colwall New Tunnel
Colwall

Evesham
Honeybourne

HEREFORD & WORCESTER

Ledbury
Ledbury Tunnel

Ashchurch

Coal Depot – NCB
Cheltenham Spa
C.S.

GLOUCESTERSHIRE

GLOUCESTER
Gloucester
GL
Over Junc.
Barnwood Junc.
7 1 6
Horton Rd. Junc.
3
2
Gloucester Yard Junc.
Tuffley
Quedgeley –Dowmac

1) Llanthony Goods
2) Gloucester New Yard
3) Wagon Repair Works
4) Barnwood UKF Fertilizers
5) Sidings & Goods
6) Railcar Services Works
7) Llanthony – Blue Circle Cement Terminal

Newnham Tun.

Standish Junc.

Coal Depot –Stonehouse Coal Co.
Stonehouse

Stroud

Sapperton Long Tunnel (1 m. 100 yds.)

Sharpness Dks.

Sapperton Summit
Sapperton Short Tunnel

Berkeley Nuclear P.S.
Berkeley Rd. Junc.

Kemble
Kemble Tun.

Coopers Scrapyard

Bremmell Siding – Esso

Tytherington –ARC
Wickwar Tunnel

WILTSHIRE

Hartwell Oils
BL Wks.

Yate Middle Junc.

AVON

SW
BREL

South Junc.

Wootton Bassett Junc.

Swindon
SWINDON
5

Westerleigh CCE Siding
Westerleigh Junc.
Chipping Sodbury Tunnel (2 m. 924 yds.)
Alderton Tunnel

Wootton Bassett –Foster Yeoman Stone Terminal

Chippenham

0   5   10 m.
(1:350,000)
0   5   10   15 km.

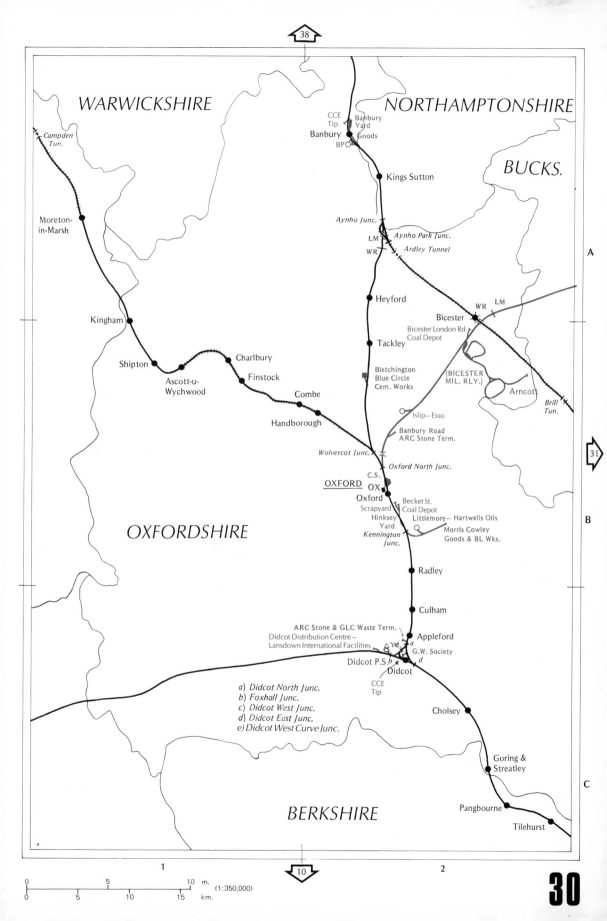

WARWICKSHIRE

NORTHAMPTONSHIRE

BUCKS.

Campden Tun.

CCE
Tip

Banbury Yard

Banbury
Goods
BPO

Kings Sutton

Moreton-
in-Marsh

Aynho Junc.

LM   *Aynho Park Junc.*
WR   *Ardley Tunnel*

A

Kingham

Heyford

WR   LM

Bicester

Bicester London Rd
Coal Depot

Shipton

Charlbury

Tackley

Finstock

Ascott-u-
Wychwood

(BICESTER
MIL. RLY.)

Arncott

Combe

Bletchington
Blue Circle
Cem. Works

*Brill
Tun.*

Handborough

Islip – Esso

Banbury Road
ARC Stone Term.

Wolvercot Junc.

31

Oxford North Junc.

C.S.

OXFORD   OX

OXFORDSHIRE

Oxford

Scrapyard

Becket St.
Coal Depot

Littlemore – Hartwells Oils

B

Hinksey
Yard

*Kennington
Junc.*

Morris Cowley
Goods & BL Wks.

Radley

Culham

ARC Stone & GLC Waste Term.

Appleford

Didcot Distribution Centre –
Lansdown International Facilities

Y   *a*

G.W. Society

Didcot P.S.

b
d

Didcot

CCE
Tip

a) *Didcot North Junc.*
b) *Foxhall Junc.*
c) *Didcot West Junc.*
d) *Didcot East Junc.*
e) *Didcot West Curve Junc.*

Cholsey

Goring &
Streatley

C

BERKSHIRE

Pangbourne

Tilehurst

1

10

2

0   5   10 m.
0   5   10   15 km.   (1:350,000)

30

BEDFORDSHIRE

Wolverton
BREL
Dunlop & Ranken
ARC Stone Terminal
Milton Keynes
Denbigh Hall Junc.
BLETCHLEY C.S.
Bletchley BY
Bletchley Stone Term.
Fenny Stratford
Fenny Stratford Flyover Junc.
Bow Brickhill
Woburn Sands
Ridgmont
Aspley Guise

Kempston Hardwick
Forders Sidings
London Brick Wks.
Stewartby
Millbrook
Lidlington
CCE Tip
Ampthill Tuns.
Elstow—Redland Stone Terminal
Biggleswade
Whittals

Flitwick
Harlington
Leagrave
Stone Term. & Scrapyard
Coal Depot (Limbury Rd.)
Goods & Car Term.
Luton
Cambridge Junc.
HI Hitchin
P.W. Yard

1) Headstone Lane
2) Harrow & Wealdstone
3) Croxley Green
4) Watford West
5) Mill Hill Broadway
6) Watford High Street
7) Watford Stadium*

A

Claydon L.N.E. Junc.
Calvert – GLC Waste Terminal
Grendon Underwood Junc.
Quainton Road*
Akeman Street—UKF Fertilizers

Linslade Tuns.
Leighton Buzzard
LEIGHTON BUZZARD N.G. RLY. (2' 0")
Blue Circle Cem. Term.
BP
Dunstable
WHIPSNADE & UMFOLOZI RLY. (2' 6")

Cheddington

Thame—BP

Coal Depot
Aylesbury
Stoke Mandeville
Little Kimble
Wendover
Monks Risborough
Princes Risborough
Chinnor Cem. Wks.
Saunderton

30

B

Tring
Tring Summit
Northchurch Tuns.
Berkhamsted
Hemel Hempstead
Apsley
King's Langley
WATFORD JUNC.
Watford Fast Tun. (1m 55yds)
Chesham
M
Great Missenden
Chalfont & Latimer
LM LT
Amersham
Chorley Wood
Watford
Croxley C.S. M
M

HERTFORDSHIRE

Harpenden

Parcels
Watford Slow Tun. (1m 230yds)
Park St.
St. Albans Abbey
St. Albans City
Bricket Wood
Coal Dep.
Garston
Watford North
CCE
WJ
Watford Junc.
Redland Aggr. Stone Term
Radlett
Elstree Tuns.
Elstree

BUCKINGHAMSHIRE

High Wycombe
Beaconsfield
Whitehouse Tun.
Seer Green
Rickmansworth
Moor Park
Northwood
Northwood Hills
Gerrards Cross
Denham Golf Club
Denham
West Ruislip

8) Watford Cardiff Road P.S.
9) Reading S. & T. Works
10) Queensbury
11) Kingsbury
12) Burnt Oak
13) Colindale
14) Canons Park

Bushey
Carpenders Park
Hatch End
Stanmore
J C.S.
14
2 10
Edgware
12 N
M 11
5
Pinner
Rayners Lane
P
1
(See Map 20)

OXON

Marlow
Bourne End
Cookham
Furze Platt
Henley-on-Thames
Shiplake
Wargrave

BERKSHIRE

Taplow
Maidenhead
Bruce Bishop
Burnham
Slough Estates
SLOUGH
Slough
Langley Total
Langley
Iver
West Drayton
Datchet

Uxbridge
GREATER LONDON

READING
RG
Earley (disused)
SO Reading Spur Junc.
Reading 9 Gds.
a
Reading West C.S.
b
WR

Twyford

WINDSOR & ETON Central

Langley Riverside
Sunnymeads
Wraysbury

Heathrow Term. 4
(See Map 19)
Heathrow Term. 1, 2 & 3
P

Ealing Bdy.

Feltham
Richmond

C

a) Reading West Junc.
b) Oxford Road Junc.
c) Reading New Junc.

1

B BAKERLOO
C CENTRAL
C CIRCLE
D DISTRICT
J JUBILEE

M METROPOLITAN
M(EL) METROPOLITAN (East London)
N NORTHERN
P PICCADILLY
V VICTORIA

11
2
15
16

0   5   10 m.
0   5   10   15 km.
(1:350,000)

A 30 B

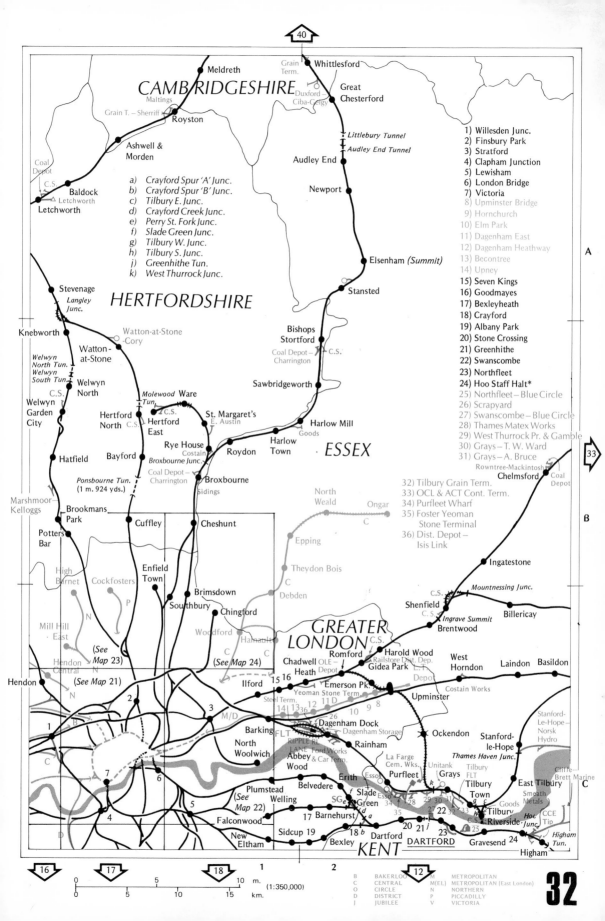

CAMBRIDGESHIRE

Meldreth
Whittlesford
Grain Term.
Great Chesterford
Duxford Ciba-Geigy
Maltings
Grain T. – Sherriff
Royston
Ashwell & Morden
Littlebury Tunnel
Audley End Tunnel
Audley End
Coal Depot
C.S.
Baldock
Letchworth
Newport

Letchworth

a) Crayford Spur 'A' Junc.
b) Crayford Spur 'B' Junc.
c) Tilbury E. Junc.
d) Crayford Creek Junc.
e) Perry St. Fork Junc.
f) Slade Green Junc.
g) Tilbury W. Junc.
h) Tilbury S. Junc.
j) Greenhithe Tun.
k) West Thurrock Junc.

Elsenham *(Summit)*

Stevenage
Langley Junc.
HERTFORDSHIRE
Stansted

Knebworth

Bishops Stortford
Coal Depot – Charrington C.S.

Welwyn North Tun.
Welwyn South Tun.
C.S.
Welwyn Garden City
Welwyn North
Watton-at-Stone -Cory
Watton-at-Stone
Molewood Tun.
Ware
C.S.
Hertford North C.S.
Hertford East
St. Margaret's
E. Austin
Sawbridgeworth

Hatfield
Bayford
Rye House
Costain
Broxbourne Junc.
Roydon
Harlow Town
Harlow Mill
Goods
ESSEX

Ponsbourne Tun. (1 m. 924 yds.)
Coal Depot – Charrington
Broxbourne
Sidings

Marshmoor-Kelloggs
Brookmans Park
Cuffley
Cheshunt
North Weald
Ongar
C

Potters Bar
Epping

High Barnet
Cockfosters
P
Enfield Town
Theydon Bois
C
Ingatestone

Mill Hill East
N
Southbury
Brimsdown
Chingford
Debden
C.S.
Mountnessing Junc.
Shenfield
C.S.
Billericay
Ingrave Summit
Brentwood

(See Map 23)
N
Hendon Central
(See Map 21)
N
(See Map 24)
C
C
Woodford
C
Hainault
C
GREATER LONDON
C.S.
Romford
Harold Wood
West Horndon
Laindon
Basildon

Hendon
N
Chadwell Heath
OLE Depot
Gidea Park
Upminster
Costain Works
Stanford-Le-Hope- Norsk Hydro

1) Willesden Junc.
2) Finsbury Park
3) Stratford
4) Clapham Junction
5) Lewisham
6) London Bridge
7) Victoria
8) Upminster Bridge
9) Hornchurch
10) Elm Park
11) Dagenham East
12) Dagenham Heathway
13) Becontree
14) Upney
15) Seven Kings
16) Goodmayes
17) Bexleyheath
18) Crayford
19) Albany Park
20) Stone Crossing
21) Greenhithe
22) Swanscombe
23) Northfleet
24) Hoo Staff Halt*
25) Northfleet – Blue Circle
26) Scrapyard
27) Swanscombe – Blue Circle
28) Thames Matex Works
29) West Thurrock Pr. & Gamble
30) Grays – T. W. Ward
31) Grays – A. Bruce
Rowntree-Mackintosh
Chelmsford
Coal Depot

32) Tilbury Grain Term.
33) OCL & ACT Cont. Term.
34) Purfleet Wharf
35) Foster Yeoman Stone Terminal
36) Dist. Depot – Isis Link

Ilford
15 16
Emerson Pk.
Yeoman Stone Term.
11 D
L.T. Depot
Steel Term.
Barking
14 13 36
12
10 9 8
M/D
FLT
Dagenham Dock
RIPPLE RD.
N. Woolwich
North Woolwich
Ford Works & Car Term.
Dagenham Storage
Rainham
Ockendon
Stanford-le-Hope
Thames Haven Junc.

Abbey Wood
La Farge Cem. Wks.
Purfleet
Unitank
Grays
Tilbury FLT
East Tilbury
Cliffe-Brett Marine

Plumstead
Welling
Belvedere
Erith
Esso
k
Tilbury Town
Smeath Metals
CCE Tip

(See Map 22)
SG
Slade Green
Esso
Goods
Tilbury Riverside
Higham Tun.

Falconwood
f
d
a
34
28
Gravesend 24
Higham

New Eltham
Sidcup 19
Bexley
18 b
Dartford
DARTFORD
20 21
22
25
23

KENT

0   5   10 m.
0   5   10   15 km.
(1:350,000)

B BAKERLOO   M METROPOLITAN
C CENTRAL   M(EL) METROPOLITAN (East London)
C CIRCLE   N NORTHERN
D DISTRICT   P PICCADILLY
J JUBILEE   V VICTORIA

33

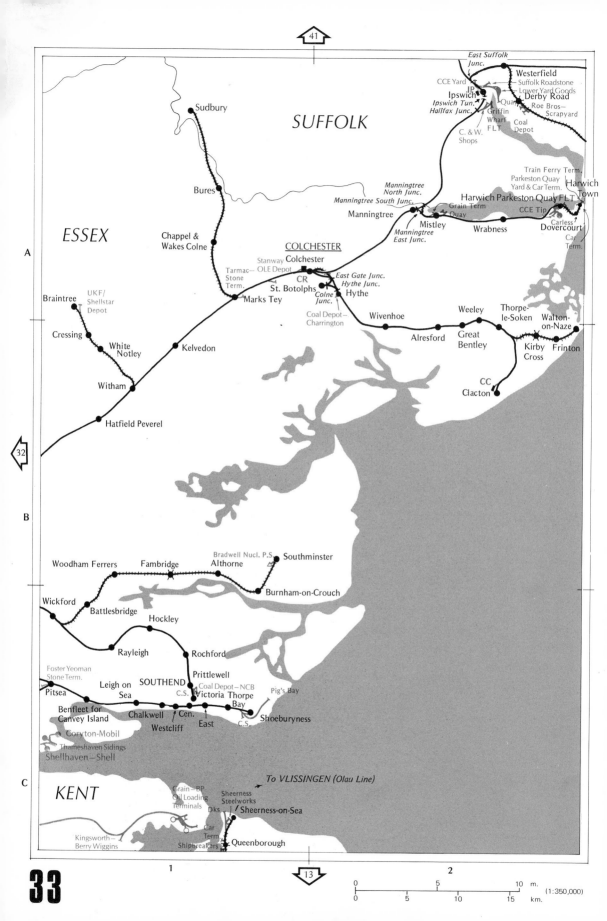

East Suffolk Junc.

Westerfield

CCE Yard — Suffolk Roadstone
IP — Lower Yard Goods
Ipswich — Derby Road
Ipswich Tun. — Quay — Roe Bros—
Halifax Junc. — Griffin — Scrapyard
Wharf — Coal
FLT — Depot
C. & W. — Train Ferry Term.
Shops — Parkeston Quay
— Yard & Car Term. — Harwich
Grain Term — Harwich Parkeston Quay FLT — Town
Quay — CCE Tip
Mistley — Carless
Manningtree North Junc. — Wrabness — Dovercourt
Manningtree — Car
North Junc. — Term.
Manningtree South Junc.
Manningtree
Manningtree
East Junc.

SUFFOLK

Sudbury

Bures

ESSEX

Chappel &
Wakes Colne

COLCHESTER
Stanway
OLE Depot — Colchester
Tarmac— — CR
Stone — St. Botolphs — East Gate Junc.
Term. — *Colne* — Hythe Junc.
Marks Tey — *Junc.* — Hythe
— Coal Depot—
— Charrington — Wivenhoe — Weeley — Thorpe-
Braintree — le-Soken — Walton-
UKF/ — Alresford — Great — on-Naze
Shellstar — Bentley — Kirby — Frinton
Depot — Cross
Cressing — CC
White — Clacton
Notley — Kelvedon

Witham

Hatfield Peverel

A

32

B

Woodham Ferrers — Fambridge — Althorne — Bradwell Nucl. P.S. — Southminster

Wickford — Burnham-on-Crouch

Battlesbridge

Hockley

Rayleigh — Rochford

Prittlewell
Foster Yeoman — Coal Depot—NCB — Pig's Bay
Stone Term. — Leigh on — SOUTHEND — Victoria — Thorpe
Pitsea — Sea — C.S. — Bay
Benfleet for — Chalkwell — Cen. — East — Shoeburyness
Canvey Island — Westcliff — C.S.
Coryton-Mobil
Thameshaven Sidings
Shellhaven—Shell

C

KENT

Grain—BP — To VLISSINGEN (Olau Line)
Oil Loading — Sheerness
Terminals — Steelworks
Dks — Sheerness-on-Sea

Kingsworth— — Car
Berry Wiggins — Term.
Shipbreakers — Queenborough

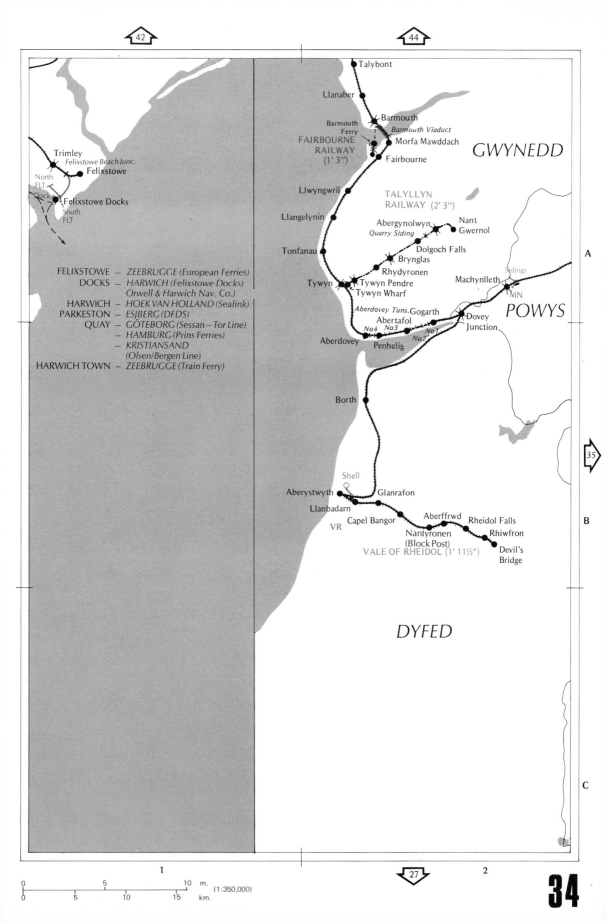

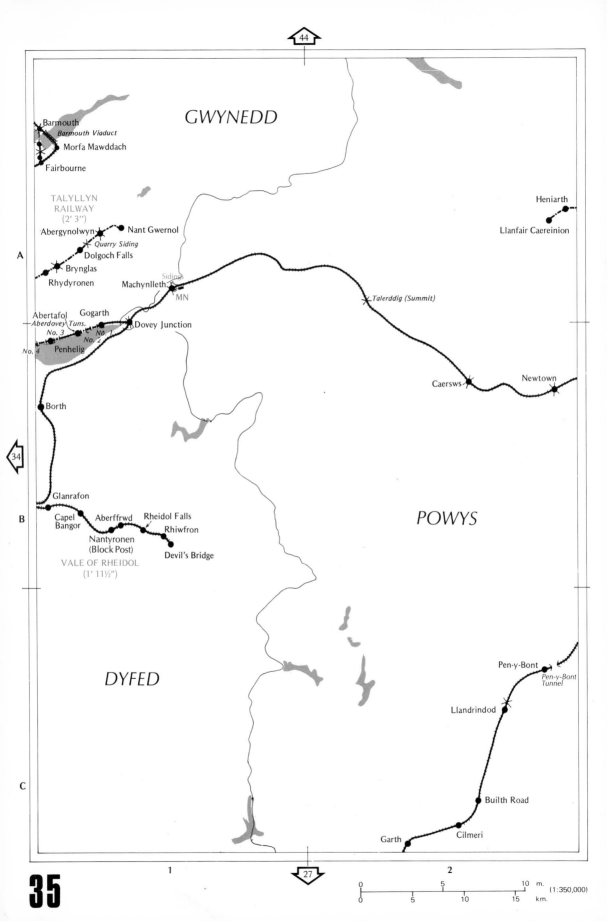

GWYNEDD

Barmouth
Barmouth Viaduct
Morfa Mawddach
Fairbourne

Heniarth

Llanfair Caereinion

TALYLLYN
RAILWAY
(2′ 3″)

Abergynolwyn · Nant Gwernol
Quarry Siding
A · Dolgoch Falls
Brynglas
Rhydyronen

Machynlleth
Sidings
MN

Talerddig (Summit)

Abertafol · Gogarth
Aberdovey Tuns.
No. 3 · No. 1
No. 2 · Dovey Junction
No. 4 · Penhelig

Caersws · Newtown

Borth

Glanrafon

POWYS

B
Capel · Aberffrwd · Rheidol Falls
Bangor · Rhiwfron
Nantyronen
(Block Post) · Devil's Bridge
VALE OF RHEIDOL
(1′ 11½″)

Pen-y-Bont
Pen-y-Bont Tunnel

Llandrindod

DYFED

C

Builth Road

Garth · Cilmeri

35

0   5   10   m. (1:350,000)
0   5   10   15   km.

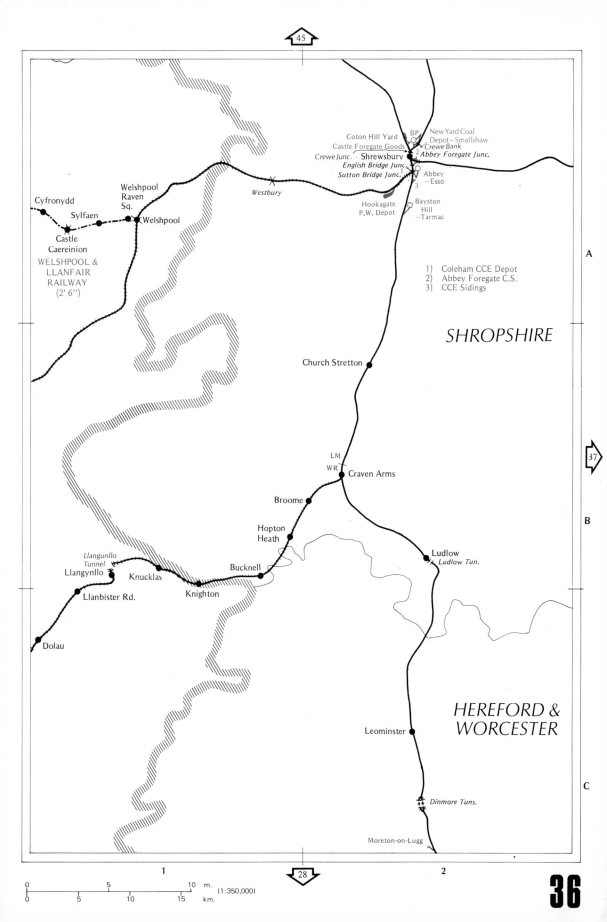

B.P.
Coton Hill Yard
Castle Foregate Goods
Crewe Junc.
Crewe Bank
New Yard Coal
Depot—Smallshaw
2
Abbey Foregate Junc.
Shrewsbury
English Bridge Junc.
Sutton Bridge Junc.
1
Abbey
—Esso
3
Westbury
Hookagate
P.W. Depot
Bayston
Hill
—Tarmac

Cyfronydd
Sylfaen
Welshpool
Raven
Sq.
Welshpool
Castle
Caereinion
WELSHPOOL &
LLANFAIR
RAILWAY
(2' 6")

1) Coleham CCE Depot
2) Abbey Foregate C.S.
3) CCE Sidings

SHROPSHIRE

Church Stretton

LM
WR
Craven Arms

Broome

Hopton
Heath

Ludlow
Ludlow Tun.

Llangunllo
Tunnel
Llangynllo
Knucklas
Bucknell

Llanbister Rd.
Knighton

Dolau

HEREFORD &
WORCESTER

Leominster

A

37

B

C

Dinmore Tuns.

Moreton-on-Lugg

1

28

2

| 0 | 5 | 10 | m. | (1:350,000) |
| 0 | 5 | 10 | 15 | km. |

36

STAFFORDSHIRE

Colwich Junc.

Shugborough Tun.

Rugeley North Junc.

Rugeley

Brereton Sidings

Rugeley

Lea Hall

Donnington

Stafford Junc.

Sidings

Penkridge

Littleton Coll. Sids.

Rowntree Mackintosh Penkridge

Littleton

CHASEWATER RAILWAY

Rom River Works

Lichfield Trent Valley

Lichfield T.V. Junc.

Mid Cannock Opencast

High Level Goods Loop Junc.

Lichfield City

Wellington Goods

Tunnel Cement Term.

Oakengates

Oakengates Tun.

Shifnal

Madeley Junc.

Cosford

Albrighton

Codsall

Bilbrook

Four Ashes – Synthetic Chemicals

Brownhills – Charringtons

Brownhills West

Essington Wood

Anglesea Sidings

Shenstone

SHROPSHIRE

Ironbridge

A

WEST MIDLANDS

Wolverhampton

Walsall

Blake Street

Butlers Lane

Four Oaks

SEVERN VALLEY RAILWAY

Bridgnorth

Eardington

Bescot

Sutton Coldfield

Wylde Green

Chester Rd.

Erdington

Coseley

Tipton

Dudley Port

Hamstead

Perry Barr

Gravelly Hill

36

Hampton Loade

Highley

Smethwick West

Rowley Regis

Oldbury

Langley Green

Witton

Aston

Stechford

Lea Hall

5

1 3

4

Cradley Heath

Lye

Old Hill
(SEE MAP 87)

Five Ways

2

7

6

Tyseley

Acocks Green

Stourbridge Town

University

(SEE MAP 88)

B

Arley

Foley Park Tun.

Stourbridge Junction

Hagley

Selly Oak

Bournville

Lifford West Junc.

King's Norton

Spring Road

Hall Green

Yardley Wood

Olton

Solihull

Northwood

Bewdley

Kidderminster

Blakedown

Northfield

East Junc.

Car Term.

BL Longbridge

Halesowen Junc.

Longbridge

Whitlock's End

Shirley

Widney Manor

Wythall

Earlswood

The Lakes

Wood End

Hartlebury

BL Cofton Hackett

Barnt Green

LM

WR

Blackwell Summit

Bromsgrove

Alvechurch

ARC Stone Term.

Redditch

Wood End Tun.

Danzey

Hallam Oil

HEREFORD & WORCESTER

Stoke Works Junc.

Henley-in-Arden

Wootton Wawen

Droitwich Spa

Coal Depot – Underwood

LM
WR

1) Birmingham New St.
2) Birmingham Moor St.
3) Duddeston
4) Adderley Park
5) Smethwick Rolfe St.
6) Small Heath
7) Bordesley

(Henley to Bearley Junc. is proposed for closure)

WORCESTER

Foregate Street

WS

Tunnel Junc.
CCE Sidings

Henwick

Yard

Shrub Hill

Metal Box Co.

Coal Depot

C

Malvern Link

Norton Junc.

Abbotswood Junc.

Pershore

37

1

2

0   5   10   m.

0   5   10   15   km.

(1:350,000)

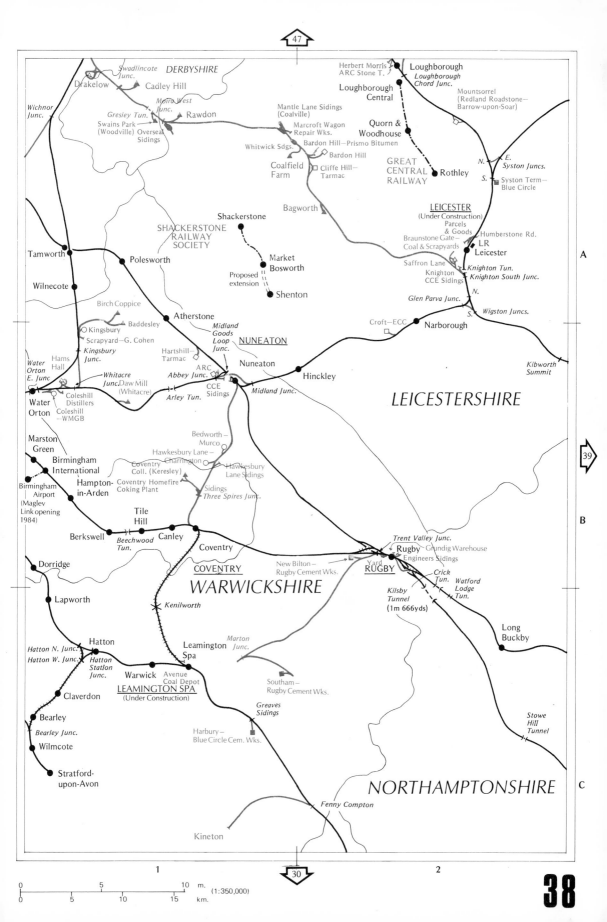

DERBYSHIRE

Swadlincote Junc.
Drakelow
Cadley Hill
Moira West Junc.
Wichnor Junc.
Gresley Tun.
Rawdon
Swains Park (Woodville) Overseal Sidings

Herbert Morris ARC Stone T.
Loughborough
Loughborough Chord Junc.
Loughborough Central
Mountsorrel (Redland Roadstone—Barrow-upon-Soar)

Mantle Lane Sidings (Coalville)
Marcroft Wagon Repair Wks.
Whitwick Sdgs.
Bardon Hill—Prismo Bitumen
Bardon Hill
Coalfield Farm
Cliffe Hill—Tarmac

Quorn & Woodhouse

Rothley

GREAT CENTRAL RAILWAY

N.
E. Syston Juncs.
S.
Syston Term—Blue Circle

Shackerstone
SHACKERSTONE RAILWAY SOCIETY
Bagworth

Tamworth
Polesworth
Market Bosworth
Proposed extension
Shenton

LEICESTER (Under Construction)
Parcels & Goods
Braunstone Gate—Coal & Scrapyards
Humberstone Rd.
LR Leicester
Saffron Lane
Knighton CCE Sidings
Knighton Tun.
Knighton South Junc.

Wilnecote

Birch Coppice
Baddesley
Kingsbury Scrapyard—G. Cohen
Kingsbury Junc.
Atherstone
Midland Goods Loop Junc.
Hartshill—Tarmac
NUNEATON
Nuneaton

Croft—ECC
Narborough

Glen Parva Junc.
N.
Wigston Juncs.
S.

LEICESTERSHIRE

Kibworth Summit

Water Orton E. Junc.
Hams Hall
Kingsbury
ARC Abbey Junc.
CCE Sidings
Whitacre Junc. Daw Mill (Whitacre)
Arley Tun.
Midland Junc.
Hinckley

Water Orton
Coleshill Distillers
Coleshill—WMGB

Marston Green
Birmingham International
Bedworth—Murco
Hawkesbury Lane—Charrington
Hawkesbury Lane Sidings
Hampton-in-Arden
Coventry Coll. (Keresley)
Coventry Homefire Coking Plant
Sidings
Three Spires Junc.

Birmingham Airport (Maglev Link opening 1984)

Tile Hill
Berkswell
Canley
Beechwood Tun.
Coventry

COVENTRY
WARWICKSHIRE

New Bilton—Rugby Cement Wks.
Yard
RUGBY
Trent Valley Junc.
Rugby
Grundig Warehouse
Engineers Sidings
Crick Tun.
Watford Lodge Tun.
Kilsby Tunnel (1m 666yds)

Long Buckby

Dorridge
Lapworth
Kenilworth

Hatton
Hatton N. Junc.
Hatton W. Junc.
Hatton Station Junc.
Leamington Spa
Marton Junc.

Warwick
Avenue Coal Depot
LEAMINGTON SPA (Under Construction)
Southam—Rugby Cement Wks.

Claverdon
Bearley
Bearley Junc.
Wilmcote
Stratford-upon-Avon

Greaves Sidings
Harbury—Blue Circle Cem. Wks.

Stowe Hill Tunnel

NORTHAMPTONSHIRE

Fenny Compton
Kineton

A

B

39

C

1   2

0   5   10 m. (1:350,000)
0 5 10 15 km.

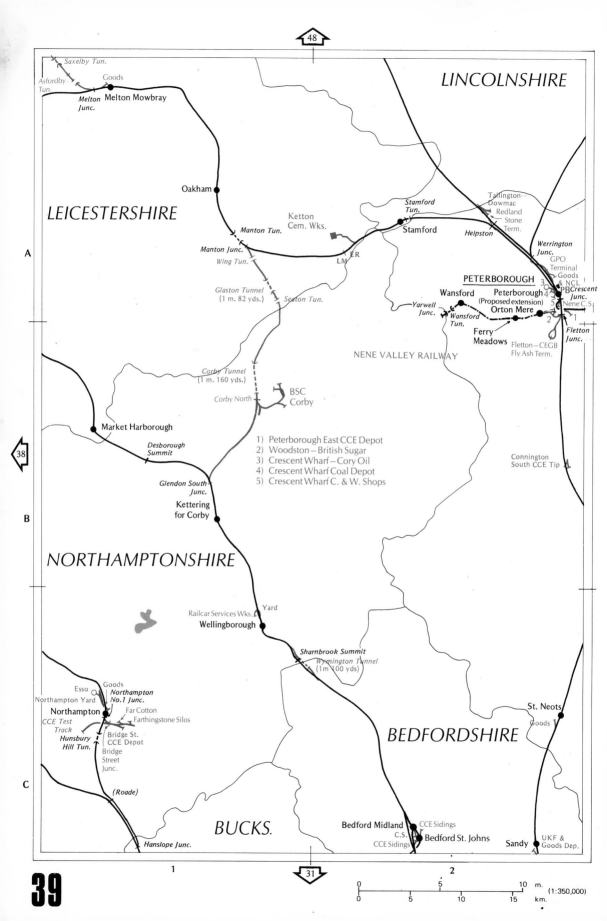

LINCOLNSHIRE

Saxelby Tun.

Asfordby Tun.

Goods

Melton Junc. Melton Mowbray

LEICESTERSHIRE

Oakham

Ketton Cem. Wks.

Stamford Tun.

Stamford

Tallington – Dowmac Redland Stone Term.

Helpston

Manton Tun.

Manton Junc.

ER

LM

Wing Tun.

A

Glaston Tunnel (1 m. 82 yds.)

Seaton Tun.

Werrington Junc.

GPO Terminal Goods & NCL

PETERBOROUGH

Wansford

Peterborough (Proposed extension)

Orton Mere

Yarwell Junc.

Wansford Tun.

3
4
PB Crescent Junc.
5 2 Nene C.S.
1

Ferry Meadows

NENE VALLEY RAILWAY

Fletton – CEGB Fly Ash Term.

Fletton Junc.

Corby Tunnel (1 m. 160 yds.)

Corby North

BSC Corby

Market Harborough

Desborough Summit

1) Peterborough East CCE Depot
2) Woodston – British Sugar
3) Crescent Wharf – Cory Oil
4) Crescent Wharf Coal Depot
5) Crescent Wharf C. & W. Shops

Connington South CCE Tip

Glendon South Junc.

Kettering for Corby

B

NORTHAMPTONSHIRE

Railcar Services Wks.

Yard

Wellingborough

Sharnbrook Summit

Wymington Tunnel (1m 100 yds)

St. Neots

Goods

BEDFORDSHIRE

Esso

Goods

Northampton No.1 Junc.

Northampton Yard

Northampton

CCE Test Track

Hunsbury Hill Tun.

Far Cotton

Farthingstone Silos

Bridge St. CCE Depot

Bridge Street Junc.

C

(Roade)

Hanslope Junc.

BUCKS.

Bedford Midland

C.S.

CCE Sidings

Bedford St. Johns

CCE Sidings

Sandy

UKF & Goods Dep.

1

2

0   5   10 m.   (1:350,000)
0   5   10   15 km.

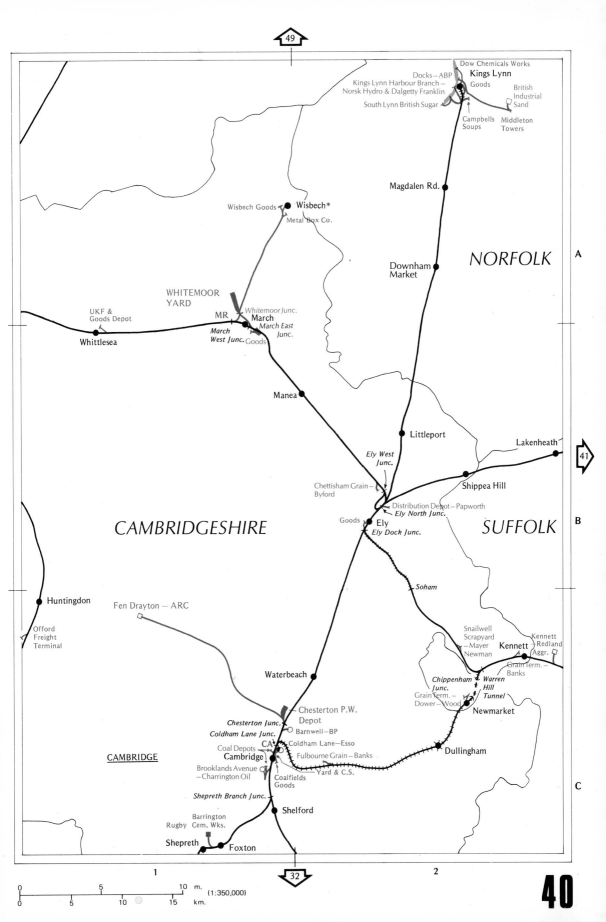

Dow Chemicals Works
Docks — ABP
Kings Lynn Harbour Branch — **Kings Lynn**
Norsk Hydro & Dalgetty Franklin   Goods
South Lynn British Sugar

British
Industrial
Sand

Campbells Soups   Middleton
                       Towers

Magdalen Rd.

NORFOLK

A

Wisbech Goods   **Wisbech***
                  Metal Box Co.

Downham
Market

WHITEMOOR
YARD

UKF &
Goods Depot

MR   **March**   *Whitemoor Junc.*
                    March East
      March   *Junc.*
Whittlesea *West Junc.* Goods

Manea

Littleport

Lakenheath

Ely West
Junc.

41

CAMBRIDGESHIRE

Chettisham Grain —
Byford   Shippea Hill

Distribution Depot — Papworth
                     Ely North Junc.
Goods **Ely**
       Ely Dock Junc.

SUFFOLK   B

Huntingdon

Fen Drayton — ARC

Soham

Offord
Freight
Terminal

Snailwell
Scrapyard
— Mayer
Newman   **Kennett** Kennett
                           Redland
                           Aggr.

Waterbeach

                           Grain Term. —
Chippenham   *Warren*   Banks
Junc.   *Hill*
Grain Term. —   *Tunnel*
Dower — Wood   **Newmarket**

Chesterton P.W.
Depot

Chesterton Junc.   Barnwell — BP
Coldham Lane Junc.

Coal Depots   **CA** Coldham Lane — Esso
Cambridge Fulbourne Grain — Banks
Brooklands Avenue   Yard & C.S.   **Dullingham**
— Charrington Oil
              Coalfields
              Goods

CAMBRIDGE

C

Shepreth Branch Junc.

Barrington
Rugby Cem. Wks.   **Shelford**

Shepreth **Foxton**

1   2

0   5   10 m.   (1:350,000)
0   5   10   15 km.

40

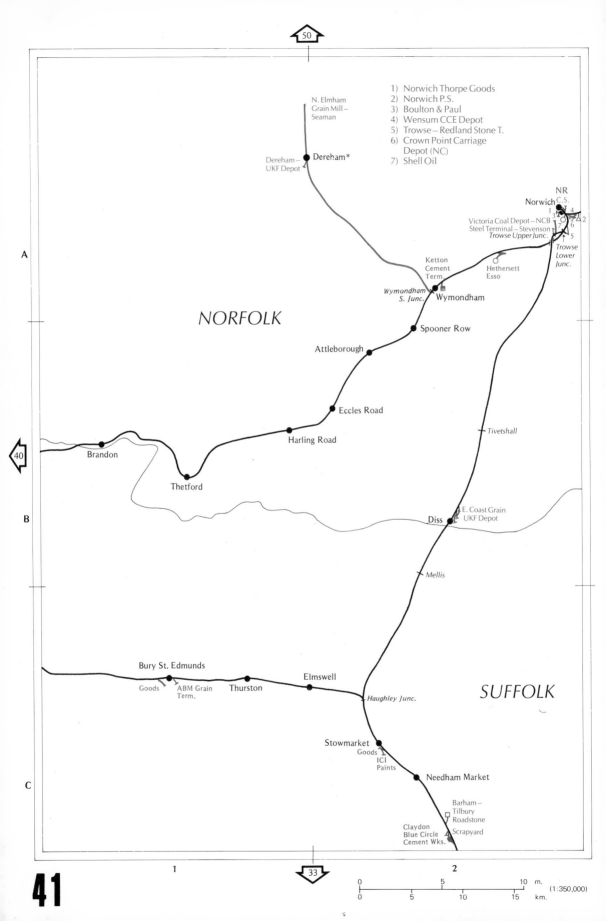

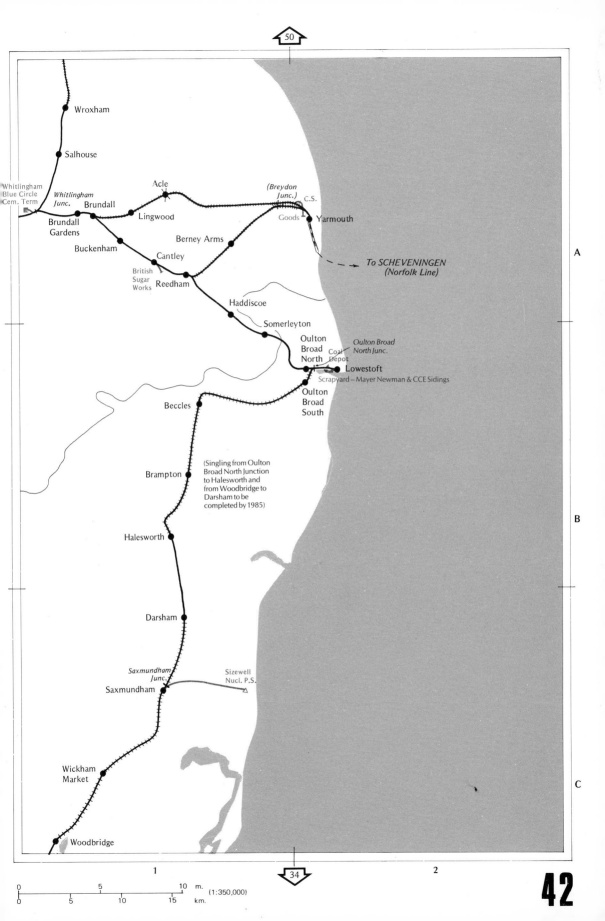

Wroxham

Salhouse

Acle

Whitlingham
Blue Circle
Cem. Term

*Whitlingham
Junc.* Brundall

Lingwood

*(Breydon
Junc.)* C.S.

Goods Yarmouth

Brundall
Gardens

Buckenham

Berney Arms

Cantley

*To SCHEVENINGEN
(Norfolk Line)*

British
Sugar
Works Reedham

Haddiscoe

Somerleyton

Oulton
Broad
North

Coal
Depot

*Oulton Broad
North Junc.*

Lowestoft

Scrapyard – Mayer Newman & CCE Sidings

Oulton
Broad
South

Beccles

Brampton

(Singling from Oulton
Broad North Junction
to Halesworth and
from Woodbridge to
Darsham to be
completed by 1985)

Halesworth

Darsham

*Saxmundham
Junc.*

Sizewell
Nucl. P.S.

Saxmundham

Wickham
Market

Woodbridge

1

2

A

B

C

0   5   10   m.   (1:350,000)
0   5   10   15   km.

42

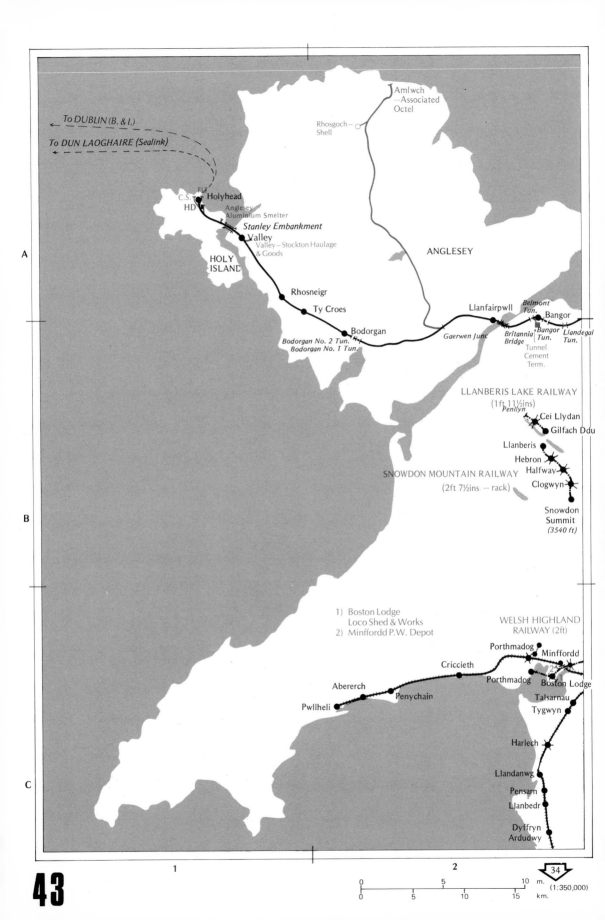

To DUBLIN (B. & I.)

To DUN LAOGHAIRE (Sealink)

Amlwch
—Associated
Octel

Rhosgoch —
Shell

ANGLESEY

F.I.
C.S. Holyhead
HD

Anglesey
Aluminium Smelter

Stanley Embankment

Valley
Valley – Stockton Haulage
& Goods

HOLY
ISLAND

A

Rhosneigr

Ty Croes

Llanfairpwll

Belmont
Tun.
Bangor

Bodorgan

Bodorgan No. 2 Tun.
Bodorgan No. 1 Tun.

Gaerwen Junc

Britannia
Bridge

Bangor
Tun.

Llandegai
Tun.

Tunnel
Cement
Term.

LLANBERIS LAKE RAILWAY
(1ft 11½ins)

Penllyn

Cei Llydan

Gilfach Ddu

Llanberis

Hebron

Halfway

SNOWDON MOUNTAIN RAILWAY

(2ft 7½ins — rack)

Clogwyn

B

Snowdon
Summit
(3540 ft)

1) Boston Lodge
Loco Shed & Works
2) Minffordd P.W. Depot

WELSH HIGHLAND
RAILWAY (2ft)

Porthmadog

Minffordd

Criccieth

Porthmadog

Boston Lodge

Abererch

Talsarnau

Penychain

Tygwyn

Pwllheli

Harlech

Llandanwg

Pensarn

C

Llanbedr

Dyffryn
Ardudwy

34

(1:350,000)

0   5   10 m.

0   5   10   15 km.

43

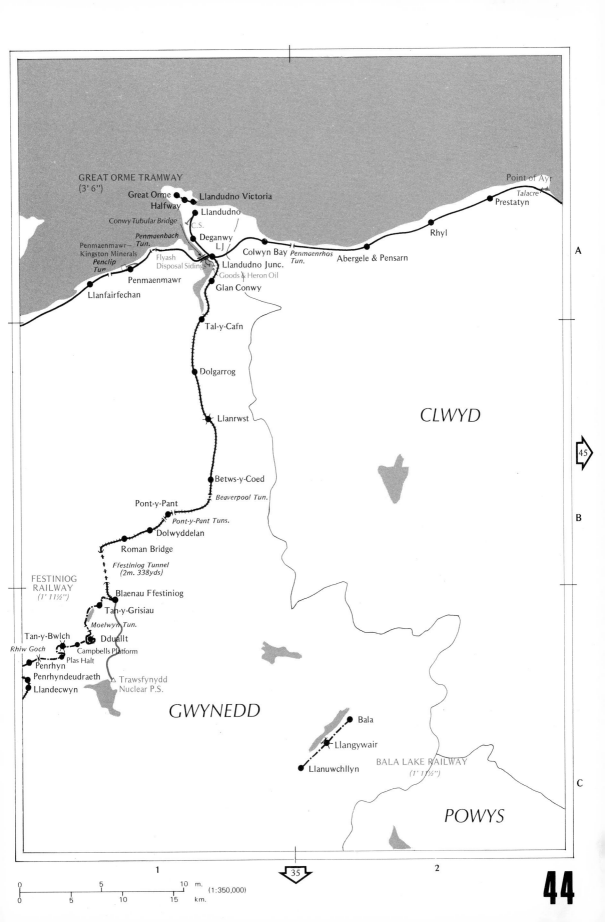

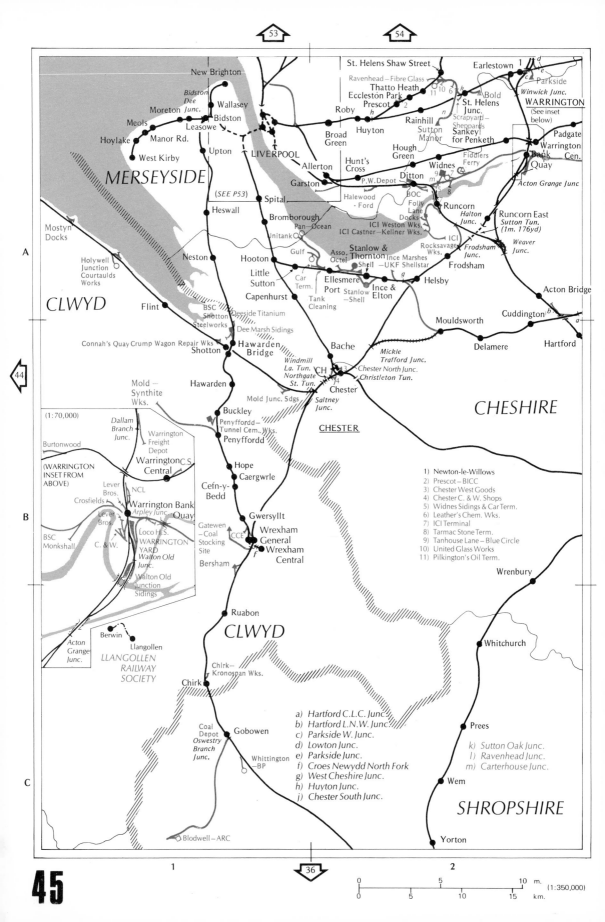

New Brighton

Bidston Dee Junc.
Wallasey
Bidston
St. Helens Shaw Street
Ravenhead – Fibre Glass
Thatto Heath
Eccleston Park
Prescot
Earlestown
Parkside
Winwick Junc.
WARRINGTON
(See inset below)

Moreton
Leasowe
Roby
Rainhill
St. Helens Junc.
Shepards
Bold
Meols
Upton
Huyton
Sutton Manor
Sankey for Penketh
Manor Rd.
LIVERPOOL
Broad Green
Hough Green
Fiddlers Ferry
Padgate
Hoylake
West Kirby
Allerton
Hunt's Cross
Widnes
Warrington Cen.
Bank Quay
MERSEYSIDE
Garston
P.W. Depot
Ditton
Acton Grange Junc.

(SEE P53)
Spital
Halewood – Ford
BOC
Folly Lane Docks
Runcorn
Runcorn East
Sutton Tun.
(1m. 176yd)

Heswall
Bromborough
Pan – Ocean
Halton Junc.
Mostyn Docks
Unitank
ICI Weston Wks.
ICI Castner – Kellner Wks.
Rocksavage Wks.
ICI
Frodsham Junc.
Weaver Junc.

Holywell Junction
Courtaulds Works
Gulf
Asso. Octel
Stanlow & Thornton
Shell
Ince Marshes
– UKF Shellstar
Frodsham Junc.
Frodsham

A
Neston
Hooton
Car Term.
Ellesmere Port
Stanlow – Shell
Ince & Elton
g
Helsby
Acton Bridge

CLWYD
Little Sutton
Tank Cleaning
Mouldsworth
Cuddington
Hartford

Flint
Capenhurst
BSC Shotton Steelworks
Deeside Titanium
Dee Marsh Sidings
Bache
Delamere

Connah's Quay Crump Wagon Repair Wks.
Shotton
Hawarden Bridge
Windmill La. Tun.
Northgate St. Tun.
CH
Mickle Trafford Junc.
Chester North Junc.
Christleton Tun.
CHESHIRE

Hawarden
Mold – Synthite Wks.
Mold Junc. Sdgs.
Saltney Junc.
Chester
CHESTER

(1:70,000)
Buckley
Penyffordd – Tunnel Cem. Wks.
Penyffordd

(WARRINGTON INSET FROM ABOVE)
Dallam Branch Junc.
Warrington Freight Depot
Hope
Caergwrle

Burtonwood
Warrington Central
C.S.
NCL
Cefn-y-Bedd
1) Newton-le-Willows
2) Prescot – BICC
3) Chester West Goods
4) Chester C. & W. Shops
5) Widnes Sidings & Car Term.
6) Leather's Chem. Wks.
7) ICI Terminal
8) Tarmac Stone Term.
9) Tanhouse Lane – Blue Circle
10) United Glass Works
11) Pilkington's Oil Term.

Lever Bros.
Crosfields
Lever Bros.
Warrington Bank Quay
Arpley Junc.
B
Gwersyllt
Gatewen – Coal Stocking Site
CCE
Wrexham General
Wrexham Central
Bersham

BSC Monkshall
C. & W.
Loco H.S.
WARRINGTON YARD
Walton Old Junc.
Walton Old Junction Sidings
f
Wrenbury

Acton Grange Junc.
Berwin
Llangollen
CLWYD
Ruabon
Whitchurch

LLANGOLLEN RAILWAY SOCIETY
Chirk – Kronospan Wks.

Chirk
Prees

Coal Depot
Oswestry Branch Junc.
Gobowen
Whittington – BP

a) Hartford C.L.C. Junc.
b) Hartford L.N.W. Junc.
c) Parkside W. Junc.
d) Lowton Junc.
e) Parkside Junc.
f) Croes Newydd North Fork
g) West Cheshire Junc.
h) Huyton Junc.
j) Chester South Junc.

k) Sutton Oak Junc.
l) Ravenhead Junc.
m) Carterhouse Junc.

Wem

SHROPSHIRE
Blodwell – ARC

Yorton

45

44

36

1   2

0   5   10 m.
0   5   10   15 km.
(1:350,000)

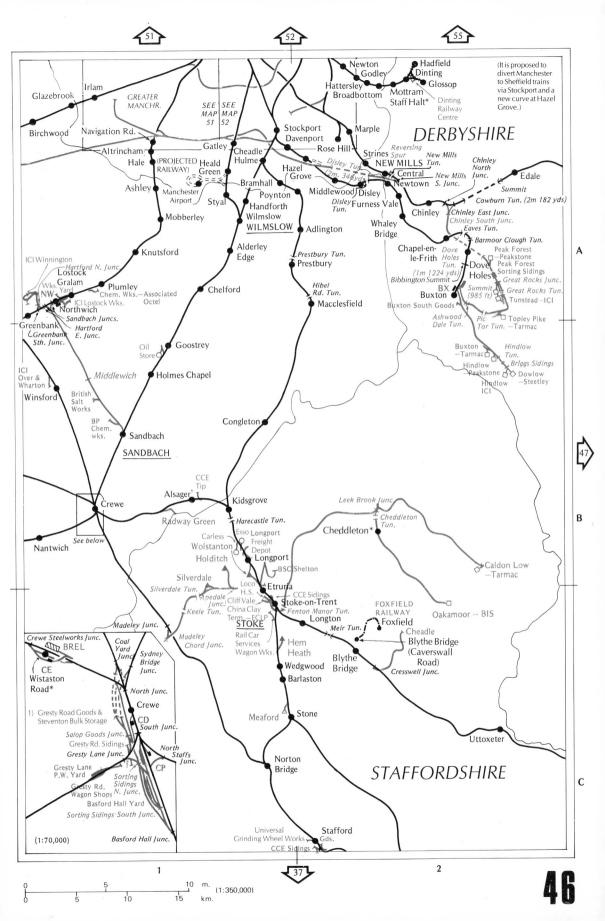

Glazebrook
Irlam
Birchwood

GREATER MANCHR.

SEE MAP 51   SEE MAP 52

Newton   Godley   Hadfield   Dinting
Hattersley   Glossop
Broadbottom   Mottram   Dinting Railway Centre
Staff Halt*

DERBYSHIRE

Navigation Rd.
Altrincham   Gatley   Stockport Davenport   Marple
Hale   Cheadle Hulme   Rose Hill
(PROJECTED RAILWAY)   Heald Green   Strines   Reversing Spur
Ashley   Hazel Grove   New Mills Tun.   Chinley North Junc.
Manchester Airport   Bramhall   **NEW MILLS** Central   Edale
Styl   Poynton   Middlewood   Newtown   New Mills S. Junc.   Summit
Mobberley   Handforth   Disley   Cowburn Tun. (2m 182 yds)
Wilmslow   Disley Tun.   Furness Vale   Chinley
WILMSLOW   Adlington   Whaley   Chinley East Junc.
Knutsford   Alderley Edge   Bridge   Chinley South Junc.
Eaves Tun.
Prestbury Tun.   Barmoor Clough Tun.
(It is proposed to divert Manchester to Sheffield trains via Stockport and a new curve at Hazel Grove.)

ICI Winnington   Hartford N. Junc.   Prestbury   Chapel-en-le-Frith   Dove Holes Tun.   Peak Forest   Peakstone
Lostock   Gralam   Yard   Hibel Rd. Tun.   (1m 1224 yds)   Peak Forest Sorting Sidings
Plumley   Chem. Wks.—Associated Octel   Bibbington Summit   Great Rocks Junc.
Northwich   ICI Lostock Wks.   Macclesfield   BX   Summit (985 ft)   Great Rocks Tun.
Greenbank   Sandbach Juncs.   Chelford   **Buxton**   Tunstead—ICI
Greenbank Sth. Junc.   Hartford E. Junc.   Buxton South Goods   *Ashwood Dale Tun.*   Pic Tor Tun. —Tarmac   Topley Pike
ICI Over & Wharton   Oil Store   Goostrey   Buxton—Tarmac   Hindlow Tun.   Briggs Sidings
Winsford   *Middlewich*   Holmes Chapel   Hindlow—Peakstone   Dowlow—Steetley
British Salt Works   Hindlow ICI
BP Chem. wks.   Congleton

Sandbach
SANDBACH

CCE Tip
Alsager   Kidsgrove   Leek Brook Junc.
Crewe   *Radway Green*   *Harecastle Tun.*   Cheddleton   *Cheddleton Tun.*
See below   Carless   Esso   Longport
Nantwich   Wolstanton   Freight Depot   Cheddleton*   Caldon Low —Tarmac
Holditch   Longport
Silverdale   BSC Shelton
Silverdale Tun.   Loco H.S.   Etruria   CCE Sidings   FOXFIELD RAILWAY
Apedale Junc.   Cliff Vale   **Stoke-on-Trent**   Foxfield   Oakamoor — BIS
Keele Tun.   China Clay Term. —ECLP   *Fenton Manor Tun.*
Madeley Junc.   **STOKE**   Longton   *Meir Tun.*   Cheadle
Rail Car Services Wagon Wks.   Blythe Bridge (Caverswall Road)
Madeley Chord Junc.   Hem Heath   Cresswell Junc.
Blythe Bridge

Crewe Steelworks Junc.   Coal Yard Junc.   Wedgwood
BREL   Sydney Bridge Junc.   Barlaston
CE Wistaston Road*   North Junc.   Meaford   Stone
1) Gresty Road Goods & Steventon Bulk Storage   Crewe   Uttoxeter
Salop Goods Junc.   CD   South Junc.   North Staffs Junc.
Gresty Rd. Sidings   Norton Bridge
Gresty Lane Junc.   CP
Gresty Lane P.W. Yard   **STAFFORDSHIRE**
Gresty Rd. Wagon Shops   Sorting Sidings N. Junc.
Basford Hall Yard
Sorting Sidings South Junc.
(1:70,000)   Basford Hall Junc.   Universal Grinding Wheel Works   Stafford Gds.
CCE Sidings

0 ——— 5 ——— 10 m.   (1:350,000)
0 — 5 — 10 — 15 km.

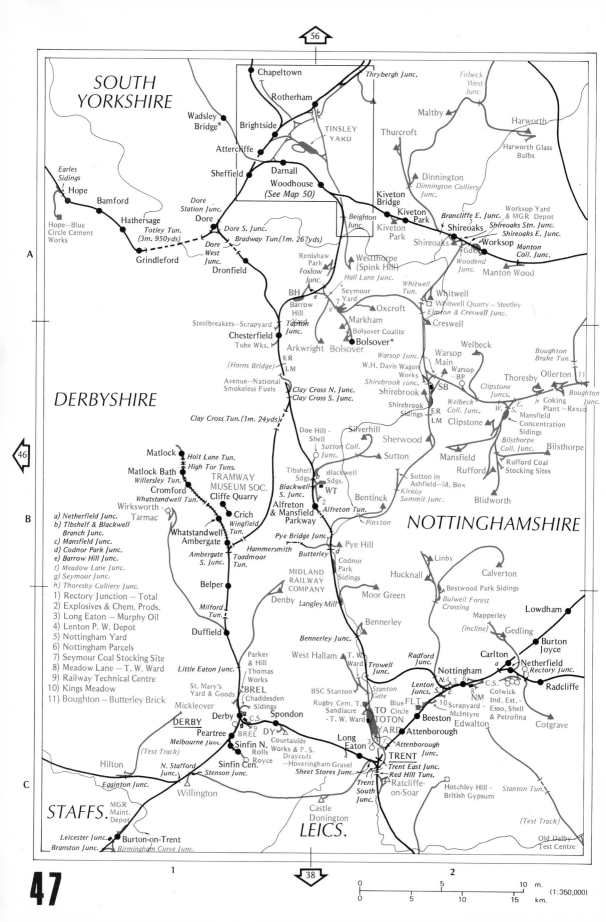

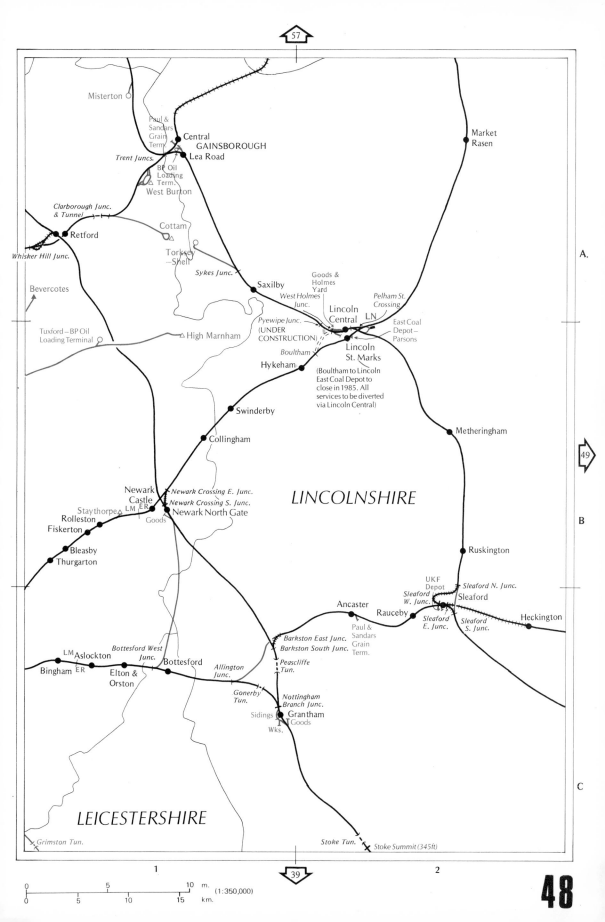

Misterton

Paul &
Sandars
Grain
Term.

Central
GAINSBOROUGH
Lea Road

Trent Juncs.

BP Oil
Loading
Term.
West Burton

*Clarborough Junc.
& Tunnel*

Cottam

Retford

Torksey
—Shell

Whisker Hill Junc.

Bevercotes

Tuxford – BP Oil
Loading Terminal

△ High Marnham

Sykes Junc.

Saxilby

Goods &
Holmes
Yard

*West Holmes
Junc.*

Lincoln
Central

*Pelham St.
Crossing*

LN

East Coal
Depot –
Parsons

Pyewipe Junc.
(UNDER
CONSTRUCTION)

Boultham

Lincoln
St. Marks

Hykeham

(Boultham to Lincoln
East Coal Depot to
close in 1985. All
services to be diverted
via Lincoln Central)

Swinderby

Collingham

Metheringham

Market
Rasen

A.

49

LINCOLNSHIRE

Newark
Castle

Newark Crossing E. Junc.

LM
ER

Newark Crossing S. Junc.

Staythorpe △

Goods

Newark North Gate

Rolleston
Fiskerton

Bleasby
Thurgarton

Ruskington

UKF
Depot

Sleaford N. Junc.

*Sleaford
W. Junc.*

Sleaford

B

Ancaster

Rauceby

*Sleaford
E. Junc.*

*Sleaford
S. Junc.*

Heckington

LM
Aslockton
ER

*Bottesford West
Junc.*

Bingham

Elton &
Orston

Bottesford

*Allington
Junc.*

Barkston East Junc.
Barkston South Junc.

*Peascliffe
Tun.*

Paul &
Sandars
Grain
Term.

*Gonerby
Tun.*

*Nottingham
Branch Junc.*

Sidings

LEICESTERSHIRE

Grantham

Goods

Wks.

C

✗ *Grimston Tun.*

Stoke Tun.

✗ *Stoke Summit (345ft)*

0   5   10 m.
(1:350,000)
0   5   10   15 km.

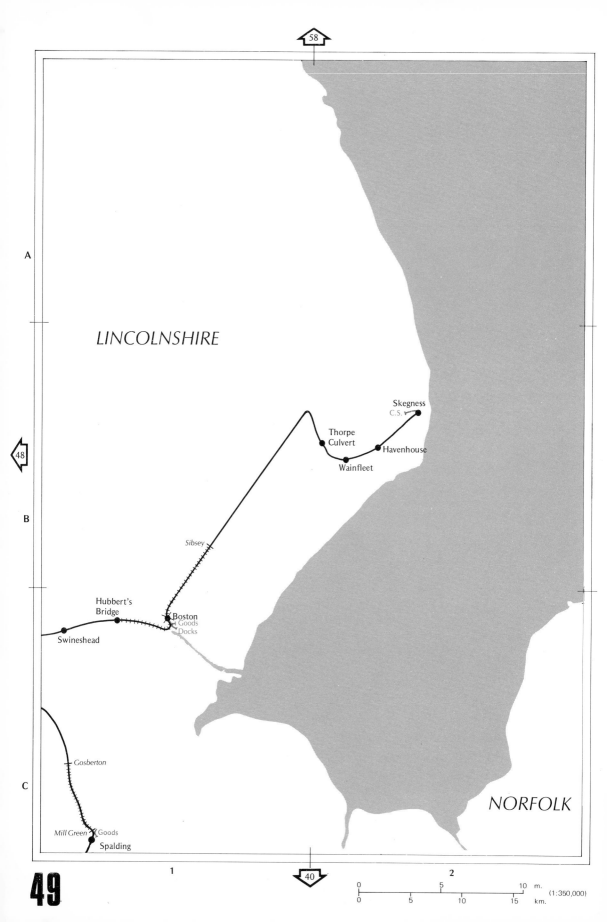

58

A

LINCOLNSHIRE

Skegness
C.S.

48

Thorpe
Culvert

Havenhouse

Wainfleet

B

Sibsey

Hubbert's
Bridge

Boston
Goods
Docks

Swineshead

C

Gosberton

NORFOLK

Mill Green Goods

Spalding

49

1

40

2

0   5   10 m.

0   5   10   15
km.

(1:350,000)

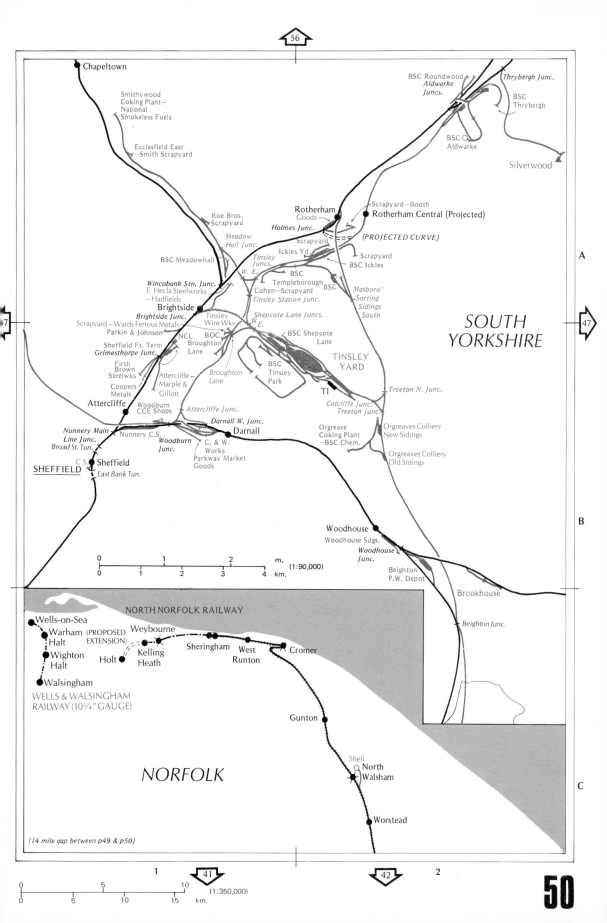

Chapeltown

Smithywood
Coking Plant—
National
Smokeless Fuels

Ecclesfield East
—Smith Scrapyard

BSC Roundwood
Aldwarke
Juncs.

Thrybergh Junc.

BSC
Thrybergh

BSC
Aldwarke

Silverwood

Roe Bros.
Scrapyard

Rotherham
Goods

Scrapyard—Booth

Rotherham Central (Projected)

*Meadow
Hall Junc.*

Holmes Junc.

(PROJECTED CURVE)

BSC Meadowhall

Scrapyard

Ickles Yd.

Scrapyard
BSC Ickles

*Tinsley Juncs.
W. E.*

Wincobank Stn. Junc.
E. Hecla Steelworks
—Hadfields

BSC
Templeborough
Cohen—Scrapyard
Tinsley Station Junc.

BSC

*Masboro'
Sorting
Sidings
South*

**SOUTH
YORKSHIRE**

Brightside

Brightside Junc.

Tinsley
Wire Wks.

Shepcote Lane Juncs.

W. E.

BSC Shepcote
Lane

A

Scrapyard—Wards Ferrous Metals—
Parkin & Johnson

NCL

BOC Broughton
Lane

**TINSLEY
YARD**

Sheffield Ft. Term.
Grimesthorpe Junc.

Firth
Brown
Steelwks.

*Broughton
Lane*

BSC
Tinsley
Park

47

47

Coopers
Metals

Attercliffe

Attercliffe
—Marple &
Gillott

Woodburn
CCE Shops

Attercliffe Junc.

Darnall W. Junc.

TI

Treeton N. Junc.

*Catcliffe Junc.
Treeton Junc.*

**Nunnery Main
Line Junc.**
Broad St. Tun.

Nunnery C.S.

*Woodburn
Junc.*

Darnall

C. & W.
Works
Parkway Market
Goods

Orgreave
Coking Plant
—BSC Chem.

Orgreaves Colliery
New Sidings

Orgreaves Colliery
Old Sidings

SHEFFIELD

C.S.

Sheffield

East Bank Tun.

Woodhouse

Woodhouse Sdgs.

**Woodhouse
Junc.**

B

Beighton
P.W. Depot

0   1   2   m.   (1:90,000)

0   1   2   3   4   km.

Brookhouse

Beighton Junc.

NORTH NORFOLK RAILWAY

Wells-on-Sea

Warham
Halt

(PROPOSED
EXTENSION)

Weybourne

Sheringham

West
Runton

Cromer

Wighton
Halt

Holt

Kelling
Heath

Walsingham

**WELLS & WALSINGHAM
RAILWAY (10¼" GAUGE)**

Gunton

Shell
North
Walsham

NORFOLK

C

(14 mile gap between p49 & p50)

Worstead

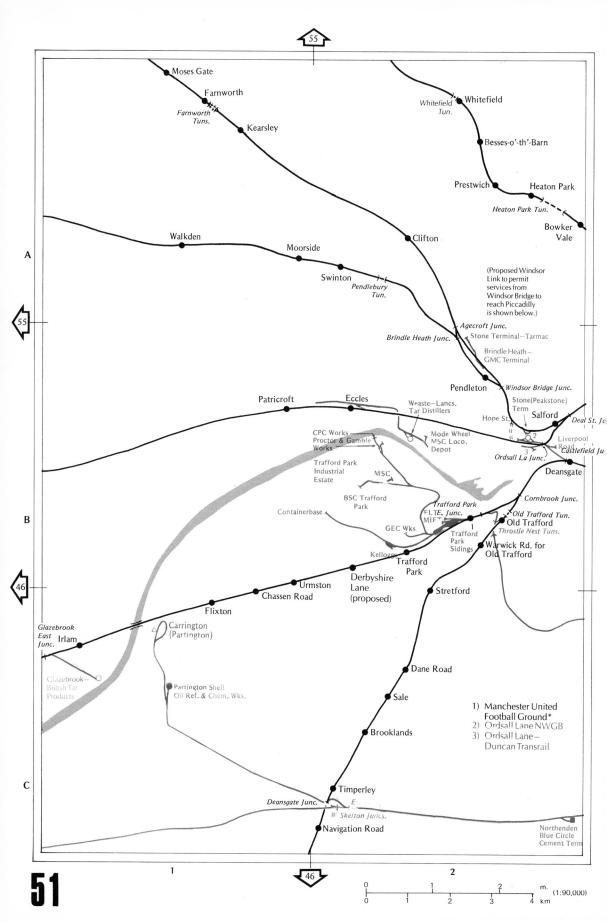

Moses Gate

Farnworth

Farnworth Tuns.

Kearsley

Whitefield Tun. Whitefield

Besses-o'-th'-Barn

Prestwich

Heaton Park

Heaton Park Tun.

Bowker Vale

Walkden

Moorside

Clifton

Swinton

Pendlebury Tun.

(Proposed Windsor Link to permit services from Windsor Bridge to reach Piccadilly is shown below.)

A

Agecroft Junc.

Stone Terminal—Tarmac

Brindle Heath Junc.

Brindle Heath—GMC Terminal

Pendleton

Windsor Bridge Junc.

Stone (Peakstone) Term

Salford

Deal St. Jc

Patricroft

Eccles

Weaste—Lancs. Tar Distillers

Hope St.

Liverpool Road

Castlefield Ju

CPC Works
Proctor & Gamble Works

Mode Wheel
MSC Loco. Depot

Ordsall La Junc.

Trafford Park Industrial Estate

MSC

Deansgate

BSC Trafford Park

Cornbrook Junc.

B

Containerbase

Trafford Park
FLT *E. Junc.*
MIFT

Old Trafford Tun.
Old Trafford
Throstle Nest Tuns.

GEC Wks.

Trafford Park Sidings

Kelloggs

Warwick Rd. for Old Trafford

Trafford Park

Derbyshire Lane (proposed)

Urmston

Chassen Road

Stretford

Flixton

Glazebrook East Junc.

Irlam

Carrington (Partington)

Glazebrook—British Tar Products

Partington Shell Oil Ref. & Chem. Wks.

Dane Road

Sale

Brooklands

1) Manchester United Football Ground*
2) Ordsall Lane NWGB
3) Ordsall Lane—Duncan Transrail

C

Timperley

Deansgate Junc. E

W Skelton Juncs.

Navigation Road

Northenden Blue Circle Cement Term

0   1   2   m.   (1:90,000)
0   1   2   3   4   km

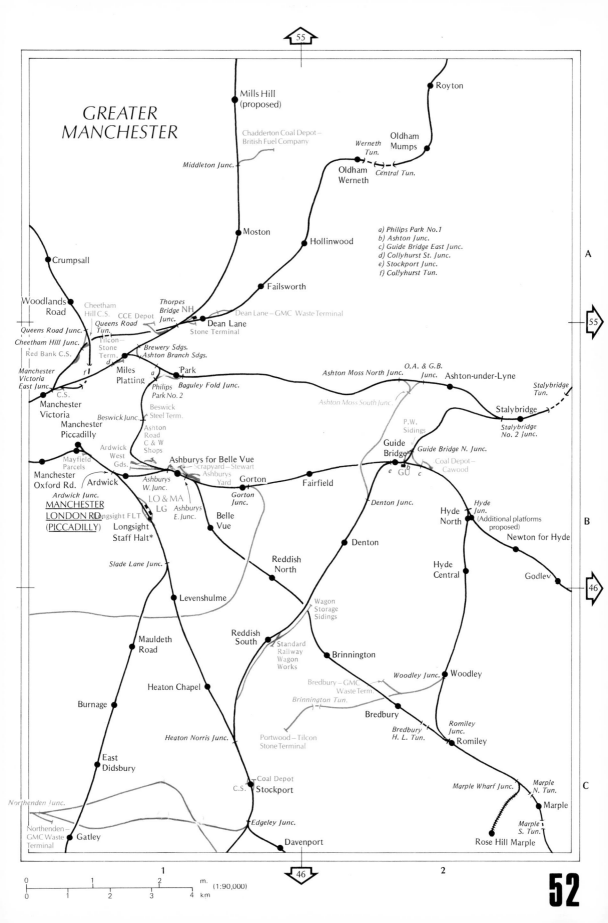

GREATER
MANCHESTER

Royton

Mills Hill
(proposed)

Chadderton Coal Depot –
British Fuel Company

Middleton Junc.

Oldham
Mumps

*Werneth
Tun.*

Oldham
Werneth

Central Tun.

Moston

Hollinwood

a) Philips Park No.1
b) Ashton Junc.
c) Guide Bridge East Junc.
d) Collyhurst St. Junc.
e) Stockport Junc.
f) Collyhurst Tun.

Crumpsall

Failsworth

Woodlands
Road

*Cheetham
Hill C.S.*

CCE Depot

*Thorpes
Bridge
Junc.*

NH

Dean Lane – GMC Waste Terminal

Queens Road Junc.

*Queens Road
Tun.*

Dean Lane
Stone Terminal

Cheetham Hill Junc.

*Tilcon–
Stone
Term.*

Red Bank C.S.

Brewery Sdgs.

Ashton Branch Sdgs.

Ashton Moss North Junc.

*O.A. & G.B.
Junc.*

Ashton-under-Lyne

*Stalybridge
Tun.*

*Manchester
Victoria
East Junc.*

d

Park

Baguley Fold Junc.

Ashton Moss South Junc.

C.S.

f

Miles
Platting

a

Manchester
Victoria

Philips
Park No.2

Beswick
Steel Term.

Stalybridge

*Stalybridge
No.2 Junc.*

Manchester
Piccadilly

Beswick Junc.

Ashton
Road
C & W
Shops

*P.W.
Sidings*

Guide
Bridge

Guide Bridge N. Junc.

*Coal Depot –
Cawood*

Mayfield
Parcels

*Ardwick
West
Gds.*

Ashburys for Belle Vue

Scrapyard – Stewart

Ashburys
Yard

Gorton

Fairfield

e

GU

b

c

Manchester
Oxford Rd.

Ardwick

*Ashburys
W. Junc.*

*Gorton
Junc.*

Ardwick Junc.

LO & MA
LG

*Ashburys
E. Junc.*

Denton Junc.

Hyde
North

*Hyde
Jun.*
(Additional platforms
proposed)

MANCHESTER
LONDON RD
(PICCADILLY)

Longsight FLT

Longsight
Staff Halt*

Belle
Vue

Denton

Newton for Hyde

Slade Lane Junc.

Reddish
North

Hyde
Central

Godley

Levenshulme

*Wagon
Storage
Sidings*

Mauldeth
Road

Reddish
South

Standard
Railway
Wagon
Works

Brinnington

Woodley Junc.

Woodley

Heaton Chapel

*Bredbury – GMC
Waste Term.*

Brinnington Tun.

Burnage

Bredbury

*Romiley
Junc.*

*Bredbury
H. L. Tun.*

Romiley

Heaton Norris Junc.

Portwood – Tilcon
Stone Terminal

East
Didsbury

Marple Wharf Junc.

*Marple
N. Tun.*

Northenden Junc.

C.S.

Coal Depot

Stockport

Marple

*Northenden –
GMC Waste
Terminal*

Gatley

Edgeley Junc.

*Marple
S. Tun.*

Rose Hill Marple

Davenport

0   1   2 m. (1:90,000)
0 1 2 3 4 km

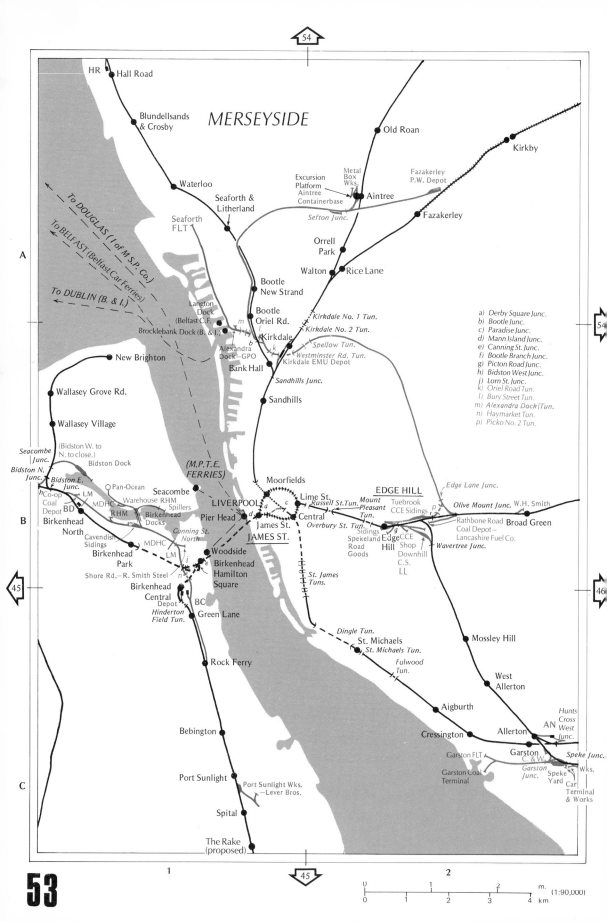

HR • Hall Road

MERSEYSIDE

Blundellsands & Crosby

Waterloo

Old Roan

Kirkby

Seaforth & Litherland

Seaforth FLT

Excursion Platform Aintree Containerbase

Metal Box Wks.

Aintree

Sefton Junc.

Fazakerley P.W. Depot

Fazakerley

Orrell Park

Walton

Rice Lane

A

To DOUGLAS (I. of M.S.P. Co.)

To BELFAST (Belfast Car Ferries)

To DUBLIN (B. & I.)

Langton Dock (Belfast C.F.)

Brocklebank Dock (B. & I.)

m

Bootle New Strand

Bootle Oriel Rd.

Kirkdale No. 1 Tun.

Kirkdale No. 2 Tun.

Kirkdale

b

Alexandra Dock-GPO

k

Bank Hall

Spellow Tun.

Westminster Rd. Tun.

Kirkdale EMU Depot

Sandhills Junc.

Sandhills

New Brighton

a) *Derby Square Junc.*
b) *Bootle Junc.*
c) *Paradise Junc.*
d) *Mann Island Junc.*
e) *Canning St. Junc.*
f) *Bootle Branch Junc.*
g) *Picton Road Junc.*
h) *Bidston West Junc.*
j) *Lorn St. Junc.*
k) *Oriel Road Tun.*
l) *Bury Street Tun.*
m) *Alexandra Dock|Tun.*
n) *Haymarket Tun.*
p) *Picko No. 2 Tun.*

Wallasey Grove Rd.

Wallasey Village

Seacombe Junc.

(Bidston W. to N. to close.)

Bidston Dock

Bidston N. Junc.

Bidston E. Junc.

h Co-op Coal Depot

BD

LM

MDHC

Warehouse RHM

RHM

Spillers

Birkenhead Docks

Seacombe

Pan-Ocean

Moorfields

Lime St.

EDGE HILL

Edge Lane Junc.

W.H. Smith

LIVERPOOL

Pier Head

(M.P.T.E. FERRIES)

(M.P.T.E. FERRIES)

a

c

Russell St.Tun.

Mount Pleasant Tun.

Tuebrook CCE Sidings

p

Olive Mount Junc.

B

Birkenhead North

Cavendish Sidings

MDHC

LM

Canning St. North

d

Central

Central

Overbury St. Tun.

Sidings

Spekeland Road Goods

g

CCE

Shop Downhill C.S. LL

Rathbone Road Coal Depot— Lancashire Fuel Co.

Broad Green

Birkenhead Park

j

JAMES ST.

James St.

Edge Hill

Wavertree Junc.

Shore Rd.—R. Smith Steel

n

e

Woodside

Birkenhead Hamilton Square

St. James Tuns.

Birkenhead Central Depot

BC

Hinderton Field Tun.

Green Lane

Mossley Hill

Rock Ferry

Dingle Tun.

St. Michaels

St. Michaels Tun.

Fulwood Tun.

West Allerton

Bebington

Aigburth

Port Sunlight

Port Sunlight Wks. —Lever Bros.

Cressington

Allerton

AN

Hunts Cross West Junc.

Garston

Garston FLT

C. & W.

Garston Junc.

Garston Coal Terminal

Speke Junc.

Garston Yard

Speke Car Terminal & Works

Wks.

C

Spital

The Rake (proposed)

45

53

1

2

0 1 2 3 4 km

0   1   2 m.

(1:90,000)

Barrow
Roose
(SEE INSET
BELOW)

Wennington

To DOUGLAS (Sealink)

Bare Lane
Hest Bank
Morecambe
Morecambe South Junc.
Lancaster

Heysham*
Heysham Moss
Heysham
Nuclear
P.S. Siding
ICI Chemical
Works

LANCASHIRE

A

(1: 90,000)

BSC
BSC
Barrow
BW
C.S.
Barrow
Cart
Coal Depot
— British
Fuels
Caird
Foundry
Hackett
Coal
Depot
Roose
Salthouse Junc.
To DOUGLAS (I of M S.P. Co.)
Roosecote
Vickers
Ramsden Dock —
British Nuclear
Fuels
Barrow
Yard

BLACKPOOL & FLEETWOOD
TRAMWAY (PRINCIPAL STOPS)

Fleetwood
Ash St.
Knott End

Rossall
Thornton
Gate
Cleveleys
Little
Bispham
Bispham
Fleetwood
(Disused)
P.W. Yard
Burn Naze—ICI P.S.
ICI Hillhouse
Wks. - Thornton
Burn Naze

BP
C.S.
Cabin
Layton
Talbot Sq.
Tower
Manchester Sq.
Pleasure Beach
Starr
Gate
St. Annes-on-the-Sea

Poulton-le-Fylde

Blackpool
North
Depot
Blackpool South
Squires
Gate
Moss
Side

Kirkham &
Wesham
Salwick
CCE Tip
British
Nuclear
Fuels
Fylde Junc.
Deepdale Tuns.
Lanfina
Petrofina
Williams
12
Deepdale Coal Dep. — NCB
Preston
Fishergate Tun.
10
Preston South Junc.

55

Ansdell &
Fairhaven
Lytham

PRESTON
Farington Curve Junc.

*Lostock
Hall Junc.*
Lostock
Hall
Bamber
Bridge
Pleasington

B

a) *Bamfurlong Sdgs Junc.*
b) *Ince Moss Junc.*
c) *Springs Branch Junc.*
d) *Bamfurlong Junc.*
e) *Haydock Branch Junc.*
f) *Gerard's Bridge Jun.*

Croston

BL
Farington Junc.
Leyland

Euxton Junc.
Euxton ROF
Chorley Tun.
Chorley

Steamport
Southport
C.S.
Meols Cop
Birkdale
Hillside
Ainsdale
Freshfield
Formby
Hightown

Bescar
Lane
New Lane
Burscough Junc.

Rufford
Burscough Bridge
Hoscar
Parbold

Appley
Bridge
Adlington
Sidings
Blackrod
Horwich
BREL
*GREATER
MANCHESTER*
WIGAN
GMC Waste
Disposal Term.

(Emergency
Connections)
Ormskirk
Aughton Park
Town Green
ICI 5
Gathurst
*Upholland
Tun.*
CCE
Depot
C.S.
Hindley
Wallgate
Ince
*Crow Nest
Junc.*

C

Maghull
Hall Road
Old Roan
Kirkby
Rainford
Upholland
Orrell
Pemberton
N.W.
Garswood
Bryn
Ince Moss CCE Tip
b
a
d
e
3
2
1
4

MERSEYSIDE

Pilkington -
Cowley Hill Wks.
Haydock—Shell
Golborne Junc.
f
9

1) Abram Exchange Sidings
2) Bickershaw Coll.
3) Albert Opencast
4) Coop Glassworks
5) Allied Steel & Wire
6) Bamber Bridge CCE Depot
  & Grain Term. — Whittle
7) Lostock Hall C & W
8) Wigan N.W. Goods
9) Ashton-in-Makerfield —
  Lowton Metals
10) Preston GPO Terminal
11) Dock St. Sidings
12) Preston Docks
  Exchange Sidings

0   5   10 m.
0   5   10   15 km.
(1:350,000)

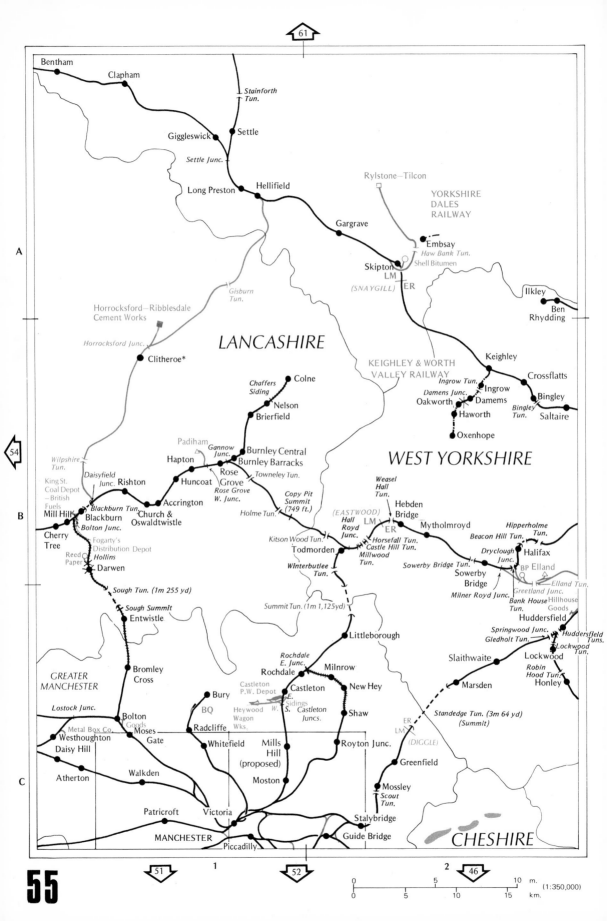

Bentham

Clapham

Stainforth Tun.

Settle

Giggleswick

Settle Junc.

Long Preston

Hellifield

Gargrave

Rylstone–Tilcon

YORKSHIRE DALES RAILWAY

Embsay
Haw Bank Tun.
Shell Bitumen

Skipton
LM
(SNAYGILL) ER

Ilkley

Ben Rhydding

Gisburn Tun.

LANCASHIRE

Horrocksford–Ribblesdale Cement Works

Horrocksford Junc.

Clitheroe*

Keighley

Crossflatts

KEIGHLEY & WORTH VALLEY RAILWAY

Ingrow Tun.
Ingrow
Damens Junc.
Oakworth Damems
Haworth

Bingley
Bingley Tun.
Saltaire

Oxenhope

Chaffers Siding

Colne

Nelson

Brierfield

Padiham
Gannow Junc.
Burnley Central
Burnley Barracks

Hapton
Rose Grove
Huncoat
Rose Grove W. Junc.
Towneley Tun.

WEST YORKSHIRE

Wilpshire Tun.

Daisyfield Junc.
Rishton
King St. Coal Depot – British Fuels
Accrington
Church & Oswaldtwistle

Blackburn Tun.
Mill Hill Blackburn
Bolton Junc.

Cherry Tree

Fogarty's Distribution Depot

Reed Paper
Hollins
Darwen

Copy Pit Summit (749 ft.)
Holme Tun.

Kitson Wood Tun.
Todmorden

Weasel Hall Tun.
Hebden Bridge

(EASTWOOD)
Hall Royd Junc.
LM
ER
Mytholmroyd

Horsefall Tun.
Castle Hill Tun.
Millwood Tun.

Winterbutlee Tun.

Hipperholme Tun.
Beacon Hill Tun.

Dryclough Junc.
Halifax

Sowerby Bridge Tun.
Sowerby Bridge

Milner Royd Junc.

BP Elland
Greetland Junc.
Elland Tun.

Sough Tun. (1m 255 yd)

Sough Summit
Entwistle

Summit Tun. (1m 1,125yd)

Bank House Tun.
Hillhouse Goods
Huddersfield

Springwood Junc.
Gledholt Tun.
Huddersfield Tuns.
Lockwood
Lockwood Tun.

Littleborough

Slaithwaite

Robin Hood Tun.
Honley
Lockwood

Bromley Cross

GREATER MANCHESTER

Lostock Junc.

Rochdale E. Junc.
Rochdale
Milnrow

New Hey

Castleton
P.W. Depot
E. Sidings
W. *Castleton Junc.*
Castleton

Marsden

Standedge Tun. (3m 64 yd) (Summit)

Bury
BQ

Heywood Wagon Wks.

Shaw

Bolton
Metal Box Co.
Moses Gate
Radcliffe

Westhoughton
Daisy Hill

Walkden

Whitefield

Mills Hill (proposed)

Moston

Royton Junc.

Greenfield

ER
LM
(DIGGLE)

Atherton

Patricroft
Victoria

Mossley
Scout Tun.

MANCHESTER
Piccadilly

Stalybridge
Guide Bridge

CHESHIRE

55

0   5   10 m.
(1:350,000)
0   5   10   15 km.

54

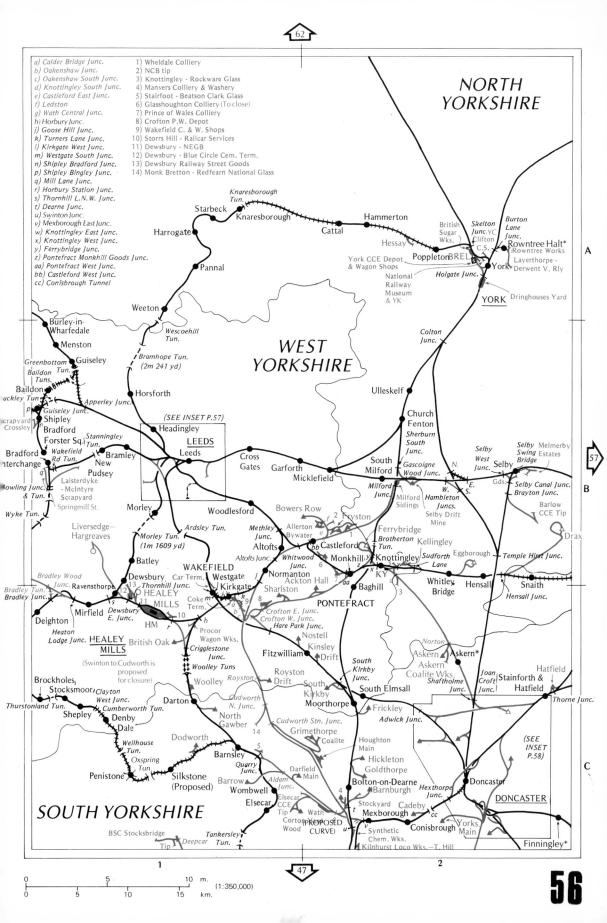

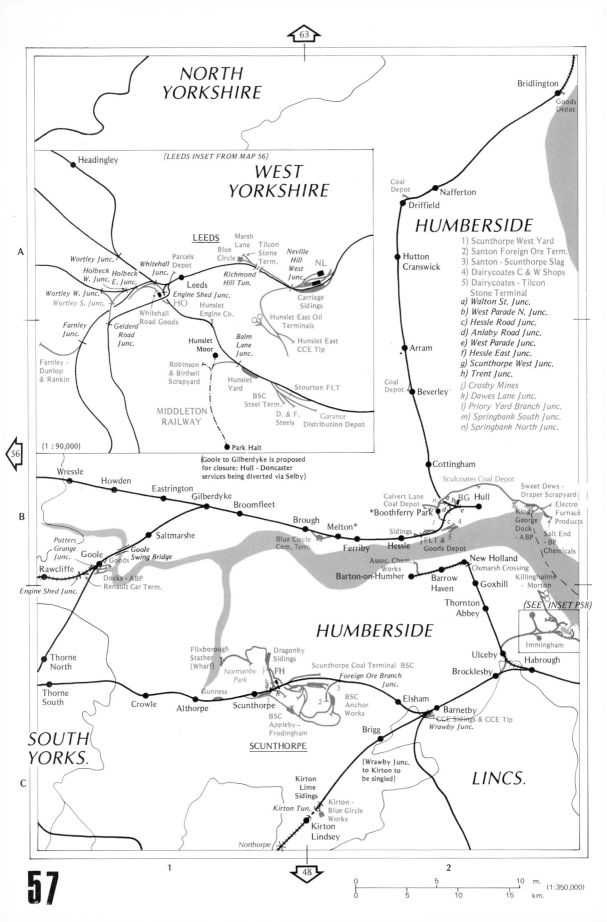

NORTH YORKSHIRE

Bridlington
Goods Depot

(LEEDS INSET FROM MAP 56)

WEST YORKSHIRE

Coal Depot

Nafferton

Driffield

HUMBERSIDE

LEEDS

Marsh Lane
Blue Circle
Tilcon Stone Term.

Parcels Depot

Whitehall Junc.

Wortley Junc.

Neville Hill West Junc.

NL

1) Scunthorpe West Yard
2) Santon Foreign Ore Term.
3) Santon - Scunthorpe Slag
4) Dairycoates C & W Shops
5) Dairycoates - Tilcon Stone Terminal
a) Walton St. Junc.
b) West Parade N. Junc.
c) Hessle Road Junc.
d) Anlaby Road Junc.
e) West Parade Junc.
f) Hessle East Junc.
g) Scunthorpe West Junc.
h) Trent Junc.
j) Crosby Mines
k) Dawes Lane Junc.
l) Priory Yard Branch Junc.
m) Springbank South Junc.
n) Springbank North Junc.

A

Headingley

Holbeck W. Junc. Holbeck E. Junc.

Wortley W. Junc.
Wortley S. Junc.

Leeds
Engine Shed Junc.
HO

Richmond Hill Tun.

Carriage Sidings

Hutton Cranswick

Farnley Junc.

Gelderd Road Junc.

Whitehall Road Goods

Hunslet Engine Co.

Hunslet East Oil Terminals

Arram

Coal Depot

Farnley - Dunlop & Rankin

Hunslet Moor

Balm Lane Junc.

Hunslet East CCE Tip

Robinson & Birdsell Scrapyard

Hunslet Yard

Stourton FLT

Beverley

MIDDLETON RAILWAY

BSC Steel Term.

D. & F. Steels

Garanor Distribution Depot

Cottingham

(1 : 90,000)

Park Halt

(Goole to Gilberdyke is proposed for closure: Hull - Doncaster services being diverted via Selby)

Sculcoates Coal Depot

Sweet Dews - Draper Scrapyard

B

56

Wressle

Howden

Eastrington

Gilberdyke

Broomfleet

Brough

Melton*

Calvert Lane Coal Depot
Boothferry Park

BG Hull

Electro Furnace Products

King George Dock - ABP

Salt End - BP Chemicals

Saltmarshe

Potters Grange Junc.

Goole
Goods

Goole Swing Bridge

Blue Circle Cem. Term.

Ferriby

Sidings

Hessle

FLT & Goods Depot

Rawcliffe

Docks - ABP
Renault Car Term.

Assoc. Chem. Works

New Holland

Oxmarsh Crossing

Engine Shed Junc.

Barton-on-Humber

Barrow Haven

Goxhill

Killingholme - Morton

Thornton Abbey

(SEE INSET P58)

HUMBERSIDE

Immingham

Thorne North

Flixborough Stather (Wharf)

Dragonby Sidings

Scunthorpe Coal Terminal BSC

Ulceby

Habrough

Normanby Park

j FH

Foreign Ore Branch Junc.

Brocklesby

Thorne South

Gunness

Crowle

Althorpe

Scunthorpe

2

BSC Anchor Works

Elsham

Barnetby

CCE Sidings & CCE Tip
Wrawby Junc.

BSC Appleby - Frodingham

Brigg

SOUTH YORKS.

SCUNTHORPE

(Wrawby Junc. to Kirton to be singled)

LINCS.

C

Kirton Lime Sidings

Kirton Tun.

Kirton - Blue Circle Works

Northorpe

Kirton Lindsey

57

48

1   2

0   5   10 m.
0   5   10   15 km.
(1:350,000)

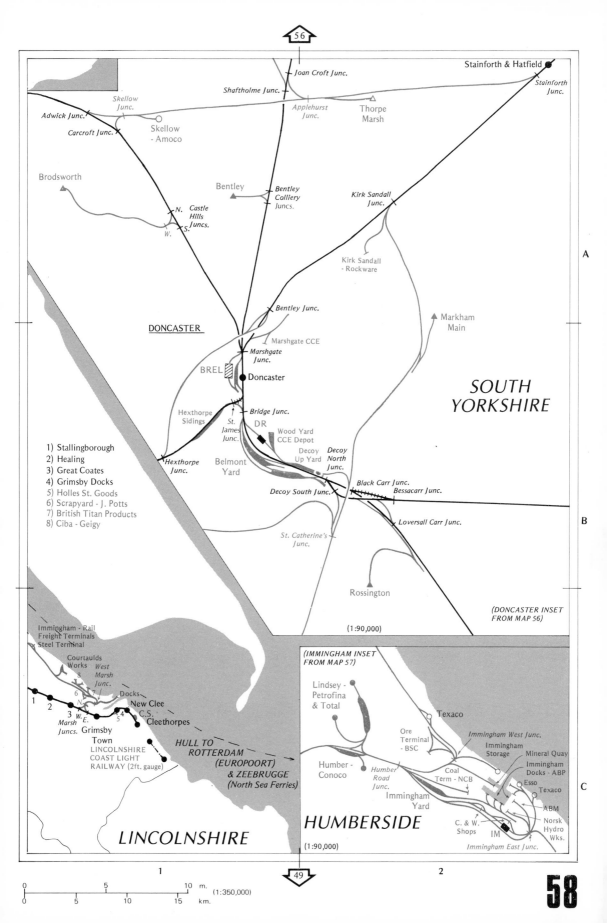

Stainforth & Hatfield

Stainforth Junc.

Joan Croft Junc.

Shaftholme Junc.

Skellow Junc.

Applehurst Junc.

Thorpe Marsh

Adwick Junc.

Skellow - Amoco

Carcroft Junc.

Brodsworth

Bentley

Bentley Colliery Juncs.

Kirk Sandall Junc.

N. *Castle Hills Juncs.*
W. S.

Kirk Sandall - Rockware

A

Bentley Junc.

Markham Main

DONCASTER

Marshgate CCE

Marshgate Junc.

SOUTH YORKSHIRE

BREL

Doncaster

Hexthorpe Sidings

Bridge Junc.

DR

St. James Junc.

Wood Yard CCE Depot

Decoy North Junc.

1) Stallingborough
2) Healing
3) Great Coates
4) Grimsby Docks
5) Holles St. Goods
6) Scrapyard - J. Potts
7) British Titan Products
8) Ciba - Geigy

Hexthorpe Junc.

Belmont Yard

Decoy Up Yard

Black Carr Junc.

Bessacarr Junc.

Decoy South Junc.

Loversall Carr Junc.

B

St. Catherine's Junc.

Rossington

(DONCASTER INSET FROM MAP 56)

(1:90,000)

Immingham - Rail Freight Terminals Steel Terminal

Courtaulds Works

West Marsh Junc.

Docks

New Clee

C.S. Cleethorpes

1 2 3 N. 4 5

Marsh Juncs. W. E.

Grimsby Town

LINCOLNSHIRE COAST LIGHT RAILWAY (2ft. gauge)

HULL TO ROTTERDAM (EUROPOORT) & ZEEBRUGGE (North Sea Ferries)

(IMMINGHAM INSET FROM MAP 57)

Lindsey - Petrofina & Total

Texaco

Ore Terminal - BSC

Immingham West Junc.

Immingham Storage

Mineral Quay

Immingham Docks - ABP

Humber - Conoco

Humber Road Junc.

Coal Term - NCB

Immingham Yard

Esso

Texaco

ABM

Norsk Hydro Wks.

C. & W. Shops

IM

Immingham East Junc.

C

HUMBERSIDE

(1:90,000)

LINCOLNSHIRE

1

2

0 — 5 — 10 m.
(1:350,000)
0 — 5 — 10 — 15 km.

58

Lakeland Maryport

Flimby

Broughton
Moor

Siddick Junc.
Derwent Junc.
Docks *Calva Junc.*
Workington Workington
BSC Works WK Goods

Harrington

Parton

Docks Whitehaven
Haig Coll. *Whitehaven Tun.*
Preston St. Goods Depot Corkickle

Marchon Chem. Wks.

*(Rope-
worked
incline)*

St. Bees

Nethertown

Braystones

Sellafield
Sellafield - British
Nuclear
Fuels

Ramsey

ISLE OF MAN RAILWAYS
(MANX ELECTRIC RAILWAY)
(3FT 0 INS DERBY CASTLE - RAMSEY)
(3FT 6 INS LAXEY - SNAEFELL)

Bellevue

Lewaigue

Cornaa Dreemskerry

Ballaglass Ballajora

Glen Mona

Snaefell Dhoon

Bungalow

Seascale

Drigg - British Drigg *Miteside*
Nuclear Fuels

Ravenglass Muncaster
Mill

*ISLE
OF MAN*

Ballaragh
Minorca
Depot
Laxey South
Fairy Cottage Cape
Ballabeg
Garwick Glen
Baldrine

*Vickers
Gun
Range
Sidings*

Eskmeals

Bootle

TO BELFAST
TO ARDROSSAN

Depot Groudle Glen
DOUGLAS CORP. HORSETRAMS Derby Castle Howstrake
(3FT 0 INS PIER - DERBY CASTLE) Douglas Onchan Head

ISLE OF MAN RAILWAYS
(STEAM OPERATED)
(3 FT 0 INS)

Port Soderick
Santon

To HEYSHAM (Sealink)
Douglas Pier

To FLEETWOOD

Colby Ballabeg
Port Erin Ballasalla
Port St. Mary Castletown

To DUBLIN

To LIVERPOOL

(All Ships I. of Man Steam Packet Co., except Heysham)

1 2

0 5 10 m.
0 5 10 15 km. (1:350,000)

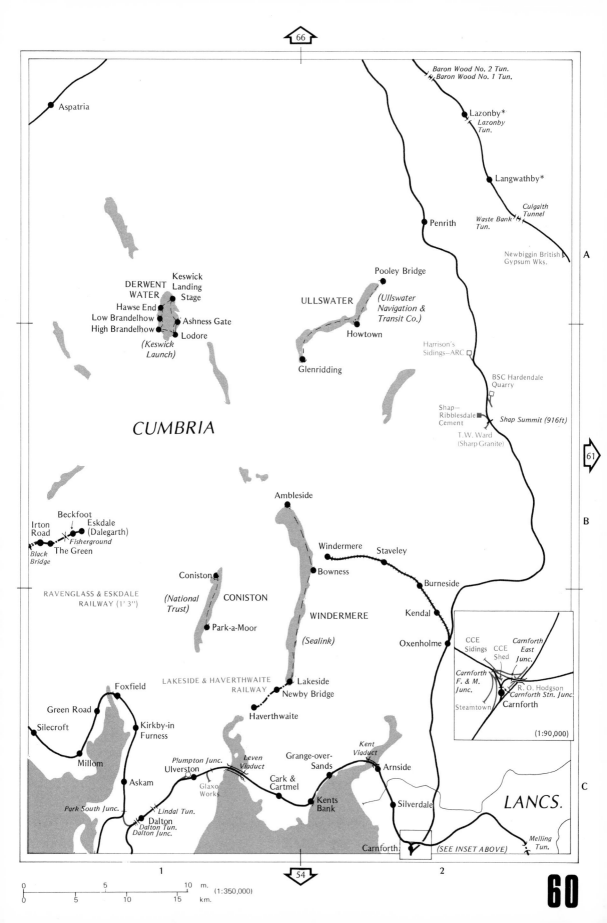

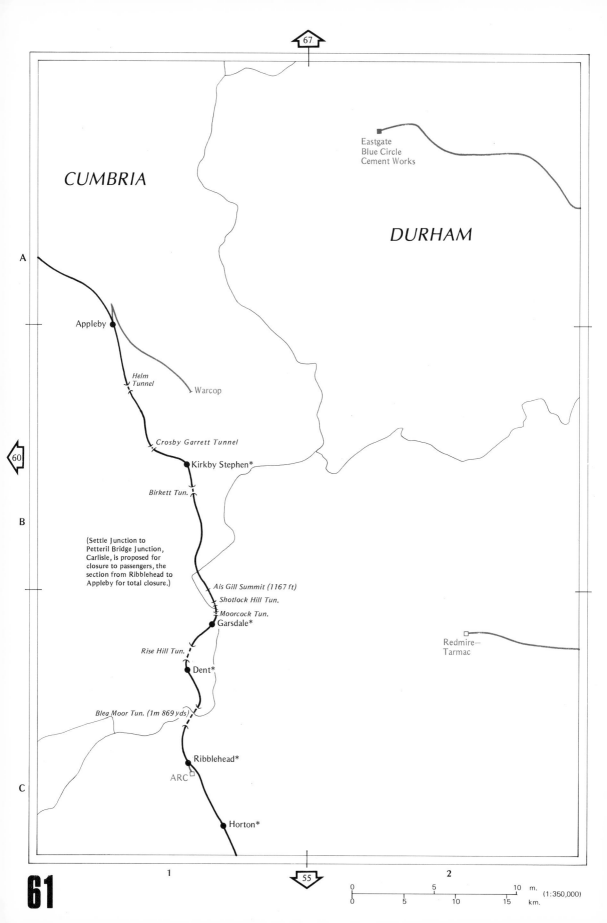

CUMBRIA

DURHAM

Eastgate
Blue Circle
Cement Works

A

Appleby

*Helm
Tunnel*

Warcop

Crosby Garrett Tunnel

60

Kirkby Stephen*

Birkett Tun.

B

(Settle Junction to
Petteril Bridge Junction,
Carlisle, is proposed for
closure to passengers, the
section from Ribblehead to
Appleby for total closure.)

Ais Gill Summit (1167 ft)
Shotlock Hill Tun.
Moorcock Tun.
Garsdale*

Redmire—
Tarmac

Rise Hill Tun.

Dent*

Blea Moor Tun. (1m 869 yds)

Ribblehead*

ARC

C

Horton*

1

55

2

0   5   10   m.   (1:350,000)
0   5   10   15   km.

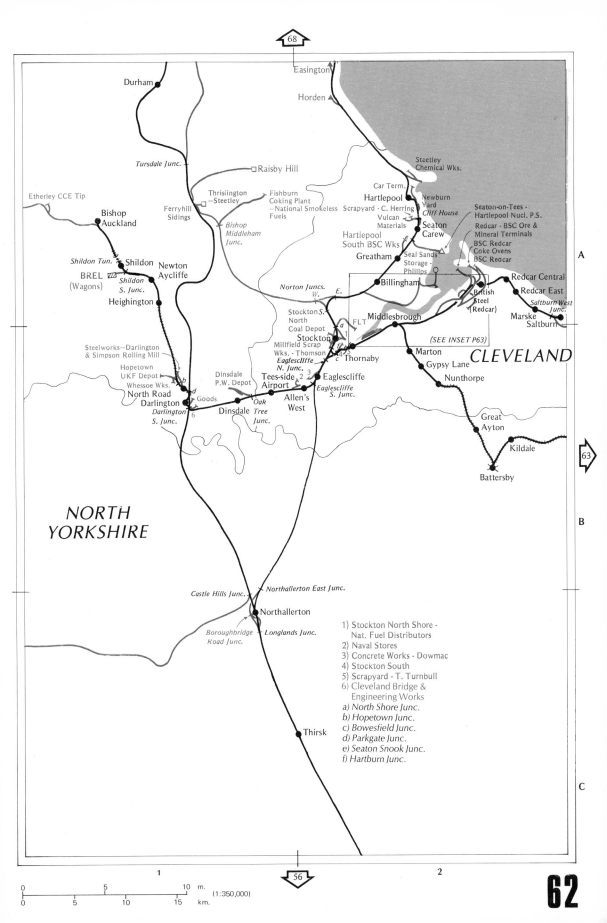

68

Durham

Easington

Horden

Tursdale Junc.

Raisby Hill

Steetley
Chemical Wks.

Etherley CCE Tip

Thrislington
—Steetley

Fishburn
Coking Plant
—National Smokeless
Fuels

Car Term.

Hartlepool

Bishop
Auckland

Ferryhill
Sidings

Bishop
Middleham
Junc.

Scrapyard - C. Herring
Vulcan
Materials

Newburn
Yard
Cliff House

Seaton-on-Tees -
Hartlepool Nucl. P.S.
Redcar - BSC Ore &
Mineral Terminals
BSC Redcar
Coke Ovens
BSC Redcar

Shildon Tun.

Shildon

Newton
Aycliffe

Hartlepool
South BSC Wks

Seaton
Carew

e

Seal Sands
Storage -
Phillips

A

BREL
(Wagons)

Shildon
S. Junc.

Greatham

Redcar Central

Redcar East

Heighington

Norton Juncs.

W.

E.

Billingham

British
Steel
(Redcar)

Saltburn West
Junc.

Steelworks—Darlington
& Simpson Rolling Mill

Stockton S.
North
Coal Depot

FLT

Middlesbrough

Marske

Saltburn

Hopetown
UKF Depot

Dinsdale
P.W. Depot

Stockton

a

1

(SEE INSET P63)

CLEVELAND

Whessoe Wks.

North Road
Darlington

b

d

Millfield Scrap
Wks. - Thomson

5

f

Marton

Eaglescliffe
N. Junc.

c

Thornaby

Gypsy Lane

Goods

Tees-side
Airport

2

3

Eaglescliffe

Nunthorpe

Darlington
S. Junc.

6

Dinsdale

Oak
Tree
Junc.

Allen's
West

Eaglescliffe
S. Junc.

Great
Ayton

Kildale

63

Battersby

NORTH
YORKSHIRE

B

Castle Hills Junc.

Northallerton East Junc.

Northallerton

1) Stockton North Shore -
Nat. Fuel Distributors
2) Naval Stores
3) Concrete Works - Dowmac
4) Stockton South
5) Scrapyard - T. Turnbull
6) Cleveland Bridge &
Engineering Works
a) North Shore Junc.
b) Hopetown Junc.
c) Bowesfield Junc.
d) Parkgate Junc.
e) Seaton Snook Junc.
f) Hartburn Junc.

Boroughbridge
Road Junc.

Longlands Junc.

Thirsk

C

1

56

2

0   5   10 m.
0   5   10   15 km.
(1:350,000)

62

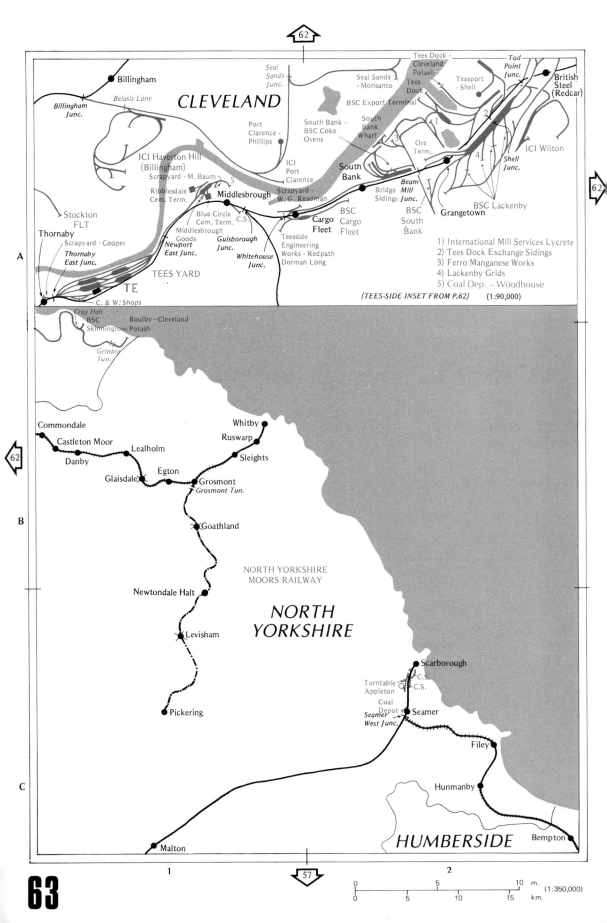

CLEVELAND

Billingham

Belasis Lane

Billingham Junc.

Seal Sands Junc.

Seal Sands - Monsanto

Tees Dock - Cleveland Potash

Tod Point Junc.

Teesport - Shell

British Steel (Redcar)

Tees Dock

BSC Export Terminal

Port Clarence - Phillips

ICI Port Clarence

South Bank - BSC Coke Ovens

South Bank Wharf

1)

2)

ICI Wilton

ICI Haverton Hill (Billingham)

Scrapyard - M. Baum

Ribblesdale Cem. Term.

Middlesbrough

Scrapyard - W. G. Readman

South Bank

Ore Term.

3)

Shell Junc.

4)

BSC Lackenby

Stockton FLT

Blue Circle Cem. Term.

C.S.

Newport East Junc.

Middlesbrough Goods

Guisborough Junc.

Cargo Fleet

Bridge Sidings

Beam Mill Junc.

BSC Cargo Fleet

BSC South Bank

Grangetown

Thornaby

Scrapyard - Cooper

Thornaby East Junc.

Whitehouse Junc.

Teesside Engineering Works - Redpath Dorman Long

5

A

TEES YARD

TE

1) International Mill Services Lycrete
2) Tees Dock Exchange Sidings
3) Ferro Manganese Works
4) Lackenby Grids
5) Coal Dep. – Woodhouse

(TEES-SIDE INSET FROM P.62)   **(1:90,000)**

C. & W. Shops

Crag Hall

BSC Skinningrove Potash

Boulby—Cleveland

Grinkle Tun.

Commondale

Castleton Moor

Danby

Lealholm

Whitby

Ruswarp

Sleights

Glaisdale

Egton

Grosmont

Grosmont Tun.

62

Goathland

B

NORTH YORKSHIRE MOORS RAILWAY

NORTH YORKSHIRE

Newtondale Halt

Levisham

Scarborough

Turntable Appleton

C.S.

C.S.

Coal Depot

Seamer West Junc.

Seamer

Pickering

Filey

C

Hunmanby

HUMBERSIDE

Malton

Bempton

63

1

2

0   5   10 m.

0   5   10   15 km.

(1:350,000)

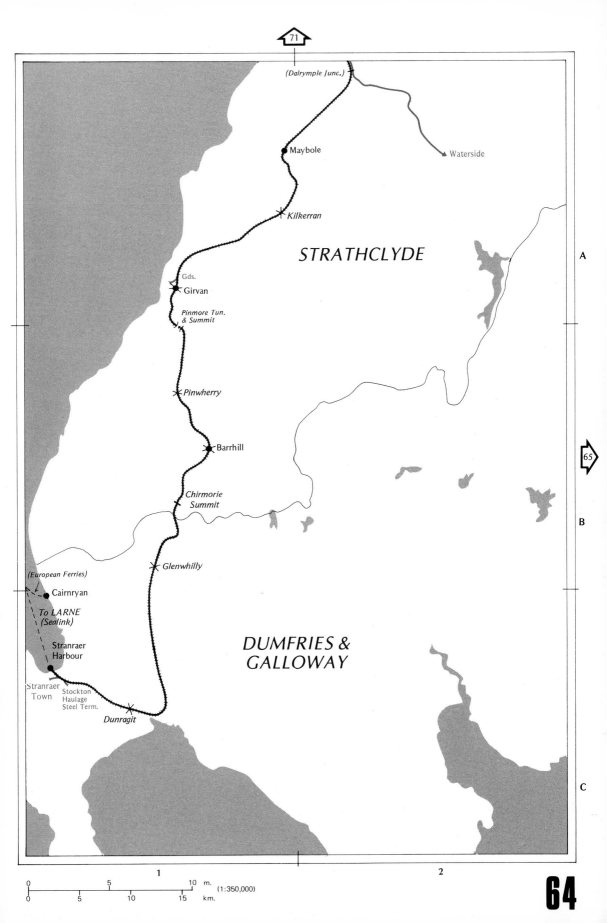

(Dalrymple Junc.)

Waterside

● Maybole

✕ *Kilkerran*

STRATHCLYDE

A

Gds.
✕ Girvan

*Pinmore Tun.
& Summit*

✕ *Pinwherry*

● Barrhill

*Chirmorie
Summit*

65

B

✕ *Glenwhilly*

(European Ferries)
● Cairnryan

*To LARNE
(Sealink)*

Stranraer
Harbour

**DUMFRIES &
GALLOWAY**

Stranraer
Town

Stockton
Haulage
Steel Term.
✕
Dunragit

C

1   2

0   5   10 m. (1:350,000)
0   5   10   15 km.

64

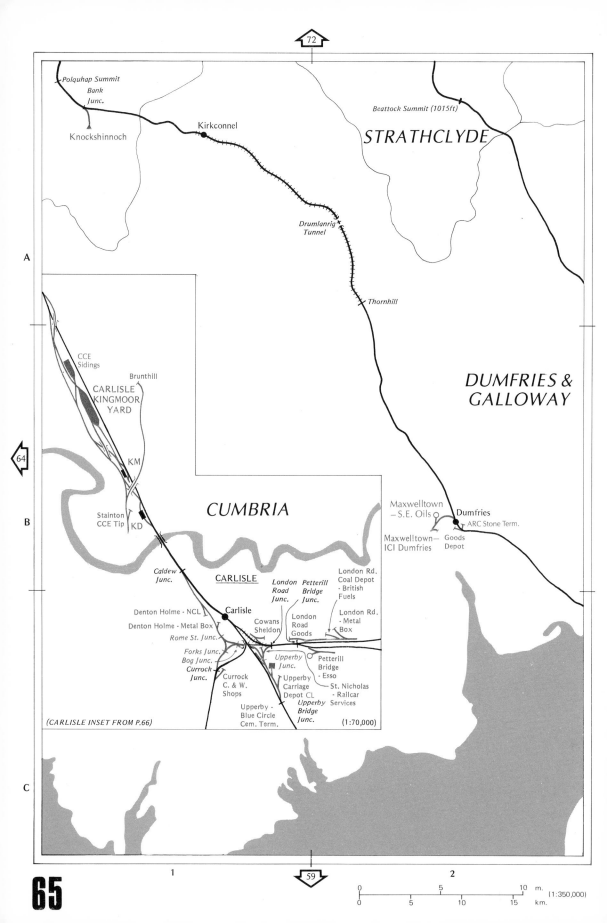

Polquhap Summit
Bank
Junc.

Knockshinnoch

Kirkconnel

Beattock Summit (1015ft)

STRATHCLYDE

*Drumlanrig
Tunnel*

A

Thornhill

**DUMFRIES &
GALLOWAY**

CCE
Sidings

Brunthill

CARLISLE
KINGMOOR
YARD

64

KM

Stainton
CCE Tip   KD

B

CUMBRIA

Maxwelltown
— S.E. Oils   Dumfries
                   ARC Stone Term.
Maxwelltown—   Goods
ICI Dumfries   Depot

*Caldew
Junc.*

<u>CARLISLE</u>

Carlisle

*London   Petterill
Road   Bridge
Junc.   Junc.*

London Rd.
Coal Depot
- British
Fuels

Denton Holme - NCL

Denton Holme - Metal Box

Rome St. Junc.

Cowans
Sheldon

London
Road
Goods

London Rd.
- Metal
Box

*Forks Junc.
Bog Junc.
Currock
Junc.*

Currock
C. & W.
Shops

*Upperby
Junc.*

Petterill
Bridge
- Esso

Upperby
Carriage
Depot CL

St. Nicholas
- Railcar
Services

Upperby -
Blue Circle
Cem. Term.

*Upperby
Bridge
Junc.*

(CARLISLE INSET FROM P.66)

(1:70,000)

C

1   59   2

0   5   10 m.
0   5   10   15   km.
                        (1:350,000)

65

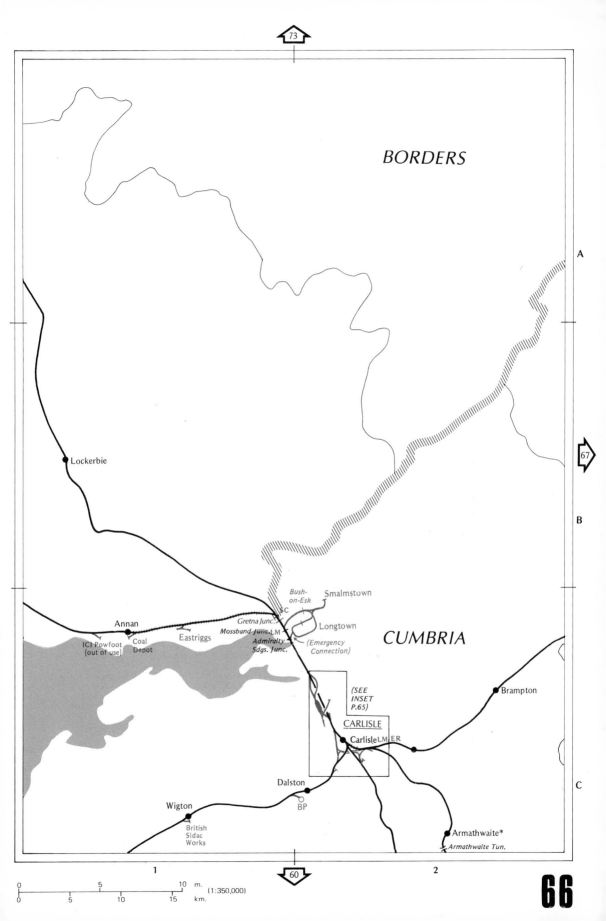

BORDERS

A

67

B

Bush-
on-Esk   Smalmstown

SC

Gretna Junc.   Longtown

CUMBRIA

Annan

LM

Mossband Junc.

ICI Powfoot   Coal   Eastriggs   Admiralty   (Emergency
(out of use)   Depot   Sdgs. Junc.   Connection)

Lockerbie

Brampton

(SEE
INSET
P.65)

CARLISLE

Carlisle LM ER

Dalston

BP   C

Wigton

British
Sidac
Works

Armathwaite*

Armathwaite Tun.

0   5   10   m.   (1:350,000)
0   5   10   15   km.

66

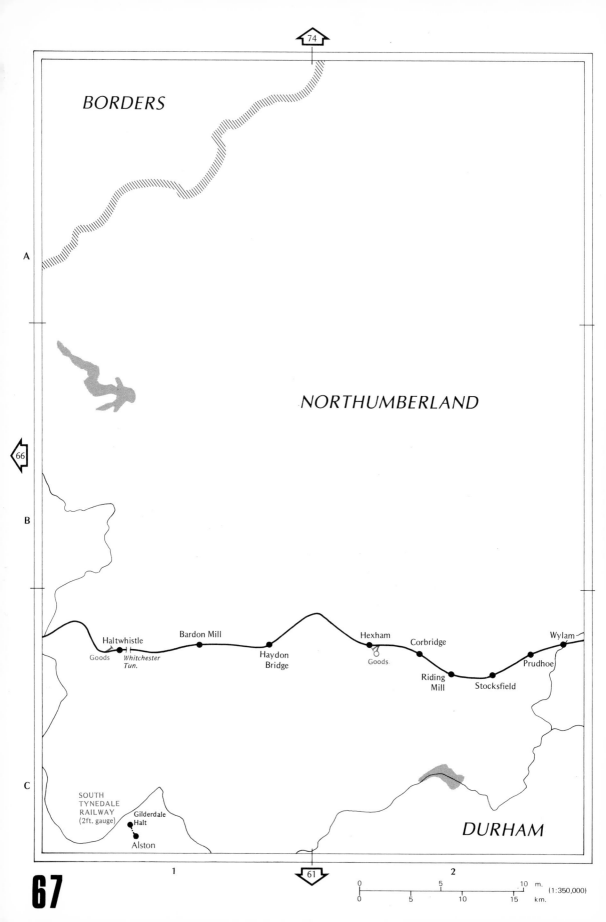

BORDERS

NORTHUMBERLAND

66

A

B

C

Haltwhistle

Goods   Whitchester
         Tun.

Bardon Mill

Haydon
Bridge

Hexham

Goods

Corbridge

Riding
Mill

Stocksfield

Prudhoe

Wylam

SOUTH
TYNEDALE
RAILWAY
(2ft. gauge)

Gilderdale
Halt

Alston

DURHAM

1   2

0   5   10 m.   (1:350,000)
0   5   10   15   km.

67

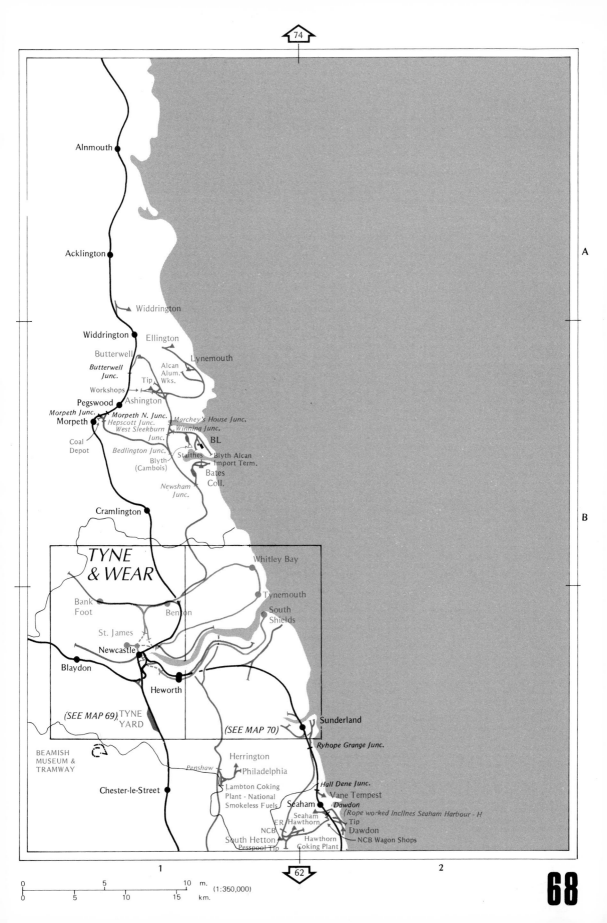

A

Alnmouth

Acklington

Widdrington

Widdrington
Ellington
Butterwell
Lynemouth
Butterwell
Junc.
Alcan
Alum.
Wks.
Workshops
Tip
Pegswood
Ashington
Morpeth Junc.
Morpeth N. Junc.
Marchey's House Junc.
Morpeth
Hepscott Junc.
Winning Junc.
West Sleekburn
Junc.
BL
Coal
Depot
Bedlington Junc.
Staithes
Blyth Alcan
Import Term.
Blyth
(Cambois)
Bates
Coll.
Newsham
Junc.

B

Cramlington

TYNE
& WEAR

Whitley Bay

Bank
Foot
Benton
Tynemouth

St. James
South
Shields

Newcastle

Blaydon

Heworth

(SEE MAP 69) TYNE
YARD
(SEE MAP 70)
Sunderland

BEAMISH
MUSEUM &
TRAMWAY
Ryhope Grange Junc.

Herrington

Penshaw
Philadelphia
Hall Dene Junc.
Vane Tempest
Chester-le-Street
Lambton Coking
Plant - National
Smokeless Fuels
Seaham
Dawdon
(Rope worked inclines Seaham Harbour - H
Seaham
Hawthorn
Tip
ER
Dawdon
NCB
NCB Wagon Shops
South Hetton
Hawthorn
Coking Plant
Pesspool Tip

0　　　　　　5　　　　　　10　m.　(1:350,000)
0　　　5　　　10　　　15　km.

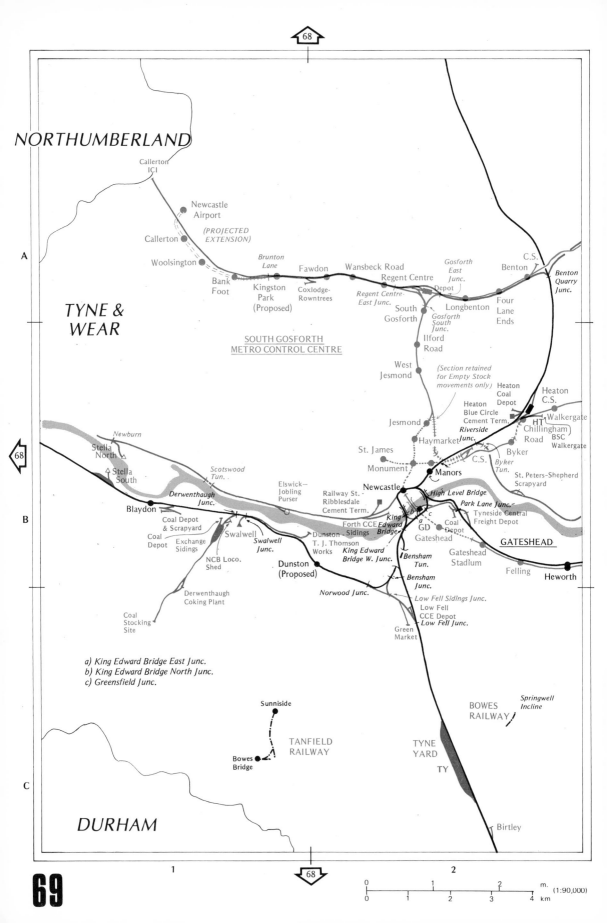

NORTHUMBERLAND

TYNE &
WEAR

Callerton ICI

Newcastle
Airport

Callerton

*(PROJECTED
EXTENSION)*

Woolsington

C.S.
Benton

*Brunton
Lane*

Fawdon

Wansbeck Road
Regent Centre

*Gosforth
East
Junc.*

*Benton
Quarry
Junc.*

Bank
Foot

Kingston
Park
(Proposed)

Coxlodge-
Rowntrees

*Regent Centre
East Junc.*

Depot

South
Gosforth

Longbenton

Four
Lane
Ends

SOUTH GOSFORTH
METRO CONTROL CENTRE

*Gosforth
South
Junc.*

Ilford
Road

West
Jesmond

*(Section retained
for Empty Stock
movements only)*

Heaton
Coal
Depot

Heaton
C.S.

Jesmond

Heaton
Blue Circle
Cement Term.

HT

Chillingham
Road

Walkergate

BSC
Walkergate

St. James

Haymarket

*Riverside
Junc.*

Byker

Monument

C.S.

*Byker
Tun.*

St. Peters-Shepherd
Scrapyard

Newcastle

Manors

Newburn

Stella
North

*Scotswood
Tun.*

Elswick—
Jobling
Purser

Railway St.-
Ribblesdale
Cement Term.

High Level Bridge

Park Lane Junc.

Tyneside Central
Freight Depot

Stella
South

*Derwenthaugh
Junc.*

Forth CCE
Sidings

*King
Edward
Bridge*

GD

Coal
Depot

Blaydon

Coal Depot
& Scrapyard

Swalwell

*Swalwell
Junc.*

Dunston
T. J. Thomson
Works

*King Edward
Bridge W. Junc.*

Gateshead

GATESHEAD

Coal
Depot

Exchange
Sidings

Dunston
(Proposed)

*Bensham
Tun.*

Gateshead
Stadium

Felling

Heworth

NCB Loco.
Shed

Norwood Junc.

*Bensham
Junc.*

Low Fell Sidings Junc.
Low Fell
CCE Depot
Low Fell Junc.

Derwenthaugh
Coking Plant

Green
Market

Coal
Stocking
Site

a) *King Edward Bridge East Junc.*
b) *King Edward Bridge North Junc.*
c) *Greensfield Junc.*

Sunniside

*Springwell
Incline*

BOWES
RAILWAY

TANFIELD
RAILWAY

TYNE
YARD

TY

Bowes
Bridge

DURHAM

Birtley

69

0   1   2   3   4 km
0   1   2   3   m. (1:90,000)

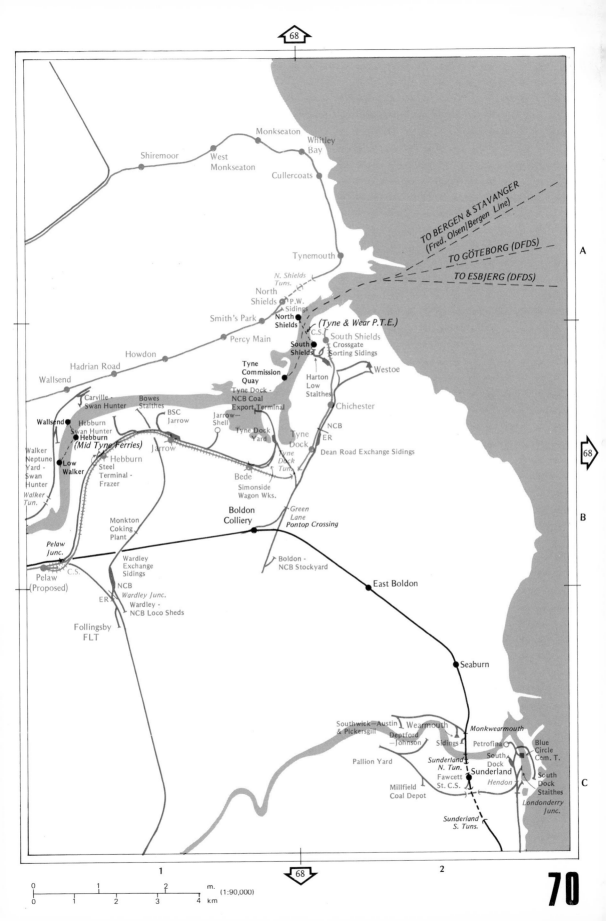

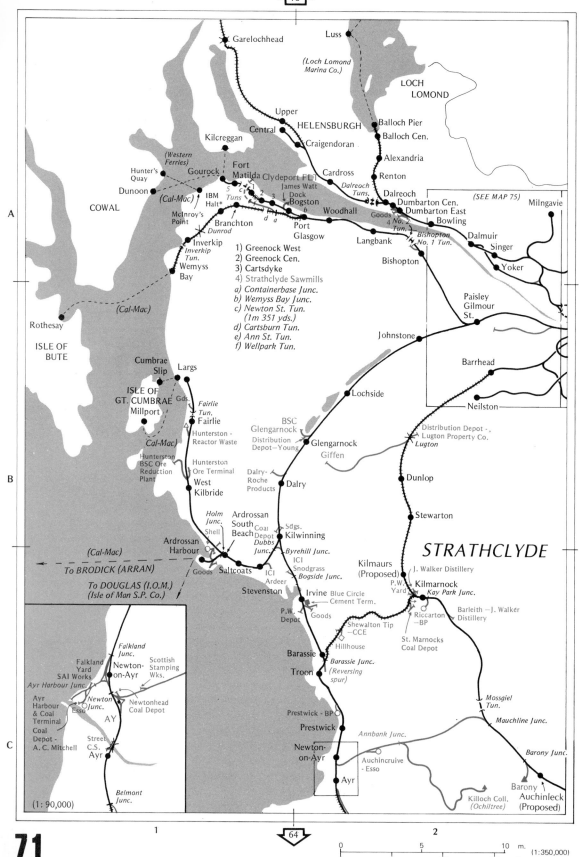

Garelochhead

Luss

(Loch Lomond Marina Co.)

LOCH LOMOND

Upper

Central

HELENSBURGH

Craigendoran

Balloch Pier

Balloch Cen.

Alexandria

Renton

Cardross

Dalreoch Tuns.

Kilcreggan

(Western Ferries)

Hunter's Quay

Gourock

Fort Matilda

Clydeport FLT

James Watt Dock

Dalreoch

Dumbarton Cen.

Dumbarton East

Bowling

(SEE MAP 75)

Milngavie

Dunoon

(Cal-Mac)

IBM Halt*

c

5 Tuns.

1

2

Bogston

3

b

Woodhall

Goods

4 No. 2 Tun.

Bishopton No. 1 Tun.

Dalmuir

Singer

Yoker

COWAL

McInroy's Point

Branchton

Dunrod

d a

Port Glasgow

Langbank

Bishopton

Paisley Gilmour St.

Inverkip

Inverkip Tun.

Wemyss Bay

1) Greenock West
2) Greenock Cen.
3) Cartsdyke
4) Strathclyde Sawmills
a) Containerbase Junc.
b) Wemyss Bay Junc.
c) Newton St. Tun. (1m 351 yds.)
d) Cartsburn Tun.
e) Ann St. Tun.
f) Wellpark Tun.

Johnstone

Barrhead

Neilston

Rothesay

ISLE OF BUTE

(Cal-Mac)

Cumbrae Slip

Largs

ISLE OF GT. CUMBRAE

Millport

Gds.

Fairlie Tun.

Fairlie

Lochside

BSC Glengarnock

Distribution Depot—Young

Glengarnock

Giffen

Distribution Depot - Lugton Property Co.

Lugton

(Cal-Mac)

Hunterston - Reactor Waste

Hunterston BSC Ore Reduction Plant

Hunterston Ore Terminal

West Kilbride

Dalry-Roche Products

Dalry

Dunlop

Stewarton

STRATHCLYDE

Holm Junc. Shell

Ardrossan South Beach

Coal Depot Dubbs Junc.

Sdgs.

Kilwinning

Byrehill Junc.

ICI Snodgrass

Bogside Junc.

Kilmaurs (Proposed)

J. Walker Distillery

P.W. Yard

Kilmarnock

Kay Park Junc.

Ardrossan Harbour

(Cal-Mac)

To BRODICK (ARRAN)

To DOUGLAS (I.O.M.) (Isle of Man S.P. Co.)

Goods

Saltcoats

ICI Ardeer

Stevenston

Irvine

Blue Circle Cement Term.

P.W. Depot

Goods

Shewalton Tip —CCE

Hillhouse

Riccarton —BP

St. Marnocks Coal Depot

Barleith —J. Walker Distillery

Barassie

Barassie Junc. (Reversing spur)

Troon

Mossgiel Tun.

Mauchline Junc.

Falkland Junc.

Falkland Yard SAI Works

Newton-on-Ayr

Scottish Stamping Wks.

Ayr Harbour Junc.

Esso

Newton Junc.

AY

Newtonhead Coal Depot

Ayr Harbour & Coal Terminal Coal Depot - A. C. Mitchell

Street C.S. Ayr

Prestwick - BP

Prestwick

Annbank Junc.

Newton-on-Ayr

Auchincruive - Esso

Barony Junc.

(1: 90,000)

Belmont Junc.

Ayr

Killoch Coll. (Ochiltree)

Barony Auchinleck (Proposed)

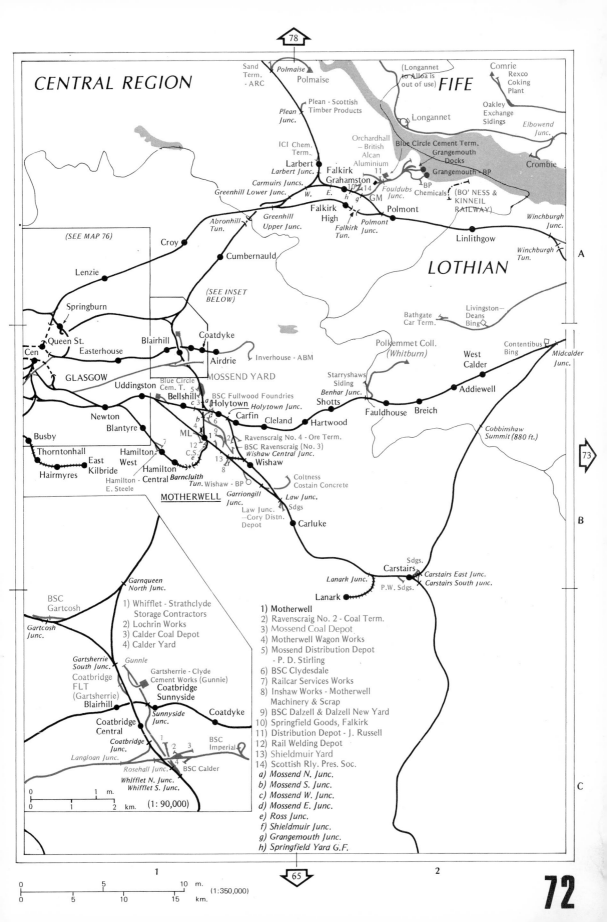

CENTRAL REGION

FIFE

Sand Term. - ARC
Polmaise
Polmaise

(Longannet to Alloa is out of use)

Comrie
Rexco Coking Plant

Plean - Scottish Timber Products

Longannet

Oakley Exchange Sidings

Plean Junc.

Elbowend Junc.

ICI Chem. Term.

Orchardhall – British Alcan Aluminium

Blue Circle Cement Term. Grangemouth Docks

Crombie

Larbert
Larbert Junc.

Falkirk Grahamston

11

Grangemouth - BP

Carmuirs Juncs.

W. E. GM
Fouldubs Junc.

BP Chemicals

Greenhill Lower Junc.

10 14
h g

(BO' NESS & KINNEL RAILWAY)

Abronhill Tun.

Greenhill Upper Junc.

Falkirk High

Polmont

Winchburgh Junc.

Croy

Falkirk Tun.

Polmont Junc.

Linlithgow

LOTHIAN

Cumbernauld

Winchburgh Tun.

A

(SEE MAP 76)

Lenzie

(SEE INSET BELOW)

Springburn

Bathgate Car Term.

Livingston – Deans Bing

Contentibus Bing

Midcalder Junc.

Queen St.
Cen

Easterhouse

Blairhill

Coatdyke

Polkemmet Coll. *(Whitburn)*

West Calder

GLASGOW

Airdrie

Inverhouse - ABM

MOSSEND YARD

Starryshaws Siding

Addiewell

Uddingston

Blue Circle Cem. T. 5

BSC Fullwood Foundries

Benhar Junc.

Bellshill

c 3 Holytown

Holytown Junc.

Shotts

Fauldhouse

Breich

Newton

Blantyre

b 4 6

Carfin

Cleland

Hartwood

Cobbinshaw Summit (880 ft.)

Busby

ML

9 1

a

Ravenscraig No. 4 - Ore Term.

Thorntonhall

12 2

BSC Ravenscraig (No. 3)

Hamilton West

C.S. e

Wishaw Central Junc.

73

Hairmyres

East Kilbride

13

8

Wishaw

Hamilton Central *Barncluith*

Tun. Wishaw - BP

Coltness Costain Concrete

Hamilton E. Steele

MOTHERWELL

Garriongill Junc.

Law Junc.

Sdgs.

Law Junc. -Cory Distn. Depot

Carluke

B

Sdgs.

Carstairs

Lanark Junc.

Carstairs East Junc.
Carstairs South Junc.

P.W. Sdgs.

Lanark

BSC Gartcosh

1) Whifflet - Strathclyde Storage Contractors
2) Lochrin Works
3) Calder Coal Depot
4) Calder Yard

1) **Motherwell**
2) Ravenscraig No. 2 - Coal Term.
3) Mossend Coal Depot
4) Motherwell Wagon Works
5) Mossend Distribution Depot - P. D. Stirling
6) BSC Clydesdale
7) Railcar Services Works
8) Inshaw Works - Motherwell Machinery & Scrap
9) BSC Dalzell & Dalzell New Yard
10) Springfield Goods, Falkirk
11) Distribution Depot - J. Russell
12) Rail Welding Depot
13) Shieldmuir Yard
14) Scottish Rly. Pres. Soc.

Gartcosh Junc.

Gartsherrie South Junc.
Coatbridge FLT (Gartsherrie)
Blairhill

Gunnie

Gartsherrie - Clyde Cement Works (Gunnie)

Coatbridge Sunnyside

Coatbridge Central

Sunnyside Junc.

Coatdyke

Coatbridge Junc.

1

BSC Imperial

Langloan Junc.

2 3

Rosehall Junc.

4 BSC Calder

Whifflet N. Junc.
Whifflet S. Junc.

a) *Mossend N. Junc.*
b) *Mossend S. Junc.*
c) *Mossend W. Junc.*
d) *Mossend E. Junc.*
e) *Ross Junc.*
f) *Shieldmuir Junc.*
g) *Grangemouth Junc.*
h) *Springfield Yard G.F.*

0   1 m.
0   1   2 km.

(1: 90,000)

C

0   5   10 m.
(1:350,000)

0   5   10 m.
0   5   10   15 km.

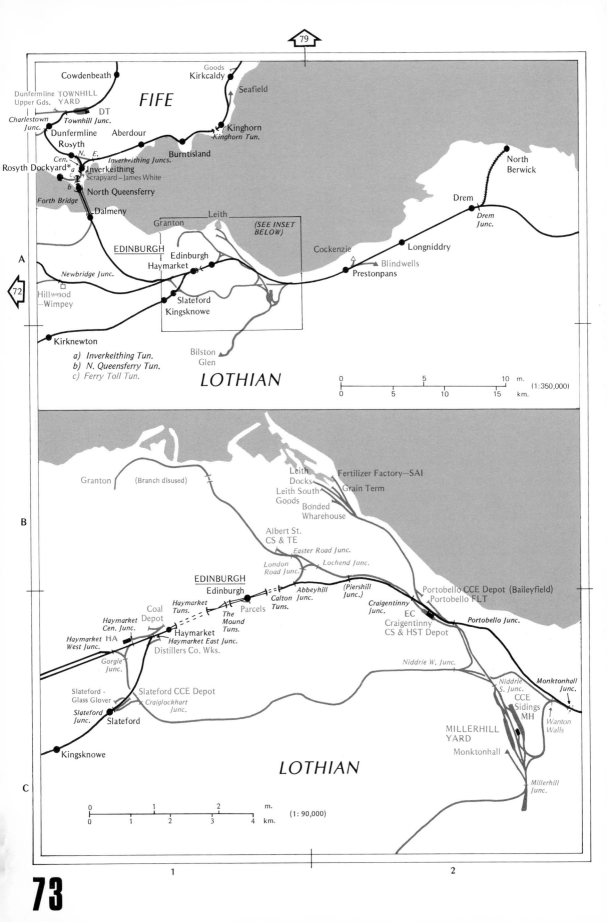

Cowdenbeath

Goods
Kirkcaldy
Seafield

FIFE

Dunfermline TOWNHILL
Upper Gds. YARD
DT
Charlestown Junc. *Townhill Junc.*
Dunfermline Aberdour
Rosyth Kinghorn
Kinghorn Tun.
N. E. Burntisland
Cen. *Inverkeithing Juncs.*
Rosyth Dockyard* *a* Inverkeithing
Scrapyard – James White North
Berwick
b North Queensferry
Forth Bridge Drem
Dalmeny *Drem Junc.*

Granton Leith
EDINBURGH *(SEE INSET BELOW)*
Edinburgh Cockenzie Longniddry
Haymarket Blindwells
A *Newbridge Junc.* Prestonpans

72 Hillwood
Wimpey
Slateford
Kingsknowe

Kirknewton

a) Inverkeithing Tun.
b) N. Queensferry Tun.
c) Ferry Toll Tun.

Bilston
Glen

LOTHIAN

0   5   10   m.
0   5   10   15   km.
(1:350,000)

Granton (Branch disused)

Leith
Docks
Leith South
Goods
Bonded
Wharehouse

Fertilizer Factory—SAI
Grain Term

Albert St.
CS & TE
Easter Road Junc.

B *London* *Lochend Junc.*
Road Junc.

EDINBURGH
Edinburgh
Abbeyhill Portobello CCE Depot (Baileyfield)
Haymarket *Junc.* *(Piershill* Portobello FLT
Tuns. Calton *Junc.)*
Coal *The* *Tuns.* *Craigentinny* EC *Portobello Junc.*
Depot *Mound* Parcels *Junc.* Craigentinny
Haymarket HA *Tuns.* CS & HST Depot
Haymarket *Cen. Junc.*
West Junc. Haymarket
Haymarket East Junc.
Gorgie Distillers Co. Wks.
Junc. *Niddrie W. Junc.*
Niddrie *Monktonhall*
Slateford – Slateford CCE Depot *S. Junc.* *Junc.*
Glass Glover *Craiglockhart* CCE
Slateford *Junc.* Sidings
Junc. Slateford MH *Wanton*
Walls
Kingsknowe MILLERHILL
YARD
Monktonhall
LOTHIAN
C *Millerhill*
Junc.

0   1   2   m.
0   1   2   3   4   km.
(1: 90,000)

1   2

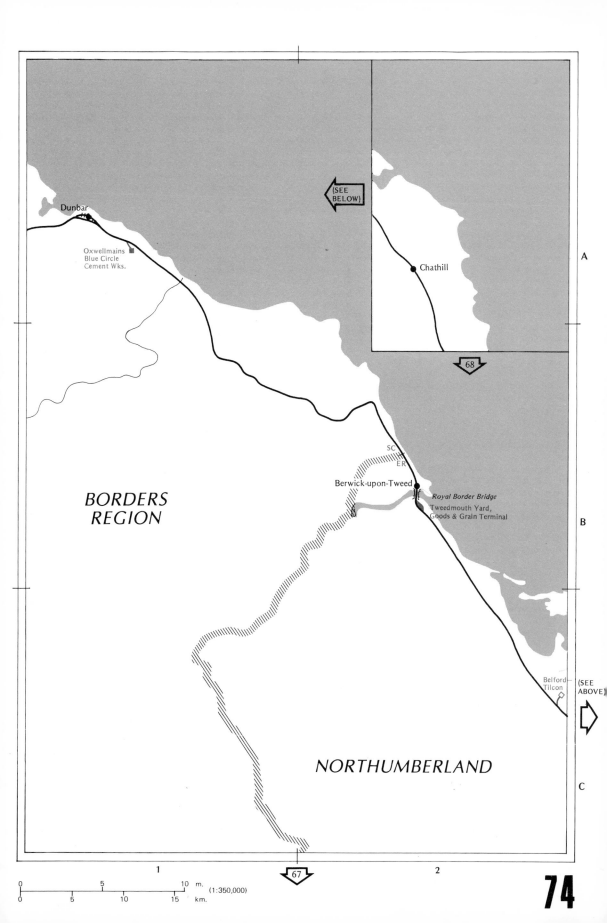

(SEE BELOW)

Dunbar

Oxwellmains
Blue Circle
Cement Wks.

Chathill

A

68

SC
ER

Berwick-upon-Tweed

Royal Border Bridge
Tweedmouth Yard,
Goods & Grain Terminal

B

BORDERS
REGION

Belford
Tilcon

(SEE
ABOVE)

NORTHUMBERLAND

C

1

67

2

0   5   10 m. (1:350,000)
0 5 10 15 km.

74

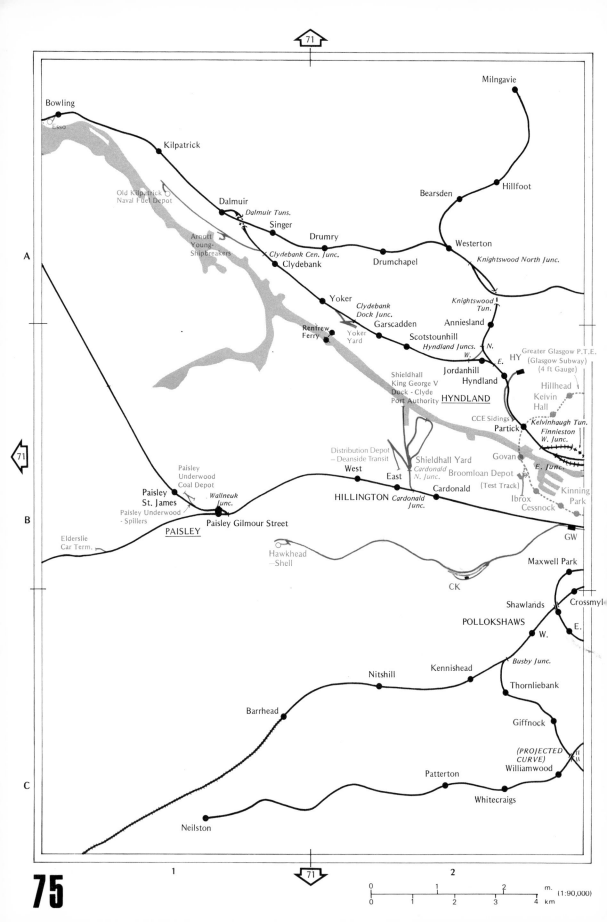

Milngavie

Bowling
Esso

Kilpatrick

Hillfoot

Bearsden

Westerton

Old Kilpatrick
Naval Fuel Depot

Dalmuir

Dalmuir Tuns.

Singer

Drumry

Knightswood North Junc.

Arnott
Young
Shipbreakers

Clydebank Cen. Junc.

Clydebank

Drumchapel

A

Yoker

*Clydebank
Dock Junc.*

Garscadden

*Knightswood
Tun.*

Anniesland

Renfrew
Ferry

*Yoker
Yard*

Scotstounhill

Hyndland Juncs. N.

W.

E.

HY

Greater Glasgow P.T.E.
(Glasgow Subway)
(4 ft Gauge)

Shieldhall
King George V
Dock - Clyde
Port Authority

Jordanhill

Hyndland

HYNDLAND

Hillhead

Kelvin
Hall

CCE Sidings

Kelvinhaugh Tun.

Partick

*Finnieston
W. Junc.*

71

Distribution Depot
– Deanside Transit

Shieldhall Yard

*Cardonald
N. Junc.*

Govan

E. Junc.

Broomloan Depot
(Test Track)

Kinning
Park

West

East

Cardonald

Paisley
Underwood
Coal Depot

*Wallneuk
Junc.*

HILLINGTON

*Cardonald
Junc.*

Ibrox
Cessnock

Paisley
St. James

Paisley Underwood
- Spillers

PAISLEY

Paisley Gilmour Street

B

GW

Elderslie
Car Term.

Hawkhead
–Shell

Maxwell Park

CK

Crossmyl

Shawlands

E.

POLLOKSHAWS

W.

Kennishead

Busby Junc.

Thornliebank

Nitshill

Barrhead

Giffnock

*(PROJECTED
CURVE)*

Williamwood

C

Patterton

Whitecraigs

Neilston

75

1

2

m. (1:90,000)

0   1   2   3   4   km

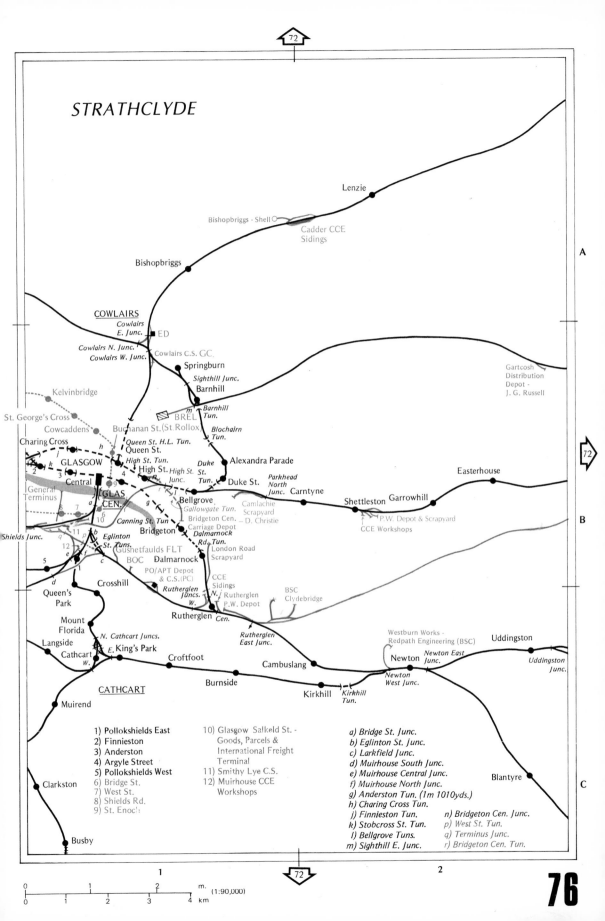

STRATHCLYDE

Lenzie

Bishopbriggs - Shell

Cadder CCE
Sidings

A

Bishopbriggs

COWLAIRS
Cowlairs
E. Junc.   ED
Cowlairs N. Junc.
Cowlairs W. Junc.   Cowlairs C.S. GC.
Springburn

Gartcosh
Distribution
Depot -
J. G. Russell

Sighthill Junc.
Barnhill

BREL   m   Barnhill
Tun.

72

Kelvinbridge

St. George's Cross   Buchanan St. (St. Rollox)   Blochairn
Tun.

Cowcaddens   Queen St. H.L. Tun.
Queen St.

Charing Cross   h   High St. Tun.   Duke
St. Tun.   Alexandra Parade

GLASGOW   j
k   High St.   High St. Junc.   Duke St.   Parkhead
North
Junc.   Carntyne   Easterhouse

General
Terminus   Central   9   Canning St. Tun.   Bellgrove   Shettleston   Garrowhill

GLAS.
CEN.   g   Gallowgate Tun.
Bridgeton Cen.   Camlachie
Scrapyard
– D. Christie   P.W. Depot & Scrapyard
B

Shields Junc.   11   b   Canning St. Tun.   Bridgeton   Carriage Depot   CCE Workshops

12   q   p   Eglinton
St. Tuns.   Dalmarnock
Rd. Tun.   London Road
Scrapyard

e   f   Gushetfaulds FLT
BOC   Dalmarnock   BSC
Clydebridge

5   c   PO/APT Depot
& C.S.(PC)   CCE
Sidings

d   Crosshill   Rutherglen
Juncs.   N.   Rutherglen
W.   Rutherglen P.W. Depot

Queen's
Park   Rutherglen
Cen.

Mount
Florida   Rutherglen
East Junc.   Westburn Works -
Redpath Engineering (BSC)   Uddingston

Langside   N. Cathcart Juncs.
Cathcart   E. King's Park   Croftfoot   Cambuslang   Newton   Newton East
Junc.   Uddingston
Junc.

CATHCART   W.   Burnside   Kirkhill   Newton
West Junc.

Muirend   Kirkhill
Tun.

Clarkston   Blantyre
C

Busby

1) Pollokshields East
2) Finnieston
3) Anderston
4) Argyle Street
5) Pollokshields West
6) Bridge St.
7) West St.
8) Shields Rd.
9) St. Enoch

10) Glasgow Salkeld St. -
    Goods, Parcels &
    International Freight
    Terminal
11) Smithy Lye C.S.
12) Muirhouse CCE
    Workshops

a) Bridge St. Junc.
b) Eglinton St. Junc.
c) Larkfield Junc.
d) Muirhouse South Junc.
e) Muirhouse Central Junc.
f) Muirhouse North Junc.
g) Anderston Tun. (1m 1010yds.)
h) Charing Cross Tun.
j) Finnieston Tun.
k) Stobcross St. Tun.
l) Bellgrove Tuns.
m) Sighthill E. Junc.

n) Bridgeton Cen. Junc.
p) West St. Tun.
q) Terminus Junc.
r) Bridgeton Cen. Tun.

0   1   2   m. (1:90,000)
0   1   2   3   4 km

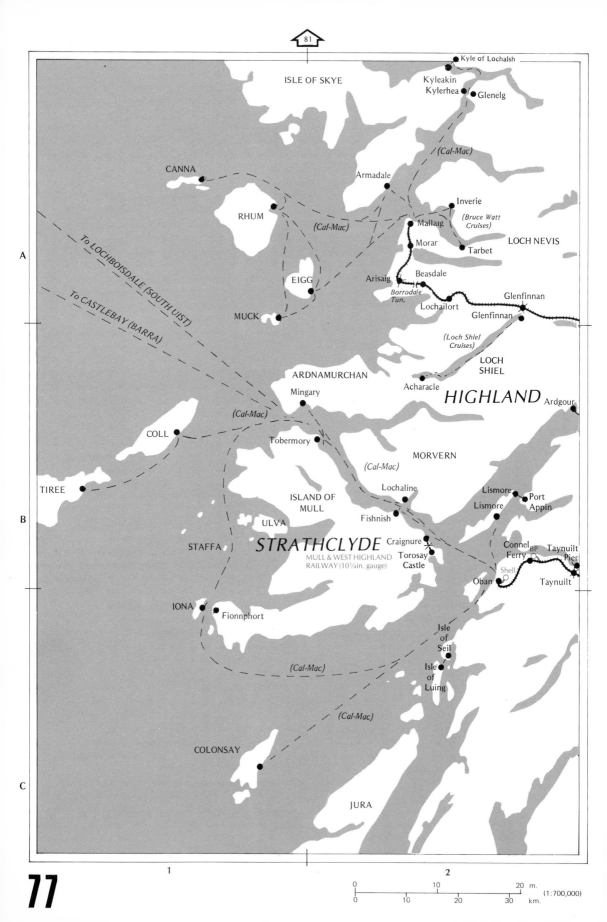

ISLE OF SKYE

Kyle of Lochalsh

Kyleakin
Kylerhea
Glenelg

CANNA

RHUM

(Cal-Mac)

Armadale

Inverie

(Bruce Watt Cruises)

LOCH NEVIS

Mallaig

Morar

Tarbet

A

EIGG

Arisaig
Beasdale

Borrodale Tun.

Lochailort

Glenfinnan

Glenfinnan

MUCK

(Loch Shiel Cruises)

LOCH SHIEL

To LOCHBOISDALE (SOUTH UIST)

To CASTLEBAY (BARRA)

ARDNAMURCHAN

Mingary

Acharacle

HIGHLAND

Ardgour

(Cal-Mac)

COLL

Tobermory

MORVERN

(Cal-Mac)

TIREE

Lochaline

ISLAND OF MULL

Lismore

Port Appin

Lismore

B

ULVA

Fishnish

STAFFA

STRATHCLYDE

Craignure

Connel Ferry

BP

Taynuilt Pier

MULL & WEST HIGHLAND
RAILWAY (10¼in. gauge)

Torosay Castle

Shell

Taynuilt

Oban

IONA

Fionnphort

Isle of Seil

Isle of Luing

(Cal-Mac)

(Cal-Mac)

COLONSAY

C

JURA

1

2

0   10   20 m.

0   10   20   30 km.

(1:700,000)

HIGHLAND

Slochd

Slochd Summit (1315ft) Carrbridge

Boat of Garten
STRATHSPEY
RAILWAY

AVIEMORE

Aviemore

GRAMPIAN A

Kincraig

Kingussie

Newtonmore

Dalwhinnie

Annat (Corpach
Paper Mill) -
Scottish Pulp
& Paper
FW

Spean
Bridge
Roy
Bridge

Tulloch
Fersit Tun.

Locheilside
Banavie
Corpach
West
Highland
Oil
Fort William
Mallaig Junc. Yard & Goods
Lochaber - British
Alcan Aluminium
*Mallaig
Junc.*

Druimuachdar Summit (1484ft)

Blair Atholl
*Killiecrankie
Tun.*

Pitlochry

Ballinluig

Corran

Corrour
Corrour Summit (1350ft)

*Cruach Snow
Shed*
Rannoch

TAYSIDE

*Inver
Tun.*

Dunkeld B
*Kingswood
Tun.*

LOCH
ETIVE
Lochetivehead
(D. Kennedy)

Bridge
of Orchy

Dail

Craig
Inverliever

Tyndrum Summit (840ft.)
West Highland County March Summit (1024ft)
Tyndrum
Upper

Tyndrum
Lower
Crianlarich Lower -
Scottish Pulp & Paper
Dalmally
Crianlarich

STRATHCLYDE

Ardlui

Gleneagles

79

Stronachlachar
LOCH KATRINE

Arrochar &
Tarbet
Inversnaid
Tarbet
Trossachs
Pier
*Strathclyde
Water
Dept.)*

LOCH
LOMOND
Glen Douglas
*Whistlefield
Summit*
Rowardennan
*(Loch Lomond
Marina Co.)*
Luss

Dunblane

*Kippenross
Tun.*
Goods &
Motorail T.
Stirling
MOD
Depot

CENTRAL

Menstrie—Distillers
Cambus
(Alloa to Longannet
is disused)

Alloa
Yard

Cambus—Distillers

FIFE C

Garelochhead

HELENSBURGH
Upper
Central

Balloch
Pier

71 1

72 2

0   10   20 m.
0   10   20   30 km.
(1 : 700,000)

78

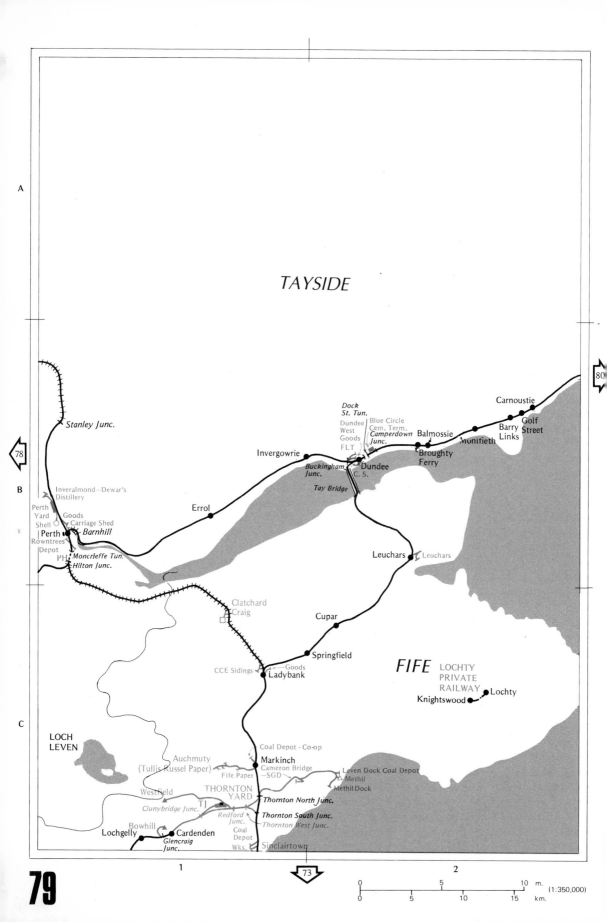

TAYSIDE

Stanley Junc.

Carnoustie

Dock St. Tun.
Dundee West Goods FLT
Blue Circle Cem. Term.
Camperdown Junc.
Balmossie
Golf Street
Barry Links
Monifieth
Broughty Ferry

Invergowrie
Buckingham Junc.
Dundee
C.S.
Tay Bridge

Inveralmond—Dewar's Distillery
Perth Yard Goods
Shell
Carriage Shed
Perth
Barnhill
Rowntrees Depot
PH
Moncrieffe Tun.
Hilton Junc.

Errol

Leuchars
Leuchars

Clatchard Craig

Cupar

CCE Sidings
Goods
Springfield

FIFE
LOCHTY PRIVATE RAILWAY
Lochty
Knightswood

LOCH LEVEN

Auchmuty (Tullis Russel Paper)
Coal Depot - Co-op
Markinch
Cameron Bridge —SGD
Fife Paper
Leven Dock Coal Depot
Methil
Methil Dock

Westfield
THORNTON YARD
Clunybridge Junc.
TJ
Thornton North Junc.
Thornton South Junc.
Thornton West Junc.
Redford Junc.
Coal Depot
Bowhill
Lochgelly
Cardenden
Glencraig Junc.
Wks.
Sinclairtown

79

0   5   10 m.
0   5   10   15 km.
(1:350,000)

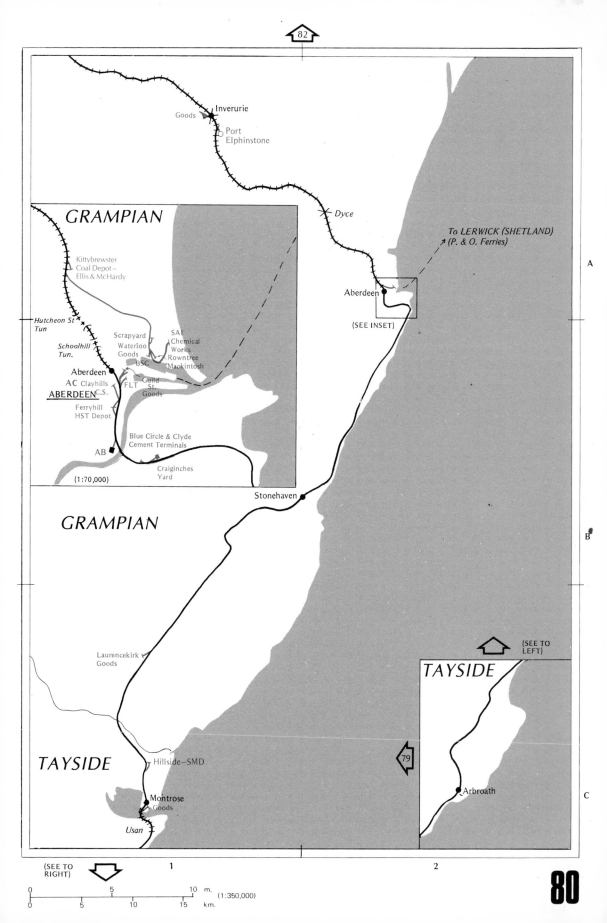

Goods • Inverurie
○ Port
Elphinstone

Dyce

To LERWICK (SHETLAND)
(P. & O. Ferries)

A

Aberdeen ●

(SEE INSET)

GRAMPIAN

Kittybrewster
Coal Depot –
Ellis & McHardy

Hutcheon St
Tun.

Schoolhill
Tun.

Scrapyard
Waterloo
Goods

SAI
Chemical
Works
Rowntree
Mackintosh

BSC

Aberdeen ●
AC Clayhills
C.S.
ABERDEEN FLT
Guild
St.
Goods
Ferryhill
HST Depot

Blue Circle & Clyde
Cement Terminals

AB ■

(1:70,000)

Craiginches
Yard

GRAMPIAN

Stonehaven ●

B

Laurencekirk
Goods

(SEE TO
LEFT)

TAYSIDE

TAYSIDE

79

Hillside—SMD

Arbroath

C

Montrose
Goods

Usan

(SEE TO
RIGHT)

1

2

0   5   10 m.   (1:350,000)
0   5   10   15   km.

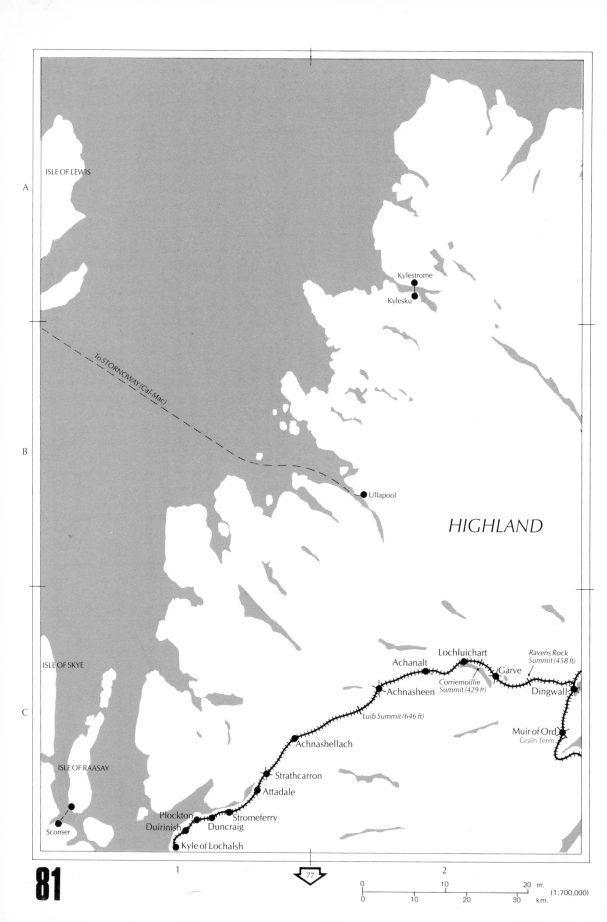

ISLE OF LEWIS

A

Kylestrome
Kylesku

To STORNOWAY (Cal-Mac)

B

● Ullapool

HIGHLAND

ISLE OF SKYE

Lochluichart
Achanalt   *Ravens Rock
                             Summit (458 ft)*
                    Garve
         Achnasheen   *Corriemoillie
                      Summit (429 ft)*
C   Dingwall

                      Luib Summit (646 ft)

         Achnashellach
                                Muir of Ord
                                Grain Term.
ISLE OF RAASAY
            Strathcarron
            Attadale
     Plockton
Duirinish   Duncraig Stromeferry
Sconser
         Kyle of Lochalsh

1   77   2

0   10   20 m.
0   10   20   30
                        km.
                        (1:700,000)

To TORSHAVN (Faroes) (Strandfaraskip Landsins)
To STROMNESS (Orkney) (P & O Ferries)

Scrabster
Thurso • Goods
Georgemas Junc.
Scotscalder
Goods Wick

A

Altnabreac
Forsinard *County March Summit (708 ft)*

Kinbrace

Kildonan
Helmsdale

Lairg *Summit (488 ft)*
BP
Rogart Golspie
Brora

B

Invershin
Culrain
Ardgay
Coal Depot

Tain
Fearn Goods

Alness
Goods Invergordon
McK. Shand Distillery
Evanton-Dunlop & Rankin

Burghead — SMD
Roseisle — SMD
Coal Depot Elgin East Goods
Alves Elgin

Carriage Depot
Coal Depot
Inverness Yard & Cement Term.
Harbour — Esso
Highland Bitumen
Lentran
Rose St. Millburn
IS Gds *Culloden Moor*
Inverness
Welsh's Bridge Junc.

Nairn Forres

Keith *Keith Junc.* Chivas Distillery
Coal Depot

C

Dufftown

Moy

Tomatin

GRAMPIAN

Huntly

Kennethmont Insch

1
78
0   10   20 m.
0   10   20   30 km.   (1:700,000)

2
80

82

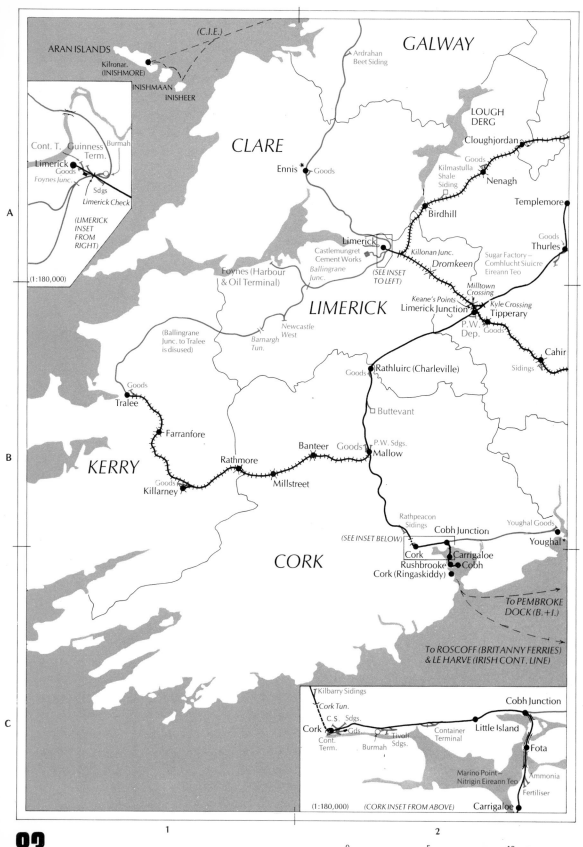

ARAN ISLANDS

Kilronar.
(INISHMORE)

INISHMAAN
INISHEER

(C.I.E.)

GALWAY

LOUGH
DERG

Ardrahan Beet Siding

Cloughjordan

CLARE

Cont. T. Guinness
Term.
Burmah
Limerick
Goods
Foynes Junc.
Sdgs
Limerick Check
(LIMERICK INSET FROM RIGHT)
(1:180,000)

Ennis *
Goods

Kilmastulla
Shale Siding

Goods

Nenagh

Templemore

Birdhill

Thurles
Goods

A

Limerick
(SEE INSET TO LEFT)

Castlemungret
Cement Works
Ballingrane Junc.

Killonan Junc.

Dromkeen

Sugar Factory –
Comhlucht Siuicre
Eireann Teo

Foynes (Harbour
& Oil Terminal)

LIMERICK

Milltown
Crossing

Keane's Points
Limerick Junction

Kyle Crossing
Tipperary

*(Ballingrane
Junc. to Tralee
is disused)*

Newcastle
West

Barnargh
Tun.

P.W.
Dep.
Goods

Cahir

Sidings

Rathluirc (Charleville)
Goods

B

Goods

Tralee

KERRY

Farranfore

Rathmore

Banteer
Goods

P.W. Sdgs.

Buttevant

Mallow

Killarney
Goods

Millstreet

CORK

Rathpeacon
Sidings

Youghal Goods

Cobh Junction
(SEE INSET BELOW)

Youghal *

Cork
Rushbrooke
Cork (Ringaskiddy)

Carrigaloe
Cobh

*To PEMBROKE
DOCK (B.+I.)*

*To ROSCOFF (BRITANNY FERRIES)
& LE HARVE (IRISH CONT. LINE)*

Kilbarry Sidings

Cork Tun.

C.S. Sdgs.

Cork
Cont.
Term.

Gds.

Burmah

Tivoli
Sdgs.

Container
Terminal

Cobh Junction

Little Island

C

Fota

Marino Point –
Nitrigin Eireann Teo

Ammonia

Fertiliser

(1:180,000) *(CORK INSET FROM ABOVE)*

Carrigaloe

83

1

2

0   5   10   m.
| | | (1:1,070,000)
0   5   10   15   km.

Geashill • Droichead Nua (Newbridge) • Shankhill • Bray
Portarlington • Cherryville Junc. • Goods • Curragh* • Bray Head Tuns. • C.S. • Greystones
Kildare • Kilcoole

Portlaoise
P.W. Depot • Goods
Roscrea • Athy • Wicklow
Goods • Athy Asbestos Works

KILDARE

WICKLOW

Ballybrophy • Rathdrum
Lisduff • Rathdrum Tun.

Avoca*

LAOIS • Goods • Carlow • Arklow
Shelton Abbey Fertilizer Works
Nitrigin Eireann Teo
Goods

KILKENNY • **CARLOW**

Kilkenny • Muine Bheag (Bagenalstown) • Gorey
Goods • Lavistown Junc.

(WATERFORD INSET FROM BELOW)

Bennettsbridge
P.W. Sidings • Goods • Waterford
West Junc. • Abbey Junc.
Thomastown • Enniscorthy
Wharf • Bell Line Container Terminal
Enniscorthy Tun. (1:180,000)

TIPPERARY

New Ross Goods • New Ross* • Killurin Tun.
Ferrycarrig Tun. • Goods
Clonmel • Kilsheelan • Mullinavat • Snowhill Tun. • Wexford • To FISHGUARD (Sealink)
Goods • Carrick on Suir • **WEXFORD** • Wexford South • Rosslare Strand • To PEMBROKE DOCK (B+I)
Campile • Ballycullane
Wellington Bridge • Rosslare Harbour Pier
Waterford • Bridgetown • Rosslare Harbour (Mainland) • To LE HAVRE & CHERBOURG (Irish Continental Line)
(SEE INSET TO RIGHT)

WATERFORD • Ballygeary C.S. & Stabling Point

DUBLIN

Howth Junction • Sutton
Kilbarrack • Bayside • Howth
DUBLIN CONNOLLY • Raheny
Harmonstown
Clonsilla • Killester
Ashtown • Liffey Junc. • Glasnevin Junc. • North Strand Junc. • Fairview Depot
Sdgs. • Cross Guns Tun. • Newcomen Junc. • East Wall Junc. • Asahi Chemicals Term. • To DOUGLAS (I. of M.S.P. Co.)
Cabra Cement Term. • Dublin Connolly • Texaco • B & I Container Terminal • To LIVERPOOL (B+I)
Phoenix Park Tun. • Tara St. • North Wall Goods • To HOLYHEAD (B+I)
Islandbridge Junc. • Dublin Heuston • Dublin Pearse • Alexandra Road Gypsum Terminal
Inchicore • Depot Works • Lansdowne Road • To HOLYHEAD (Sealink)
Sandymount
Sydney Parade
Booterstown
Salthill • Dun Laoghaire
Blackrock • Sandycove
Monkstown & Seapoint
Glenageary • Dalkey • Dalkey Tun.

a) West Road Junc.
b) Church Road Junc.

1) Carriage Sidings
2) Bell Line Container Terminal
3) Parcels & Mail Terminal
4) Guinness Terminal
5) North Wall Container Terminals
6) Grand Canal St. Carriage Sidings

0 2 4 m. (1:180,000)
0 2 4 6 km.

(DUBLIN INSET FROM MAP 86)

0 5 10 m. (1:1,070,000)
0 5 10 15 km.

84

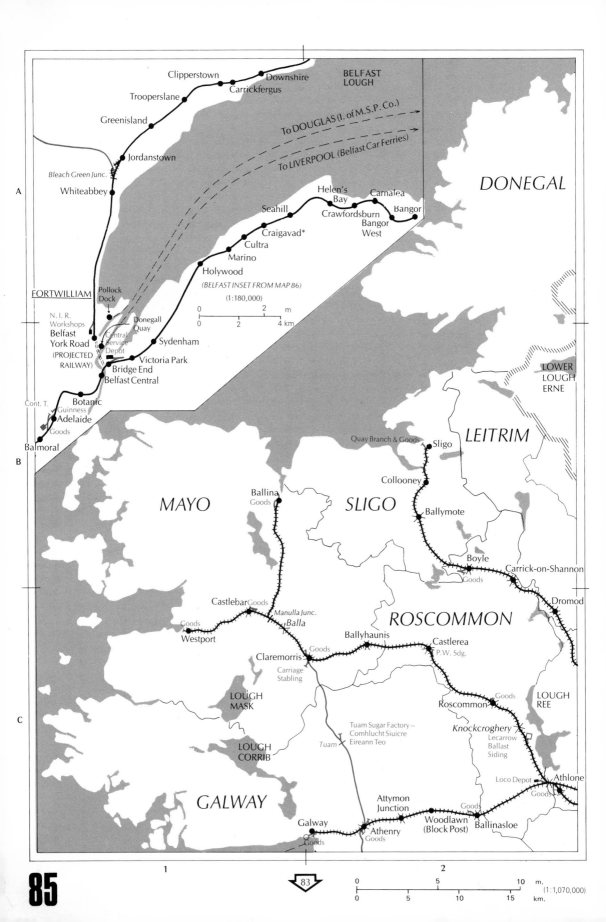

Belfast Inset

CLIPPERSTOWN
Downshire
Carrickfergus
Trooperslane
Greenisland
Jordanstown
Bleach Green Junc.
Whiteabbey

BELFAST LOUGH

To DOUGLAS (I. of M.S.P. Co.)
To LIVERPOOL (Belfast Car Ferries)

DONEGAL

Helen's Bay
Carnalea
Seahill
Crawfordsburn
Bangor
Craigavad*
Bangor West
Cultra
Marino
Holywood

(BELFAST INSET FROM MAP 86)
(1:180,000)

0   2   m
0   2   4 km

FORTWILLIAM
Pollock Dock
N.I.R. Workshops
Belfast York Road
(PROJECTED RAILWAY)
Central Service Depot
Donegall Quay
Sydenham
Victoria Park
Bridge End
Belfast Central
Cont. T.
Botanic
Guinness
Adelaide
Goods
Balmoral

LOWER LOUGH ERNE

Quay Branch & Goods
Sligo

LEITRIM

MAYO

Ballina
Goods

SLIGO

Collooney

Ballymote

Boyle
Goods
Carrick-on-Shannon

Dromod

Castlebar
Goods
Manulla Junc.
Balla

ROSCOMMON

Goods
Westport

Ballyhaunis

Castlerea
P.W. Sdg.

LOUGH REE

Claremorris
Goods
Carriage Stabling

Roscommon
Goods

Knockcroghery
Lecarrow Ballast Siding

LOUGH MASK

LOUGH CORRIB

Tuam Sugar Factory –
Comhlucht Siuicre
Eireann Teo
Tuam

Loco Depot
Athlone
Goods

GALWAY

Attymon Junction

Woodlawn
(Block Post)
Ballinasloe
Goods

Galway
Goods
Athenry
Goods

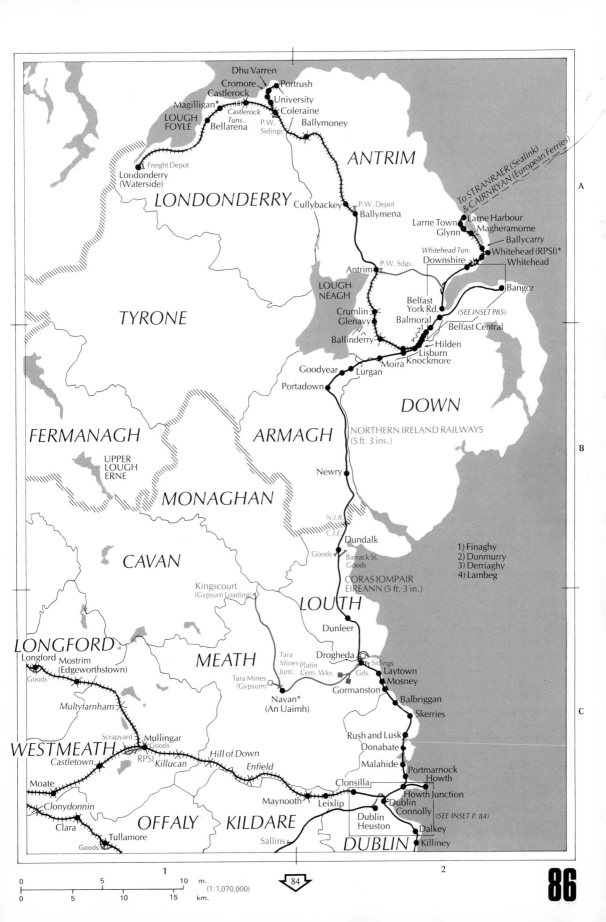

Dhu Varren
Portrush
Cromore
Castlerock
Magilligan*
Castlerock
Tuns.
Bellarena
University
Coleraine
P.W. Sidings
Ballymoney

LOUGH
FOYLE

Freight Depot
Londonderry
(Waterside)

LONDONDERRY

ANTRIM

To STRANRAER (Sealink)
& CAIRNRYAN (European Ferries)

A

Cullybackey
P.W. Depot
Ballymena

Larne Town
Glynn
Larne Harbour
Magheramorne
Ballycarry

Whitehead Tun.
Downshire
Whitehead (RPSI)*
Whitehead

TYRONE

Antrim
P.W. Sdgs.

Bangor

LOUGH
NEAGH

Crumlin
Glenavy
Ballinderry

Belfast
York Rd.
Balmoral
2 1
3 4
Hilden
Lisburn
Knockmore
Moira

(SEE INSET P.85)
Belfast Central

DOWN

Goodyear
Portadown
Lurgan

NORTHERN IRELAND RAILWAYS
(5 ft. 3 ins.)

B

FERMANAGH

UPPER
LOUGH
ERNE

ARMAGH

Newry

MONAGHAN

N.I.R.
C.I.E.

CAVAN

Dundalk
Goods
Barrack St.
Goods

1) Finaghy
2) Dunmurry
3) Derriaghy
4) Lambeg

CORAS IOMPAIR
EIREANN (5 ft. 3 in.)

Kingscourt
(Gypsum Loading)

LOUTH

Dunleer

LONGFORD

Longford
Mostrim
(Edgeworthstown)
Goods

MEATH

Tara
Mines
Junc.
Platin
Cem. Wks.
Drogheda
Gds.
Sidings
Laytown
Mosney

C

Tara Mines
(Gypsum)
Navan*
(An Uaimh)

Gormanston
Balbriggan
Skerries

Multyfarnham

Scrapyard
Mullingar
Goods
RPSI
Killucan

Hill of Down
Enfield

Rush and Lusk
Donabate
Malahide
Portmarnock
Howth

WESTMEATH
Castletown

Moate
Clonydonnin

Clonsilla
Maynooth
Leixlip

Howth Junction
Dublin
Connolly
(SEE INSET P. 84)

Dublin
Heuston

Clara
Tullamore
Goods

OFFALY   KILDARE

Sallins

Dalkey
Killiney

DUBLIN

1   5   10 m.
(1:1,070,000)
0   5   10   15 km.

84

86

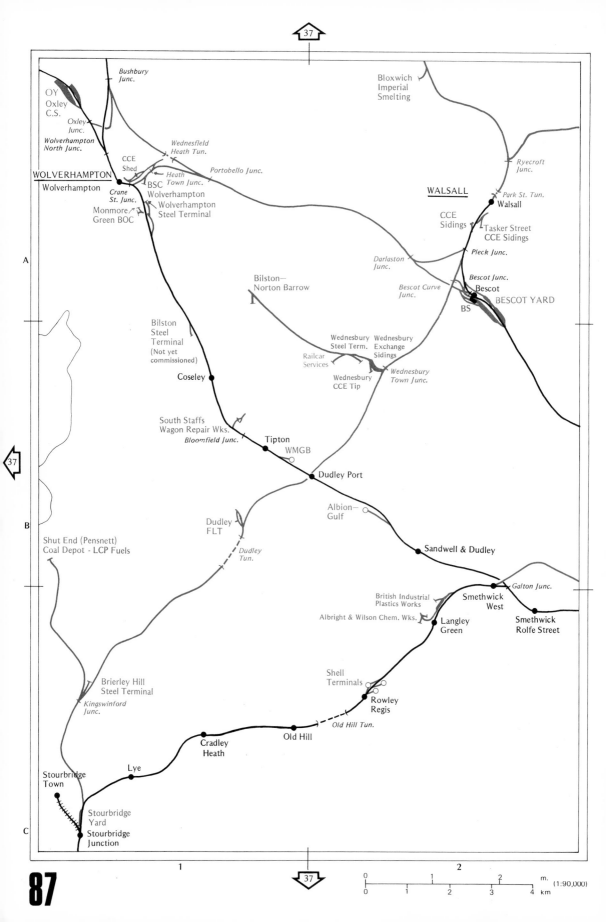

Bushbury
Junc.

Bloxwich
Imperial
Smelting

OY
Oxley
C.S.

Oxley
Junc.

Wolverhampton
North Junc.

Wednesfield
Heath Tun.

Portobello Junc.

Ryecroft
Junc.

WOLVERHAMPTON

CCE
Shed

Heath
Town Junc.

Park St. Tun.

WALSALL

Wolverhampton

Crane
St. Junc.

BSC
Wolverhampton
Steel Terminal

Walsall

CCE
Sidings

Tasker Street
CCE Sidings

Monmore
Green BOC

Wolverhampton
Steel Terminal

Pleck Junc.

Darlaston
Junc.

Bescot Junc.

A

Bilston—
Norton Barrow

Bescot Curve
Junc.

Bescot

BESCOT YARD

Bilston
Steel
Terminal
(Not yet
commissioned)

BS

Wednesbury
Steel Term.

Wednesbury
Exchange
Sidings

Coseley

Railcar
Services

Wednesbury
Town Junc.

South Staffs
Wagon Repair Wks.

Wednesbury
CCE Tip

Bloomfield Junc.

Tipton

WMGB

Dudley Port

Albion—
Gulf

Dudley
FLT

B

Dudley
Tun.

Shut End (Pensnett)
Coal Depot - LCP Fuels

Sandwell & Dudley

Galton Junc.

British Industrial
Plastics Works

Smethwick
West

Albright & Wilson Chem. Wks.

Langley
Green

Smethwick
Rolfe Street

Brierley Hill
Steel Terminal

Shell
Terminals

Kingswinford
Junc.

Rowley
Regis

Old Hill Tun.

Cradley
Heath

Old Hill

Lye

Stourbridge
Town

Stourbridge
Yard

C

Stourbridge
Junction

87

1

2

m.   (1:90,000)

0   1   2
0   1   2   3   4   km

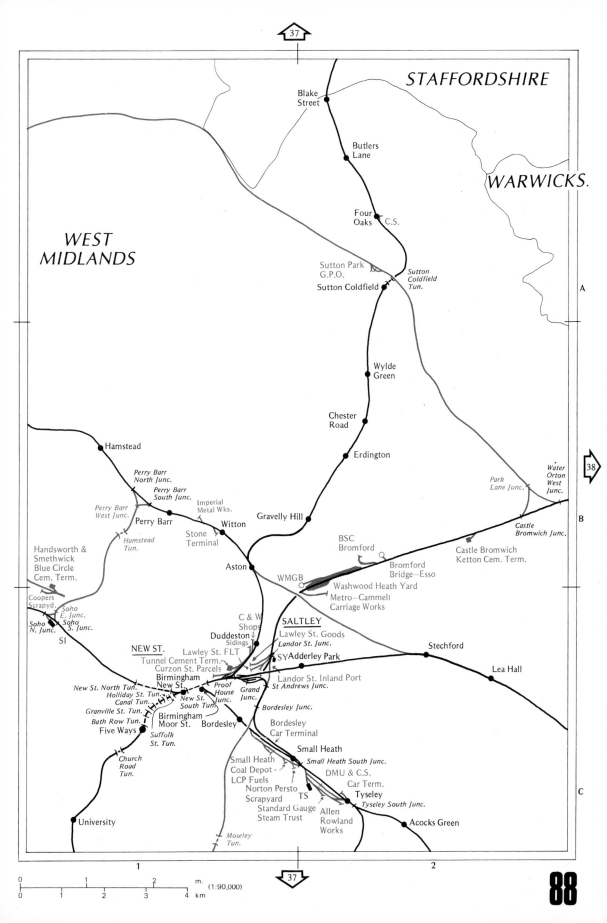

STAFFORDSHIRE

WARWICKS.

Blake
Street

Butlers
Lane

Four
Oaks   C.S.

WEST
MIDLANDS

Sutton Park
G.P.O.
Sutton Coldfield   *Sutton
Coldfield
Tun.*

A

Wylde
Green

Chester
Road

Erdington

Hamstead

*Perry Barr
North Junc.*

*Perry Barr
South Junc.*

*Perry Barr
West Junc.*

Imperial
Metal Wks.

Perry Barr

Witton   Gravelly Hill

*Water
Orton West
Junc.*

*Park
Lane Junc.*

B

*Castle
Bromwich Junc.*

*Hamstead
Tun.*

Stone
Terminal

Handsworth &
Smethwick
Blue Circle
Cem. Term.

Aston

BSC
Bromford

WMGB

Bromford
Bridge—Esso

Castle Bromwich
Ketton Cem. Term.

Coopers
Scrapyd.   *Soho
E. Junc.*   *Soho
S. Junc.*

*Soho
N. Junc.*

Washwood Heath Yard
Metro—Cammell
Carriage Works

S1

C & W
Shops

Duddeston
Sidings

SALTLEY

Lawley St. Goods

Landor St. Junc.

NEW ST.   Lawley St. FLT
Tunnel Cement Term.
Curzon St. Parcels

SY Adderley Park   Stechford

Lea Hall

Birmingham
New St.

New St. North Tun.
Holliday St. Tun.
Canal Tun.
Granville St. Tun.
Bath Row Tun.
Five Ways

Proof
House
Junc.   Grand
Junc.

Landor St. Inland Port
St Andrews Junc.

*New St.
South Tun.*

Birmingham
Moor St.   Bordesley

Bordesley Junc.

*Church
Road
Tun.*

*Suffolk
St. Tun.*

Bordesley
Car Terminal

Small Heath

Small Heath
Coal Depot -
LCP Fuels
Norton Persto
Scrapyard
Standard Gauge
Steam Trust

Small Heath South Junc.

DMU & C.S.
Car Term.
Tyseley

Tyseley South Junc.

TS

C

University

*Moseley
Tun.*

Allen
Rowland
Works

Acocks Green

0   1   2   m.   (1:90,000)
0   1   2   3   4   km

INDEX TO PASSENGER STATIONS

For list abbreviations see end of Passenger Station Index
(*Indicates unadvertised or excursion station)

NAME	RAILWAY CODE	PAGE NO.	PAGE REF.
Abbey Wood	SO	32	C2
Aber	WR	28	C1
Abercynon	WR	27	C2
Aberdare*	WR	27	B2
Aberdeen	SC	80	B1
Aberdour	SC	73	A1
Aberdovey	LM	34	B2
Abererch	LM	43	C2
Aberffrwd	LM	34	B2
Abergavenny	WR	28	B1
Abergele & Pensarn	LM	44	A2
Abergynolwyn	TL	34	A2
Abertafol	LM	34	B2
Aberystwyth	LM	34	B2
Accrington	LM	55	B1
Achanalt	SC	81	C2
Achnasheen	SC	81	C2
Achnashellach	SC	81	C1
Acklington	ER	68	A1
Acle	ER	42	A1
Acocks Green	LM	88	C2
Acton Bridge	LM	45	A2
Acton Central	LM	20	B2
Acton Main Line	WR	20	B2
Acton Town	LT	20	C2
Adderley Park	LM	88	C2
Addiewell	SC	72	B2
Addiscombe	SO	17	B2
Addlestone	SO	15	C1
Adelaide	NI	85	B1
Adisham	SO	13	A2
Adlington (Cheshire)	LM	46	A2
Adlington (Lancs.)	LM	54	C2
Aigburth	LM	53	C2
Ainsdale	LM	54	C1
Aintree	LM	53	A2
Airdrie	SC	72	B1
Albany Park	SO	32	C2
Albrighton	LM	37	A1
Alderley Edge	LM	46	A1
Aldermaston	WR	10	A2
Aldershot	SO	11	A1
Aldgate	LT	21	B2
Aldgate East	LT	21	B2
Aldrington	SO	12	C1
Aldwych	LT	21	B2
Alexandra Palace	ER	23	C2
Alexandra Parade	SC	76	B1
Alexandria	SC	71	A2
Alfreton & Mansfield Parkway	LM	47	B2
Allen's West	ER	62	B2
Allerton	LM	53	C2
Alness	SC	82	C1
Alnmouth	ER	68	A1
Alperton	LT	20	B1
Alresford (Essex)	ER	33	B2
Alresford (Hants.)	MH	10	B2
Alsager	LM	46	B2
Althorne	ER	33	B1
Althorpe	ER	57	C1
Altnabreac	SC	82	A1
Altofts	ER	56	B1
Alton	SO	11	B1
Altrincham	LM	46	A1
Alvechurch	LM	37	B2
Ambergate	LM	47	B1
Amberley	SO	11	C2
Amersham	LM/LT	31	C2
Ammanford	WR	27	B1
Ampress Works*	SO	6	A1
Ancaster	ER	48	C2
Anderston	SC	76	B1
Andover	SO	10	B1
Anerley	SO	18	A1
Angel	LT	21	B2
Angel Road	ER	24	C1
Angmering	SO	11	C2
Annan	SC	66	C1
Anniesland	SC	75	B2
Ansdell & Fairhaven	LM	54	B1
Antrim	NI	86	A2
Appleby	LM	61	A1
Appledore	SO	13	B1
Appleford	WR	30	C2
Appley Bridge	LM	54	C2
Apsley	LM	31	B2
Arbroath	SC	80	C2
Archway	LT	21	A2
Ardgay	SC	82	B1
Ardlui	SC	78	C1
Ardrossan Harbour	SC	71	C1
Ardrossan South Beach	SC	71	C1
Ardwick	LM	52	B1
Argyle Street	SC	76	B1
Arisaig	SC	77	A2
Arklow	CI	84	A2
Arley	SV	37	B1
Armathwaite*	LM	66	C2
Arnos Grove	LT	23	C2
Arnside	LM	60	C2
Arram	ER	57	B2
Arrochar & Tarbet	SC	78	C1
Arsenal	LT	21	A2
Arundel	SO	11	C2
Ascot	SO	11	A1
Ascott-under-Wychwood	WR	30	B1
Ash	SO	11	A1
Ashburys for Belle Vue	LM	52	B1
Ashford (Kent)	SO	13	B2
Ashford (Surrey)	SO	15	A1
Ashley	LM	46	A1
Ash Street	BF	54	A1
Ashtead	SO	11	A2
Ashton-under-Lyne	LM	52	B2
Ashtown	CI	84	C1
Ashurst	SO	12	B2
Ash Vale	SO	11	A1
Ashwell & Morden	ER	32	A1
Askam	LM	60	C1
Askern*	ER	56	C2
Aslockton	ER	48	C1
Aspatria	LM	60	A1
Aspley Guise	LM	31	A1
Aston	LM	88	B1
Athenry	CI	85	C2
Atherstone	LM	38	A1
Atherton	LM	55	C1
Athlone	CI	85	C2
Athy	CI	84	A1
Attadale	SC	81	C1
Attenborough	LM	47	C2
Attercliffe	ER	50	B1
Attleborough	ER	41	B2
Attymon Junction	CI	85	C2
Auchinleck (Proposed)	SC	71	C2
Audley End	ER	32	A2
Aughton Park	LM	54	C2
Aviemore	SC/SY	78	A2
Avoca*	CI	84	A2
Avoncliff	WR	9	A1
Avonmouth	WR	28	C2
Axminster	WR	4	A1
Aylesbury	LM	31	B1
Aylesford	SO	12	A2
Aylesham	SO	13	A2
Ayr	SC	71	C1
Bache	LM	45	B2
Bagshot	SO	11	A1
Baildon	ER	56	B1
Baker Street	LT	21	B1
Bala	BA	44	C2
Balbriggan	CI	86	C2
Balcombe	SO	12	B1
Baldock	ER	32	A1
Baldrine	ME	59	C2
Balham	SO/LT	17	A1
Ballabeg	ME	59	C2
Ballaglass	ME	59	B2
Ballajura	ME	59	B2
Ballaragh	ME	59	C2

NAME	RAILWAY CODE	PAGE NO.	PAGE REF.
Ballasalla	ME	59	C1
Ballina	CI	85	B1
Ballinasloe	CI	85	C2
Ballinderry	NI	86	B2
Balloch Central	SC	71	A2
Balloch Pier	SC	71	A2
Ballybrophy	CI	84	A1
Ballycarry	NI	86	A2
Ballycullane	CI	84	B1
Ballyhaunis	CI	85	C2
Ballymena	NI	86	A2
Ballymoney	NI	85	A2
Ballymote	CI	85	B2
Balmoral	NI	85	B1
Balmossie	SC	79	B2
Bamber Bridge	LM	54	B2
Bamford	LM	47	A1
Banavie	SC	78	B1
Banbury	LM	30	A2
Bangor (Co. Down)	NI	86	C2
Bangor (Gwynedd)	LM	43	A2
Bangor West	NI	86	C2
Bank	SO/LT	21	B2
Bank Hall	LM	53	B1
Bank Foot	TW	69	A1
Banstead	SO	17	C1
Banteer	CI	83	B2
Barassie	SC	71	C2
Barbican	LM/LT	21	B2
Bardon Mill	ER	67	C1
Bare Lane	LM	54	A2
Bargoed	WR	28	B1
Barking	ER/LT	22	B2
Barkingside	LT	22	A2
Barlaston	LM	46	C1
Barming	SO	13	A1
Barmouth	LM	34	A2
Barmouth Ferry	FB	34	A2
Barnehurst	SO	32	C2
Barnes	SO	20	C2
Barnes Bridge	SO	20	C2
Barnetby	ER	57	C2
Barnham	SO	11	C2
Barnhill	SC	76	B1
Barnsley	ER	56	C1
Barnstaple	WR	6	B2
Barnt Green	LM	37	B2
Barons Court	LT	21	C1
Barrhead	SC	75	A2
Barrhill	SC	64	B1
Barrow Haven	ER	57	B2
Barrow-in-Furness	LM	54	A1
Barry	WR	7	A1
Barry Docks	WR	7	A1
Barry Island	WR	7	A1
Barry Links	SC	79	B2
Barton-on-Humber	ER	57	B2
Basildon	ER	32	C2
Basingstoke	SO	10	A2
Bat & Ball	SO	12	A2
Bath Spa	WR	9	A1
Batley	ER	56	B1
Battersby	ER	62	B2
Battersea Park	SO	21	C1
Battle	SO	13	C1
Battlesbridge	ER	33	C1
Bayford	ER	32	B1
Bayside	CI	84	B2
Bayswater	LT	21	B1
Beaconsfield	LM	31	C1
Bearley	LM	38	C1
Bearsden	SC	75	A2
Bearsted	SO	13	A1
Beasdale	SC	77	A2
Beaulieu Road	SO	10	C1
Bebington	LM	53	C1
Beccles	ER	42	B1
Beckenham Hill	SO	18	A1
Beckenham Junction	SO	18	A1
Beckfoot	RE	60	B1
Becontree	LT	32	C1
Beddington Lane	SO	17	B2
Bede	TW	70	B1
Bedford St. Johns	LM	39	C2
Bedhampton	SO	11	C1
Bedminster	WR	8	B2
Bedwyn	WR	10	A1
Beeston	LM	47	C2
Bekesbourne	SO	13	A2
Belfast Central	NI	85	B1
Belfast York Road	NI	85	B1
Bellarena*	NI	86	A1
Bellevue	ME	59	B2
Belle Vue	LM	52	B1
Bellgrove	SC	76	B1
Bellingham	SO	18	A1
Bellshill	SC	72	B1
Belmont	SO	17	C1
Belper	LM	47	C1
Belsize Park	LT	21	A1
Beltring	SO	12	A2
Belvedere	SO	32	C2
Bempton	ER	63	C2
Benfleet for Canvey I.	ER	33	C1
Ben Rhydding	ER	55	A2
Bentham	LM	55	A1
Bentley	SO	11	B1
Benton	TW	69	A2
Bere Alston	WR	2	B2
Bere Ferrers	WR	2	B2
Berkshamsted	LM	31	B2
Berkswell	LM	38	B1
Berney Arms	ER	42	A1
Berrylands	SO	16	B2
Berwick (Sussex)	SO	12	C2
Berwick-upon-Tweed	ER	74	B2
Bescar Lane	LM	54	C2
Bescot	LM	87	A2
Besses-o'-th'-Barn	LM	51	A2
Betchworth	SO	11	A2
Bethnal Green	ER/LT	22	B1
Betws-y-Coed	LM	44	B1
Beverley	ER	57	B2
Bewdley	SV	37	B1
Bexhill	SO	13	C1
Bexley	SO	32	C2
Bexleyheath	SO	32	C2
Bicester	LM	30	A2
Bickley	SO	18	B2
Bidston	LM	45	A1
Biggleswade	ER	31	A2
Bilbrook	LM	37	A1
Billericay	ER	32	C2
Billingham	ER	63	A1
Billingshurst	SO	11	B2
Bingham	LM	48	C1
Bingley	ER	55	B2
Birchgrove	WR	28	C1
Birchington-on-Sea	SO	14	A1
Birchwood	LM	46	A1
Birdhill	CI	83	A2
Birkbeck	SO	18	B1
Birkdale	LM	54	C1
Birkenhead Central	LM	53	C1
Birkenhead Hamilton Square	LM	53	B1
Birkenhead North	LM	53	B1
Birkenhead Park	LM	53	B1
Birmingham Airport	BM	38	B1
Birmingham International	LM/BM	38	B1
Birmingham Moor Street	LM	88	C1
Birmingham New Street	LM	88	C1
Bishop Auckland	ER	62	A1
Bishopbriggs	SC	76	A1
Bishops Lydeard	WS	8	B7
Bishops Stortford	ER	32	B2
Bishopstone	SO	12	C2
Bishopton	SC	71	A2
Bispham	BF	54	B1
Bitterne	SO	9	C2
Blackburn	LM	55	B1
Blackfriars	SO/LT	21	B2
Blackheath	SO	22	C1
Blackhorse Road	ER/LT	22	A1
Blackpool North	LM	54	B1

90

NAME	RAILWAY CODE	PAGE NO.	PAGE REF.	NAME	RAILWAY CODE	PAGE NO.	PAGE REF.
Blackpool South	LM	54	B1	Bridgetown	CI	84	B2
Blackrock	CI	84	A2	Bridgnorth	WR	8	B1
Blackrod	LM	54	C2	Bridgwater	SV	37	B1
Blackwater	SO	11	A1	Bridlington	ER	57	A2
Blaenau Ffestiniog	LM/FR	44	C1	Brierfield	LM	55	B1
Blair Atholl	SC	78	B2	Brigg	ER	57	C2
Blairhill	SC	72	C1	Brighton	SO	12	C1
Blakedown	LM	37	B1	Brightside	ER	50	A1
Blake Street	LM	88	A2	Brimsdown	ER	24	B1
Blantyre	SC	76	C2	Brinnington	LM	52	C2
Blaydon	ER	69	B1	Bristol Parkway	WR	28	C2
Bleasby	LM	48	B1	Bristol Temple Meads	WR	8	B2
Bletchley	LM	31	A1	Britannia Halt*	TD	3	B2
Blue Anchor	WS	7	B2	Brithdir	WR	28	B1
Blundellsands & Crosby	LM	53	A1	British Steel (Redcar)	ER	63	A2
Blythe Bridge	LM	46	C2	Brixton	SO/LT	21	C2
Boat of Garten	SY	78	A2	Broadbottom	LM	46	A2
Bodiam	KS	13	B1	Broad Green	LM	53	B2
Bodmin Parkway	WR	2	B1	Broadstairs	SO	14	A1
Bodorgan	LM	43	B2	Broad Street	LM	21	B2
Bognor Regis	SO	11	C1	Brockenhurst	SO	10	C1
Bogston	SC	71	A1	Brockholes	ER	56	C1
Boldon Colliery	ER	70	B1	Brocklesby	ER	57	C2
Bolsover*	ER	47	B2	Brockley	SO	22	C1
Bolton	LM	55	C1	Bromborough	LM	45	A1
Bolton-on-Dearne	ER	56	C2	Bromley-by-Bow	LT	22	B1
Bond Street	LT	21	B1	Bromley Cross	LM	55	C1
Bookham	SO	11	A2	Bromley North	SO	18	B2
Booterstown	CI	84	C2	Bromley South	SO	18	B2
Boothferry Park*	ER	57	B2	Bromsgrove	WR	37	C2
Bootle (Cumbria)	LM	59	C2	Brondesbury	LM	21	B1
Bootle New Strand	LM	53	A1	Brondesbury Park	LM	21	B1
Bootle Oriel Road	LM	53	A1	Bronwydd Arms	GW	62	A2
Bordesley	LM	88	C1	Brooklands	LM	51	C2
Borough	LT	21	B2	Brookman's Park	ER	32	B1
Borough Green & Wrotham	SO	12	A2	Brookwood	SO	11	A1
Borth	LM	34	B2	Broome	WR	36	B2
Bosham	SO	11	C1	Broomfleet	ER	57	B1
Boston	ER	49	C1	Brora	SC	82	B1
Boston Lodge	FR	43	C2	Brough	ER	57	B2
Boston Manor	LT	20	C1	Broughty Ferry	SC	79	B2
Botanic	NI	85	B1	Broxbourne	ER	32	B1
Botley	SO	10	C2	Bruce Grove	ER	23	C2
Bottesford	ER	48	C1	Brundall	ER	42	A1
Bounds Green	LT	23	C2	Brundall Gardens	ER	42	A1
Bourne End	WR	31	C1	Bruton	WR	9	B1
Bournemouth	SO	5	A2	Bryn	LM	54	C2
Bournville	LM	37	B2	Brynglas	TL	34	A2
Bow Brickhill	LM	31	A1	Buchanan Street	GG	76	B1
Bowes Park	ER	23	C2	Buckenham	ER	42	A1
Bowker Vale	LM	51	A2	Buckfastleigh	DV	3	B1
Bowling	SC	75	A1	Buckhurst Hill	LT	24	C2
Bow Road	LT	22	B1	Buckley	LM	45	B1
Boxhill & Westhumble	SO	11	A2	Bucknell	WR	36	B1
Boyle	CI	85	B2	Bugle	WR	1	B2
Bracknell	SO	11	A1	Builth Road	LM	35	C2
Bradford Interchange	ER	56	B1	Bungalow	ME	59	C1
Bradford Forster Square	ER	56	B1	Bures	ER	33	A1
Bradford-on-Avon	WR	8	A1	Burgess Hill	SO	12	C1
Brading	SO	6	A2	Burley-in-Wharfedale	ER	56	A1
Braintree	ER	33	A1	Burmarsh Road Halt*	RH	13	B2
Bramhall	LM	46	A1	Burnage	LM	52	C1
Bramley (Hampshire)	SO	10	A2	Burneside	LM	60	C2
Bramley (W. Yorks)	ER	56	B1	Burnham	WR	31	C1
Brampton (Cumbria)	ER	66	C2	Burnham-on-Crouch	ER	33	C1
Brampton (Suffolk)	ER	42	B1	Burnley Barracks	LM	55	B1
Branchton	SC	71	A1	Burnley Central	LM	55	B1
Brandon	ER	41	B1	Burnside	SC	76	C1
Branksome	SO	5	A2	Burntisland	SC	73	A1
Bray	CI	84	A2	Burnt Oak	LT	31	C2
Braystones	LM	59	B2	Burscough Bridge	LM	54	C2
Bredbury	LM	52	C2	Burscough Junction	LM	54	C2
Breich	SC	72	B2	Bursledon	SO	10	C2
Brent Cross	LT	20	A2	Burton Joyce	LM	47	C2
Brentford	SO	20	C1	Burton-on-Trent	LM	47	C1
Brentwood	ER	32	C2	Bury	LM	55	C1
Bricket Wood	LM	31	B2	Bury St. Edmunds	ER	41	C1
Bridge End	NI	85	B1	Busby	SC	76	C1
Bridgend	WR	27	C2	Bushey	LM	31	C2
Bridge of Orchy	SC	78	B1	Bush Hill Park	ER	23	B2
Bridge Street	GG	76	B1	Butlers Lane	LM	88	A2
Bridgeton	SC	76	B1	Buxted	SO	12	B2

NAME	RAILWAY CODE	PAGE NOS.	PAGE REF.
Buxton	LM	46	A2
Byfleet & New Haw	SO	15	C1
Byker	TW	69	B2
Bynea	WR	26	B2
Cabin	BF	54	B1
Cadoxton	WR	7	A1
Caergwrle	LM	45	B1
Caerphilly	WR	28	C1
Caersws	LM	35	B2
Cahir	CI	83	B2
Caldicot	WR	28	C2
Caledonian Road	LT	21	A2
Caledonian Road & Barnsbury	LM	21	A2
Calstock	WR	2	B2
Camberley	SO	11	A1
Camborne	WR	1	C1
Cambridge	ER	40	C1
Cambridge Heath	ER	22	B1
Cambuslang	SC	76	C2
Camden Road	LM	21	B1
Camden Town	LT	21	B1
Campbells Platform	FR	44	C1
Campile	CI	84	B1
Canley	LM	38	B1
Canning Town	ER	22	B1
Cannon Street	SO/LT	21	B2
Canonbury	LM	21	A2
Canons Park	LT	31	C2
Canterbury East	SO	13	A2
Canterbury West	SO	13	A2
Cantley	ER	42	A1
Capel Bangor	LM	33	B2
Capenhurst	LM	45	A1
Carbis Bay	WR	1	A1
Cardendon	SC	79	C1
Cardiff Bute Road	WR	28	A1
Cardiff Central	WR	28	A1
Cardiff Queen Street	WR	28	A1
Cardonald	SC	75	B2
Cardross	SC	71	A2
Carfin	SC	72	B1
Cargo Fleet	ER	63	A1
Cark & Cartmel	LM	60	C1
Carlisle	LM	65	C1
Carlow	CI	84	A1
Carlton	LM	47	C2
Carluke	SC	72	B2
Carmarthen	WR	26	B2
Carnalea	NI	85	A2
Carnforth	LM	60	C2
Carnoustie	SC	79	B2
Carntyne	SC	76	B2
Carpenders Park	LM	31	C2
Carrbridge	SC	78	A2
Carrickfergus	NI	85	A1
Carrick-on-Shannon	CI	85	B2
Carrick-on-Suir	CI	84	B1
Carrigaloe	CI	83	C2
Carshalton	SO	17	B1
Carshalton Beeches	SO	17	C1
Carstairs	SC	72	B2
Cartsdyke	SC	71	A1
Castlebar	CI	85	C2
Castle Bar Park	WR	20	B1
Castle Caereinion	WL	36	A1
Castle Cary	WR	8	B2
Castleford	ER	56	B2
Castlerea	CI	85	C2
Castlerock	NI	86	A1
Castleton	LM	55	C1
Castleton Moor	ER	63	B1
Castletown	ME	59	C1
Caterham	SO	12	A1
Catford	SO	18	A1
Catford Bridge	SO	18	A1
Cathays	WR	27	A1
Cathcart	SC	76	C1
Cattal	ER	56	A2
Causeland	WR	2	B1
Cefn-Onn	WR	28	C1
Cefn-y-Bedd	LM	45	B1
Cei Llydan	LL	43	B2
Cessnock	GG	75	B2
Chadwell Heath	ER	32	C2
Chalfont & Latimer	LM/LT	31	C2
Chalk Farm	LT	21	B1
Chalkwell	ER	33	C1
Chancery Lane	LT	21	B2
Chapel-en-le-Frith	LM	46	A2
Chapelton	WR	6	B2
Chapeltown	ER	50	A1
Chappel & Wakes Colne	ER	33	A1
Charing	SO	13	A1
Charing Cross (Glasgow)	SC	76	B1
Charing Cross (London)	SO/LT	21	B2
Charlbury	WR	30	B1
Charlton	SO	22	C2
Chartham	SO	13	A2
Chassen Road	LM	51	C1
Chatham	SO	13	A1
Chathill	SC	74	A2
Cheadle Hulme	LM	46	A1
Cheam	SO	17	C1
Cheddington	LM	31	B1
Cheddleton*	LM	46	B2
Chelford	LM	46	A1
Chelmsford	ER	32	B2
Chelsfield	SO	12	A1
Cheltenham Spa	WR	29	A2
Chepstow	WR	28	C2
Cherry Tree	LM	55	B1
Chertsey	SO	15	B1
Chesham	LT	31	B2
Cheshunt	ER	24	A1
Chessington North	SO	16	C1
Chessington South	SO	16	C1
Chester	LM	45	B2
Chester-le-Street	ER	68	C1
Chesterfield	ER	47	B1
Chester Road	LM	88	B2
Chestfield & Swalecliffe	SO	13	A2
Chetnole	WR	8	C2
Chichester (Sussex)	SO	11	C1
Chichester (Tyne & Wear)	TW	70	B2
Chigwell	LT	24	C2
Chilham	SO	13	A2
Chillingham Road	TW	69	B2
Chilworth	SO	11	B2
Chingford	ER	24	C1
Chinley	LM	46	A2
Chippenham	WR	29	C2
Chipstead	SO	12	A1
Chirk	LM	45	C1
Chislehurst	SO	18	B2
Chiswick	SO	20	C2
Chiswick Park	LT	20	C2
Cholsey	WR	30	C2
Chorley	LM	54	C2
Chorley Wood	LM/LT	31	C2
Christ's Hospital	SO	11	B2
Christchurch	SU	5	A2
Church & Oswaldtwistle	LM	55	B1
Church Fenton	ER	56	B1
Church Stretton	LM	36	B2
Churston	TD	3	B2
Cilmeri	LM	35	C2
Clacton	ER	33	B2
Clandon	SO	11	A2
Clapham (Greater London)	SO	21	C2
Clapham (N. Yorks)	LM	55	A1
Clapham Common	LT	21	C2
Clapham Junction	SO	21	C1
Clapham North	LT	21	C2
Clapham South	LT	17	A1
Clapton	ER	22	A1
Clara	CI	86	C1
Clarbeston Road	WR	25	A2
Claremorris	CI	85	C2
Clarkston	SC	76	C1
Claverdon	LM	38	C2
Claygate	SO	16	C1
Cleethorpes	ER	58	C1
Cleland	SC	72	B1
Cleveleys	BF	54	B1

NAME	RAILWAY CODE	PAGE NO.	PAGE REF.
Clifton	LM	51	A2
Clifton Down	WR	8	A2
Clipperstown	NI	85	A1
Clitheroe*	LM	55	B1
Clock House	SO	18	B1
Clogwyn	SM	43	B2
Clonmel	CI	84	B1
Clonsilla	CI	84	B1
Cloughjordan	CI	83	A2
Clunderwen	WR	26	B1
Clydebank	SC	75	A1
Coatbridge Central	SC	72	C1
Coatbridge Sunnyside	SC	72	C1
Coatdyke	SC	72	C1
Cobb Junction	CI	83	C2
Cobham & Stoke d'Abernon	SO	11	A2
Cockfosters	LT	23	B1
Codsall	LM	37	A1
Cogan	WR	28	B1
Colby	ME	59	C1
Colchester	ER	33	A1
Coleraine	NI	86	A1
Colindale	LT	31	C2
Collier's Wood	LT	17	A1
Collingham	ER	48	B1
Collington	SO	12	C2
Collooney	CI	85	B2
Colne	LM	55	B1
Colwall	WR	29	A1
Colwyn Bay	LM	44	A1
Colyford	ST	4	A1
Colyton	ST	4	A1
Combe (Oxon)	WR	30	B1
Commondale	ER	63	B1
Congleton	LM	46	B1
Conisbrough	ER	56	C2
Connel Ferry	SC	77	B2
Cooden Beach	SO	12	C2
Cookham	WR	31	C1
Cooksbridge	SO	12	C1
Coombe (Cornwall)	WR	2	B1
Copplestone	WR	7	C1
Corbridge	ER	67	C2
Cork	CI	83	C2
Corkickle	LM	59	B2
Cornaa	ME	59	B2
Corpach	SC	78	B1
Corrour	SC	78	B1
Coryton	WR	28	C1
Coseley	LM	87	B1
Cosford	LM	37	A1
Cosham	SO	10	C2
Cottingham	ER	57	B2
Coulsdon South	SO	12	A1
Covent Garden	LT	21	B2
Coventry	LM	38	B1
Cowcaddens	GG	76	B1
Cowden	SO	12	B2
Cowdenbeath	SC	73	A1
Cradley Heath	LM	87	C1
Craigavad*	NI	85	A1
Craigendoran	SC	71	A1
Cramlington	ER	68	B1
Craven Arms	WR	36	B2
Crawfordsburn	NI	85	A2
Crawley	SO	12	B1
Crayford	SO	32	C2
Crediton	WR	3	A1
Cressing	ER	33	B1
Cressington	LM	53	C2
Crewe	LM	46	B1
Crewkerne	WR	8	C2
Crews Hill	ER	23	A2
Crianlarich	SC	78	C1
Criccieth	LM	43	C2
Cricklewood	LM	20	A2
Croftfoot	SC	76	C1
Crofton Park	SO	18	A1
Cromer	ER	50	C1
Cromford	LM	47	B1
Cromore	NI	86	A1
Crossflatts	ER	55	B2
Cross Gates	ER	56	B1
Crosshill	SC	76	C1
Crossmyloof	SC	75	C2
Croston	LM	54	C2
Crouch Hill	ER	21	A2
Crowborough	SO	12	B2
Crowcombe	WS	8	B1
Crowhurst	SO	13	C1
Crowle	ER	57	C1
Crowthorne	SO	11	A1
Croxley	LT	31	C2
Croxley Green	LM	31	C2
Croy	SC	72	A1
Crumlin	NI	86	A2
Crumpsall	LM	52	A1
Crystal Palace	SO	17	A2
Cuddington	LM	45	C2
Cuffley	ER	23	A2
Culham	WR	30	C2
Cullercoats	TW	70	A2
Culleybackey	NI	86	A2
Culrain	SC	82	B1
Cultra	NI	85	A1
Cumbernauld	SC	72	A1
Cupar	SC	79	C2
Curragh*	CI	84	A1
Custom House Victoria Dock	ER	22	B2
Cuxton	SO	12	A2
Cwmbran (Proposed)	WR	28	C1
Cwmdwyfran	GW	26	A2
Cyfronydd	WL	36	A1
Cynghordy	WR	27	A1
Dagenham Dock	ER	32	C2
Dagenham East	LT	32	C2
Dagenham Heathway	LT	32	C2
Daisy Hill	LM	55	C1
Dalkey	CI	84	C2
Dalmally	SC	78	C1
Dalmarnock	SC	76	B1
Dalmeny	SC	73	A1
Dalmuir	SC	75	A1
Dalreoch	SC	71	A2
Dalry	SC	71	B1
Dalston (Cumbria)	LM	66	C2
Dalston Junction	LM	21	A2
Dalston Kingsland	LM	21	A2
Dalton	LM	60	C1
Dalwhinnie	SC	78	A2
Damems	KW	55	B2
Danby	ER	63	B1
Dane Road	LM	51	C2
Danzey	LM	37	C2
Darlington	ER	62	B1
Darnall	ER	50	B1
Darsham	ER	42	C1
Dartford	SO	32	C2
Darton	ER	56	C1
Darwen	LM	55	B1
Datchet	SO	31	C2
Davenport	LM	52	C1
Dawlish	WR	3	A2
Dawlish Warren	WR	3	A2
Dduallt	FR	44	C1
Deal	SO	14	A1
Dean	SO	10	B1
Dean Lane	LM	52	A1
Deansgate	LM	51	B2
Debden	LT	24	B2
Deepdene	SO	11	A2
Deganwy	LM	44	A1
Deighton	ER	56	C1
Delamere	LM	45	B2
Denby Dale	ER	56	C1
Denham	LM	19	A1
Denham Golf Club	LM	31	C2
Denmark Hill	SO	21	C2
Dent*	LM	61	C1
Denton	LM	52	B2
Deptford	SO	22	C1
Derby	LM	47	C1
Derby Castle (Douglas)	ME	59	C1
Derby Road (Ipswich)	ER	33	A2

93

NAME	RAILWAY CODE	PAGE NO.	PAGE REF.
Derbyshire Lane (Proposed)	LM	51	B2
Dereham	ER	41	A1
Derriaghy	NI	86	B2
Devil's Bridge	LM	34	B2
Devonport	WR	2	C1
Dewsbury	ER	56	B1
Dhoon	ME	59	C2
Dhu Varren	NI	85	A2
Didcot	WR	30	C2
Dilton Marsh	WR	9	A1
Dinas	WR	27	C2
Dinas Powys	WR	8	A1
Dingle Road	WR	28	B1
Dingwall	SC	81	C2
Dinsdale	ER	62	B1
Dinting	LM	46	A2
Disley	LM	46	A2
Diss	ER	41	B2
Ditton	LM	45	A2
Dockyard	WR	2	C1
Dolau	WR	36	C1
Doleham	SO	13	C1
Dolgarrog	LM	44	B1
Dolgoch Falls	TL	34	A2
Dollis Hill	LT	20	A2
Dolwyddelan	LM	44	B1
Donabate	CI	86	C2
Doncaster	ER	58	B1
Dorchester South	SO	5	A1
Dorchester West	SO	5	A1
Dore	ER	47	A1
Dorking	SO	11	A2
Dorking Town	SO	11	A2
Dormans	SO	12	B1
Dorridge	LM	38	B1
Douglas	ME	59	C1
Dove Holes	LM	46	A2
Dovercourt	ER	33	A2
Dover Priory	SO	14	B1
Dover Western Docks	SO	14	B1
Dovey Junction	LM	34	A2
Downham Market	ER	40	A2
Downshire	NI	85	A1
Drayton Green	WR	20	B1
Drayton Park	ER	21	A2
Dreemskerry	ME	59	B2
Drem	SC	73	A2
Driffield	ER	57	A2
Drigg	LM	59	B2
Drogheda	CI	86	C2
Drogheda Nua	CI	84	A1
Droitwich Spa	WR	37	C1
Dromod	CI	85	C2
Dronfield	ER	47	A1
Drumchapel	SC	75	A2
Drumry	SC	75	A2
Dublin Connolly	CI	84	C1
Dublin Heuston	CI	84	C1
Dublin Pearse	CI	84	C1
Duddeston	LM	88	C1
Dudley Port	LM	87	B2
Duffield	LM	47	C1
Duirinish	SC	81	C1
Duke Street	SC	76	B1
Dullingham	ER	40	C2
Dumbarton Central	SC	71	A2
Dumbarton East	SC	71	A2
Dumfries	SC	65	B2
Dumpton Park	SO	14	A1
Dunbar	SC	74	A1
Dunblane	SC	78	C2
Dunbridge	SO	10	B1
Duncraig	SC	81	C1
Dundalk	CI	86	B2
Dundee	SC	79	B2
Dunfermline	SC	73	A1
Dungeness	RH	13	C2
Dunkeld	SC	78	B2
Dun Laoghaire	CI	84	C2
Dunleer	CI	86	C2
Dunlop	SC	71	B2
Dunmurry	NI	86	B2
Dunster	WS	7	B2
Dunston (proposed)	ER	69	B2
Dunton Green	SO	12	A2
Durham	ER	62	A1
Durrington-on-Sea	SO	11	C2
Dyffryn Ardudwy	LM	43	C2
Dymchurch	RH	13	B2
Eaglescliffe	ER	62	B2
Ealing Broadway	WR/LT	20	B1
Ealing Common	LT	20	B2
Eardington	SV	37	B1
Earl's Court	LT	21	C1
Earlestown	LM	45	A2
Earley	SO	11	A1
Earlsfield	SO	17	A1
Earlswood (Surrey)	SO	12	A1
Earlswood (West Midlands)	LM	37	B2
East Acton	LT	20	B2
East Boldon	ER	70	C2
Eastbourne	SO	12	C2
Eastcote	LT	19	A2
East Croydon	SO	17	B2
East Didsbury	LM	52	C1
East Dulwich	SO	21	C2
Easterhouse	SC	76	B2
East Farleigh	SO	13	A1
East Finchley	LT	21	A1
East Grinstead	SO	12	B1
East Ham	LT	22	B2
East Kilbride	SC	72	B1
Eastleigh	SO	10	C2
East Malling	SO	12	A2
East Putney	LT	21	C1
Eastrington	ER	57	B1
East Tilbury	ER	32	C2
East Worthing	SO	11	C2
Eccles	LM	51	B2
Eccles Road	ER	41	B2
Eccleston Park	LM	45	A2
Edale	LM	46	A2
Edenbridge	SO	12	A1
Edenbridge Town	SO	12	B1
Eden Park	SO	18	B1
Edge Hill	LM	53	B2
Edgware	LT	31	C2
Edgware Road	LT	21	B1
Edinburgh	SC	73	C1
Effingham Junction	SO	11	A2
Eggesford	WR	7	C1
Egham	SO	11	A2
Egton	ER	63	B1
Elephant & Castle	SO/LT	21	C2
Elgin	SC	82	C2
Ellesmere Port	LM	45	A2
Elmers End	SO	18	B1
Elm Park	LT	32	C2
Elmstead Woods	SO	18	A2
Elmswell	ER	41	C1
Elsecar	ER	56	C1
Elsenham	ER	32	A2
Elsham	ER	57	C2
Elstree	LM	31	C2
Eltham Park	SO	22	C2
Eltham Well Hall	SO	22	C2
Elton & Orston	ER	48	C1
Ely	ER	40	B2
Embankment	LT	21	B2
Emerson Park	ER	32	C2
Emsworth	SO	11	C1
Enfield Chase	ER	23	B2
Enfield Lock	ER	24	B1
Enfield Town	ER	23	B2
Ennis*	CI	83	A2
Enniscorthy	CI	84	B2
Entwistle	LM	55	C1
Epping	LT	32	B1
Epsom	SO	16	C2
Epsom Downs	SO	12	A1
Erdington	LM	88	B2
Eridge	SO	12	B2
Erith	SO	32	C2
Errol	SC	79	B1

94

NAME	RAILWAY CODE	PAGE NO.	PAGE REF.	NAME	RAILWAY CODE	PAGE NO.	PAGE REF.
Esher	SO	16	B1	Forest Hill	SO	18	A1
Eskdale (Dalegarth)	RE	60	B1	Formby	LM	54	C1
Essex Road	ER	21	B2	Forres	SC	82	C1
Etchingham	SO	12	B2	Forsinard	SC	82	A1
Etruria	LM	46	C1	Fort Matilda	SC	71	A1
Euston	LM/LT	21	B2	Fort William	SC	78	B1
Euston Square	LT	21	B2	Fota	CI	83	C2
Evesham	WR	29	A2	Four Oaks	LM	88	A2
Ewell East	SO	16	C2	Foxfield	LM	60	C1
Ewell West	SO	16	C2	Foxton	ER	40	C1
Exeter Central	WR	3	A2	Frant	SO	12	B2
Exeter St. David's	WR	3	A2	Fratton	SO	10	C2
Exeter St. Thomas	WR	3	A2	Freshfield (Merseyside)	LM	54	C1
Exmouth	WR	3	A2	Freshfield Halt (Sussex)	BL	12	B1
Exton	WR	3	A2	Freshford	WR	9	A1
Eynsford	SO	12	A2	Frimley	SO	11	A1
Failsworth	LM	52	A1	Frinton	ER	33	B2
Fairbourne	LM/FB	34	A2	Frodsham	LM	45	A2
Fairfield	LM	52	B2	Frome	WR	9	B1
Fairlie	SC	71	B1	Fulham Broadway	LT	21	C1
Fairlop	LT	24	C2	Fulwell	SO	16	A1
Fairy Cottage	ME	59	C2	Furness Vale	LM	46	A2
Falconwood	SO	22	C2	Furze Platt	WR	31	C1
Falkirk Grahamston	SC	72	A2	Gainsborough Central	ER	48	A1
Falkirk High	SC	72	A2	Gainsborough Lea Road	ER	48	A1
Falmer	SO	12	C1	Galway	CI	85	C2
Falmouth	WR	1	C2	Gants Hill	LT	22	A2
Fambridge	ER	33	B1	Garelochhead	SC	71	A1
Fareham	SO	10	C2	Garforth	ER	56	B2
Farnborough (Main)	SO	11	A1	Gargrave	LM	55	A2
Farnborough North	SO	11	A1	Garrowhill	SC	76	B2
Farncombe	SO	11	B2	Garscadden	SC	75	B2
Farnham	SO	11	B1	Garsdale*	LM	61	C1
Farningham Road	SO	12	A2	Garston (Herts.)	LM	31	B2
Farnworth	LM	51	A1	Garston (Merseyside)	LM	53	C2
Farranfore	CI	83	B1	Garswood	LM	54	C2
Farringdon	LM/LT	21	B2	Garth	LM	35	C2
Fauldhouse	SC	72	B2	Garve	SC	81	C2
Faversham	SO	13	A2	Garwick Glen	ME	59	C2
Fawdon	TW	69	A2	Gateshead	TW	69	B2
Faygate	SO	12	B1	Gateshead Stadium	TW	69	B2
Fazakerley	LM	53	A2	Gathurst	LM	54	C2
Fearn	SC	82	B1	Gatley	LM	52	C1
Felixstowe	ER	34	A1	Gatwick Airport	SO	12	B1
Felling	TW	69	B2	Georgemas Junction	SC	82	A2
Feltham	SO	15	A2	Gerrards Cross	LM	31	C2
Fenchurch Street	ER	21	B2	Gidea Park	ER	32	C2
Feniton	WR	3	A2	Giffnock	SC	75	C2
Fenny Stratford	LM	31	A1	Giggleswick	LM	55	A1
Ferriby	ER	57	B2	Gilberdyke	ER	57	B1
Ferry Meadows	NV	39	A2	Gilfach Ddu (Llanberis)	LL	43	B2
Ferryside	WR	26	B2	Gilfach Fargoed	WR	28	B1
Ffairfach	WR	27	B1	Gillingham (Dorset)	SO	9	B1
Filey	ER	63	C2	Gillingham (Kent)	SO	13	A1
Filton	WR	28	C2	Gipsy Hill	SO	17	A2
Finaghy	NI	86	B2	Girvan	SC	64	C1
Finchley Central	LT	23	C1	Glaisdale	ER	63	B1
Finchley Road	LT	21	A1	Glan Conwy	LM	44	A1
Finchley Road & Frognal	LM	21	A1	Glanrafon	LM	33	B2
Finnieston	SC	76	B1	Glasgow Central	SC	76	B1
Finningley*	ER	56	C2	Glasgow Queen Street	SC	76	B1
Finsbury Park	ER/LT	21	A2	Glazebrook	LM	46	A1
Finstock	WR	30	B1	Glenageary	CI	84	C2
Fishbourne	SO	11	C1	Glenavy	NI	86	A2
Fishersgate	SO	12	C1	Glen Mona	ME	59	C2
Fishguard Harbour	WR	25	A2	Gleneagles	SC	78	C2
Fiskerton	LM	48	B1	Glenfinnan	SC	77	A2
Fitzwilliam	ER	56	C2	Glengarnock	SC	71	B2
Five Ways	LM	88	C1	Glossop	LM	46	A2
Fleet	SO	11	A1	Gloucester	WR	29	B1
Fleetwood	BF	54	A1	Gloucester Road	LT	21	C1
Flimby	LM	59	A2	Glynde	SO	12	C1
Flint	LM	45	A1	Glynn	NI	86	B2
Flitwick	LM	31	A2	Goathland	NY	63	B1
Flixton	LM	51	C1	Gobowen	LM	45	C1
Folkestone Central	SO	13	B2	Godalming	SO	11	B2
Folkestone East*	SO	13	B2	Godley	LM	52	B2
Folkestone Harbour	SO	13	B2	Godstone	SO	12	A1
Folkestone Warren*	SO	13	B2	Gogarth	LM	34	A2
Folkestone West	SO	13	B2	Golders Green	LT	21	A1
Ford	SO	11	C2	Goldhawk Road	LT	20	C2
Forest Gate	ER	22	A2	Golf Street	SC	79	B2

NAME	RAILWAY CODE	PAGE NO.	PAGE REF.
Golspie	SC	82	B1
Gomshall	SO	11	A2
Goodge Street	LT	21	B2
Goodmayes	ER	32	C1
Goodrington Sands	TD	3	B2
Goodyear	NI	86	B2
Goole	ER	57	B1
Goostrey	LM	46	B1
Gordon Hill	ER	23	B2
Gorey	CI	84	A2
Goring & Streatley	WR	30	C2
Goring-by-Sea	SO	11	A2
Gormanston	CI	86	C2
Gorton	LM	52	B1
Gospel Oak	LM	21	A1
Gourock	SC	71	A1
Govan	GG	75	B2
Gowerton	WR	26	C2
Goxhill	ER	57	B2
Grange-over-Sands	LM	60	C2
Grange Hill	LT	24	C2
Grange Park	ER	23	B2
Grangetown (Cleveland)	ER	63	A2
Grangetown (S. Glam.)	WR	28	A1
Grantham	ER	48	C1
Grateley	SO	10	B1
Gravelly Hill	LM	88	B2
Gravesend	SO	32	C2
Grays	ER	32	C2
Great Ayton	ER	62	B2
Great Bentley	ER	33	B2
Great Chesterford	ER	32	A2
Great Coates	ER	58	C1
Greatham	ER	62	A2
Great Malvern	WR	29	A1
Great Missenden	LM	31	B1
Great Orme	GO	44	A1
Great Portland Street	LT	21	B1
Greatstone Halt	RH	13	B2
Greenbank	LM	46	A1
Greenfield	LM	55	C2
Greenford	WR/LT	20	B1
Greenhithe	SO	32	C2
Greenisland	NI	85	A1
Green Lane	LM	53	C1
Greenock Central	SC	71	A1
Greenock West	SC	71	A1
Green Park	LT	21	B1
Green Road	LM	60	C1
Greenwich	SO	22	C1
Greystones	CI	84	A2
Grimsby Docks	ER	58	C1
Grimsby Town	ER	58	C1
Grindleford	LM	47	A1
Groombridge	SO	12	B2
Grosmont	ER/NY	63	B1
Groudle Glen	ME	59	C2
Grove Park	SO	18	A2
Guide Bridge	LM	52	B2
Guildford	SO	11	A2
Guiseley	ER	56	B1
Gunnersbury	SO/LT	20	C2
Gunnislake	WR	2	B2
Gunton	ER	50	C2
Gwersyllt	LM	45	B1
Gypsy Lane	ER	62	B2
Habrough	ER	57	C2
Hackbridge	SO	17	B1
Hackney Central	ER	22	A1
Hackney Downs	ER	22	A1
Hackney Wick	ER	22	A1
Haddiscoe	ER	42	A1
Hadfield	LM	46	A2
Hadley Wood	ER	23	B1
Hadrian Road	TW	70	B1
Hagley	LM	37	B1
Hainault	LT	24	C2
Hairmyres	SC	72	B1
Hale	LM	46	A1
Halesworth	ER	42	B1
Halfway (Great Orme)	GO	44	A1
Halfway (Snowdon)	SM	43	B2
Halifax	ER	55	B2
Hall Green	LM	37	B2
Halling	SO	12	A2
Hall Road	LM	53	A1
Haltwhistle	ER	67	C1
Hamble	SO	10	C2
Hamilton Central	SC	72	B1
Hamilton West	SC	72	B1
Hammersmith	LT	20	C2
Hammerton	ER	56	A2
Hampden Park	SO	12	C2
Hampstead	LT	21	A1
Hampstead Heath	LM	21	A1
Hampton	SO	15	B2
Hampton-in-Arden	LM	38	B1
Hampton Court	SO	16	B1
Hampton Loade	SV	37	B1
Hampton Wick	SO	16	B1
Hamstead	LM	88	B1
Ham Street	SO	13	B2
Hamworthy	SO	5	A2
Handborough	WR	30	B2
Handforth	LM	46	A1
Hanger Lane	LT	20	B1
Hanwell	WR	20	B1
Hapton	LM	55	B1
Harlech	LM	43	C2
Harlesden	LM/LT	20	B2
Harling Road	ER	41	B1
Harlington	LM	31	A2
Harlow Mill	ER	32	B2
Harlow Town	ER	32	B1
Harman's Cross (proposed)	SW	5	A2
Harmonstown	CI	84	B2
Harold Wood	ER	32	C2
Harpenden	LM	31	B2
Harrietsham	SO	13	A1
Harringay	ER	21	A2
Harringay Stadium	ER	21	A2
Harrington	LM	59	A2
Harrogate	ER	56	A1
Harrow & Wealdstone	LM/LT	20	A1
Harrow-on-the-Hill	LM/LT	20	A1
Hartford	LM	45	B2
Hartlebury	LM	37	C1
Hartlepool	ER	62	A2
Hartwood	SC	72	B2
Harwich Parkeston Quay	ER	33	A2
Harwich Town	ER	33	A2
Haslemere	SO	11	B1
Hassocks	SO	12	C1
Hastings	SO	13	C1
Hatch End	LM	31	C2
Hatfield	ER	32	B1
Hatfield Peverel	ER	33	B1
Hathersage	LM	47	A1
Hattersley	LM	46	A2
Hatton	LM	38	C1
Hatton Cross	LT	19	C2
Havant	SO	11	C1
Havenhouse	ER	49	B2
Havenstreet	IW	6	A2
Haverfordwest	WR	25	B2
Haverthwaite	LH	60	C1
Hawarden	LM	45	B1
Hawarden Bridge	LM	45	B1
Haworth	KW	55	B2
Haydon Bridge	ER	67	C1
Haydons Road	SO	17	A1
Hayes (Kent)	SO	18	B2
Hayes & Harlington	WR	19	C2
Hayle	WR	1	A1
Haymarket (Edinburgh)	SC	73	C1
Haymarket (Newcastle)	TW	69	B2
Haywards Heath	SO	12	B1
Hazel Grove	LM	46	B2
Headcorn	SO	13	B1
Headingley	ER	57	A1
Headstone Lane	LM	31	C2
Heald Green	LM	46	A1
Healing	ER	58	C1
Heath High Level	WR	28	C1

NAME	RAILWAY CODE	PAGE NO.	PAGE REF.	NAME	RAILWAY CODE	PAGE NO.	PAGE REF.
Heath Low Level	WR	28	C1	Honley	ER	55	C2
Heathrow Terminals 1, 2 & 3	LT	19	C1	Honor Oak Park	SO	18	A1
Heathrow Terminal 4	LT	19	C1	Hook	SO	11	A1
Heaton Chapel	LM	52	C1	Hoo Staff Halt*	SO	32	C2
Heaton Park	LM	51	A2	Hooton	LM	45	A1
Hebburn	TW	70	B1	Hope (Clwyd)	LM	45	B1
Hebden Bridge	ER	55	B2	Hope (Derbyshire)	LM	47	A1
Hebron	SM	43	B2	Hopton Heath	WR	36	B1
Heckington	ER	48	C2	Horley	SO	12	B1
Heighington	ER	62	A1	Hornchurch	LT	32	C2
Helen's Bay	NI	85	A2	Hornsey	ER	21	A2
Helensburgh Central	SC	71	A1	Horsforth	ER	56	B1
Helensburgh Upper	SC	71	A1	Horsham	SO	11	B2
Hellifield	LM	55	A1	Horsley	SO	11	A2
Helmsdale	SC	82	B1	Horsted Keynes	BL	12	B1
Helsby	LM	45	A2	Horton*	LM	61	C1
Hemel Hempstead	LM	31	B2	Hoscar	LM	54	C2
Hendon	LM	20	A2	Hough Green	LM	45	A2
Hendon Central	LT	20	A2	Hounslow	SO	20	C1
Hengoed	WR	28	C1	Hounslow Central	LT	19	C2
Heniarth	WL	35	A2	Hounslow East	LT	20	C1
Henley-in-Arden	LM	37	C2	Hounslow West	LT	19	C2
Henley-on-Thames	WR	31	C1	Hove	SO	12	C1
Hensall	ER	56	B2	Howden	ER	57	B1
Hereford	WR	28	A2	Howdon	TW	70	B1
Herne Bay	SO	13	A2	Howstrake	ME	59	C2
Herne Hill	SO	17	A2	Howth	CI	84	B2
Hersham	SO	15	B2	Howth Junction	CI	84	B2
Herston	SW	5	A2	Hoylake	LM	45	A1
Hertford East	ER	32	B1	Hubbert's Bridge	ER	49	C1
Hertford North	ER	32	B1	Huddersfield	ER	55	C2
Hessle	ER	57	B2	Hull	ER	57	B2
Heswall	LM	45	A1	Huncoat	LM	55	B1
Hever	SO	12	B1	Hungerford	WR	10	A1
Heworth	ER/TW	69	B2	Hunmanby	ER	63	C2
Hexham	ER	67	C2	Huntingdon	ER	40	C1
Heyford	WR	30	A2	Huntly	SC	82	C2
Heysham*	LM	54	A1	Hunt's Cross	LM	45	A2
Higham	SO	32	C2	Hurst Green	SO	12	A1
Highams Park	ER	24	C1	Hutton Cranswick	ER	57	A2
High Barnet	LT	23	B1	Huyton	LM	45	A2
Highbridge	WR	8	B1	Hyde Central	LM	52	B2
High Brooms	SO	12	B2	Hyde North	LM	52	B2
Highbury & Islington	ER/LT	21	A2	Hyde Park Corner	LT	21	B1
Highgate	LT	21	A1	Hykeham	ER	48	B2
Highley	SV	37	B1	Hyndland	SC	75	B2
High Street (Glasgow)	SC	76	B1	Hythe (Essex)	ER	33	A2
High Street, Kensington	LT	21	C1	Hythe (Kent)	RH	13	B2
Hightown	LM	54	C1	IBM Halt*	SC	71	A1
High Wycombe	LM	31	C1	Ibrox	GG	75	B2
Hilden	NI	86	B2	Ickenham	LT	19	A1
Hidenborough	SO	12	A2	Ifield	SO	12	B1
Hillfoot	SC	75	A2	Ilford	ER	22	A2
Hillhead	GG	75	B2	Ilford Road	TW	69	B2
Hillingdon	LT	19	A1	Ilkley	ER	55	A2
Hillington East	SC	75	B2	Ince (Greater Manchester)	LM	54	C2
Hillington West	SC	75	B2	Ince & Elton	LM	45	A2
Hillside	LM	54	C1	Ingatestone	ER	32	B2
Hilsea	SO	10	C2	Ingrow	KW	55	B2
Hinchley Wood	SO	16	B1	Insch	SC	82	C2
Hinckley	LM	38	B2	Invergordon	SC	82	C1
Hindley	LM	54	C2	Invergowrie	SC	79	B2
Hinton Admiral	SO	6	A1	Inverkeithing	SC	73	A1
Hitchin	ER	31	A2	Inverkip	SC	71	A1
Hither Green	SO	18	A1	Inverness	SC	82	C1
Hockley	ER	33	C1	Invershin	SC	82	B1
Holborn	LT	21	B2	Inverurie	SC	80	A1
Holborn Viaduct	SO	21	B2	Ipswich	ER	33	A2
Holland Park	LT	21	B1	Irlam	LM	51	C1
Hollingbourne	SO	13	A1	Irton Road	RE	60	B1
Hollinwood	LM	52	A1	Irvine	SC	71	C2
Holloway Road	LT	21	A2	Isleworth	SO	20	C1
Holmes Chapel	LM	46	B1	Iver	WR	19	B1
Holmwood	SO	11	B2	Jarrow	TW	70	B1
Holt (proposed)	NN	50	C1	Jefferstone Lane	RH	13	B2
Holton Heath	SO	5	A2	Jesmond	TW	69	B2
Holyhead	LM	43	A1	Johnston (Dyfed)	WR	25	B2
Holytown	SC	72	B1	Johnstone	SC	71	B2
Holywood	NI	85	A1	Jordanhill	SC	75	B2
Homerton (proposed)	ER	22	A2	Jordanstown	NI	85	A1
Honeybourne	WR	29	A2	Kearsley	LM	51	A1
Honiton	WR	8	C1	Kearsney	SO	14	B1

NAME	RAILWAY CODE	PAGE NO.	PAGE REF.	NAME	RAILWAY CODE	PAGE NO.	PAGE REF.
Keighley	ER/KW	55	B2	Kiveton Bridge	ER	47	A2
Keith	SC	82	C2	Kiveton Park	ER	47	A2
Kelling Heath	NN	50	C1	Knaresborough	ER	56	A1
Kelvedon	ER	33	B1	Knebworth	ER	32	B1
Kelvinbridge	GG	76	B1	Knighton	WR	36	C1
Kelvin Hall	GG	75	B2	Knightsbridge	LT	21	C1
Kemble	WR	29	C2	Knockholt	SO	12	A2
Kempston Hardwick	LM	31	A2	Knockmore	NI	86	B2
Kempton Park*	SO	15	A2	Knottingley	ER	56	B2
Kemsing	SO	12	A2	Knucklas	WR	36	B1
Kemsley	SO	13	A1	Knutsford	LM	46	A1
Kemsley Down	SK	13	A1	Kyle of Lochalsh	SC	81	C1
Kendal	LM	60	C2	Ladbroke Grove	LT	21	B1
Kenley	SO	17	C2	Lade Halt	RH	13	C2
Kennett	ER	40	C2	Ladybank	SC	79	C1
Kennington	LT	21	C2	Ladywell	SO	22	C1
Kennishead	SC	75	C2	Laindon	ER	32	C2
Kensal Green	LM/LT	20	B2	Lairg	SC	82	A1
Kensal Rise	LM	20	B2	Lakenheath	ER	40	B2
Kensington Olympia	LM/LT	21	C1	Lakeside	LH	60	C1
Kent House	SO	18	A1	Lambeg	NI	86	B2
Kentish Town	LM	21	A1	Lambeth North	LT	21	C2
Kentish Town West	LM	21	B1	Lamphey	WR	25	B2
Kenton	LM/LT	20	A1	Lanark	SC	72	C2
Kents Bank	LM	60	C2	Lancaster	LM	54	A2
Kettering for Corby	LM	39	B1	Lancaster Gate	LT	21	B1
Kew Bridge	SO	20	C2	Lancing	SO	11	C2
Kew Gardens	SO/LT	20	C2	Langbank	SC	71	A2
Keyham	WR	2	C1	Langley	WR	31	C2
Keynsham	WR	9	A1	Langley Green	LM	87	C2
Kidbrooke	SO	22	C2	Langside	SC	76	C1
Kidderminster	LM/SV	37	B1	Langwathby*	LM	60	A2
Kidsgrove	LM	46	B2	Lansdowne Road	CI	84	C2
Kidwelly	WR	26	B2	Lapford	WR	7	C1
Kilbarrack	CI	84	B2	Lapworth	LM	38	C1
Kilburn	LT	21	A1	Larbert	SC	72	A2
Kilburn High Road	LM	21	B1	Largs	SC	71	B1
Kilburn Park	LT	21	B1	Larne Harbour	NI	86	A2
Kilcoole	CI	84	A2	Larne Town	NI	86	A2
Kildale	ER	62	B2	Latimer Road	LT	20	B2
Kildare	CI	84	A1	Lawrence Hill	WR	8	A2
Kildonan	SC	82	A1	Laxey	ME	59	C2
Kilgetty	WR	26	B1	Layton	LM	54	B1
Kilkenny	CI	84	A1	Laytown	CI	86	C2
Killarney	CI	83	B1	Lazonby*	LM	60	A2
Killester	CI	84	B2	Lea Bridge	ER	22	A1
Killiney	CI	86	C2	Leagrave	LM	31	A2
Kilmarnock	SC	71	C2	Lea Hall	LM	88	C2
Kilmaurs (proposed)	SC	71	C2	Lealholm	ER	63	B1
Kilpatrick	SC	75	A1	Leamington Spa	LM	38	C1
Kilwinning	SC	71	B1	Leasowe	LM	45	A1
Kinbrace	SC	82	A1	Leatherhead	SO	11	A2
King's Cross	ER/LT	21	B2	Ledbury	WR	29	A1
King's Cross Midland City	LM	21	B2	Lee	SO	18	A2
King's Langley	LM	31	B2	Leeds	ER	57	A1
King's Lynn	ER	40	A2	Leicester	LM	38	A2
King's Norton	LM	37	B2	Leicester Square	LT	21	B2
King's Nympton	WR	7	C1	Leigh	SO	12	B2
King's Park	SC	76	C1	Leigh-on-Sea	ER	33	C1
King's Sutton	LM	30	A2	Leighton Buzzard	LM	31	A1
Kingham	WR	30	B1	Leixlip	CI	86	C2
Kinghorn	SC	73	A1	Lelant	WR	1	A1
Kinsbury	LT	20	A2	Lelant Saltings	WR	1	A1
Kingsknowe	SC	73	C1	Lenham	SO	13	A1
Kingston	SO	16	B1	Lenzie	SC	76	A1
Kingston Park (proposed)	TW	69	A1	Leominster	WR	36	C2
Kingswear	TD	3	B2	Letchworth	ER	32	A1
Kingswood	SO	12	A1	Leuchars	SC	79	B2
Kingussie	SC	78	A2	Levenshulme	LM	52	C1
Kinning Park	GG	75	B2	Levisham	NY	63	C1
Kintbury	WR	10	A1	Lewaigue	ME	59	B2
Kirby Cross	ER	33	B2	Lewes	SO	12	C1
Kirkby (Merseyside)	LM	53	A2	Lewisham	SO	22	C1
Kirkby-in-Furness	LM	60	C1	Leyland	LM	54	B2
Kirkby Stephen*	LM	61	B1	Leyton	LT	22	A1
Kirkcaldy	SC	73	A1	Leyton Midland Road	ER	22	A1
Kirkconnel	SC	63	A1	Leytonstone	LT	22	A1
Kirkdale	LM	53	B1	Leytonstone High Road	ER	22	A1
Kirkham & Wesham	SC	54	C2	Lichfield City	LM	37	A2
Kirkhill	SC	76	C1	Lichfield Trent Valley	LM	37	A2
Kirknewton	SC	73	B1	Lidlington	LM	31	A2
Kirton Lindsey	ER	57	C2	Limerick	CI	83	A1

NAME	RAILWAY CODE	PAGE NO.	PAGE REF.	NAME	RAILWAY CODE	PAGE NO.	PAGE REF.
Limerick Junction	CI	83	B2	Lostock Gralam	LM	46	A1
Lincoln Central	ER	48	B2	Lostock Hall	LM	54	B2
Lincoln St. Marks	ER	48	B2	Lostwithiel	WR	2	B1
Lingfield	SO	12	B1	Loughborough	LM	38	A2
Lingwood	ER	42	A1	Loughborough Central	ML	38	A2
Linlithgow	SC	72	A2	Loughborough Junction	SO	21	C2
Liphook	SO	11	B1	Loughton	LT	24	B2
Lisburn	NI	86	B2	Lowdham	LM	47	C2
Liskeard	WR	2	B1	Lower Edmonton	ER	23	C2
Liss	SO	11	B1	Lower Sydenham	SO	18	A1
Little Bispham	BF	54	B1	Lowestoft	ER	42	B2
Littleborough	LM	55	C2	Ludgershall*	SO	10	A1
Littlehampton	SO	11	C2	Ludlow	WR	36	B2
Littlehaven	SO	11	B2	Lurgan	NI	86	B2
Little Island	CI	83	C2	Luton	LM	31	B2
Little Kimble	LM	31	B1	Luxulyan	WR	1	B2
Littleport	ER	40	B2	Lydney	WR	28	B2
Little Sutton	LM	45	A1	Lye	LM	87	C1
Liverpool Central	LM	53	B1	Lymington Pier	SO	6	A1
Liverpool James Street	LM	53	B1	Lymington Town	SO	6	A1
Liverpool Lime Street	LM	53	B1	Lympstone	WR	3	A2
Liverpool Moorfields	LM	53	B1	Lympstone Commando	WR	3	A2
Liverpool Street (London)	ER/LT	21	B2	Lyndhurst Road	SO	9	C1
Llanaber	LM	34	A2	Lytham	LM	54	B1
Llanbadarn	LM	34	B2	Macclesfield	LM	46	A2
Llanbedr	LM	43	C2	Machynlleth	LM	34	A2
Llanberis	SM	43	B2	Magdalen Road	ER	40	A2
Llanbister Road	WR	36	CI	Magheramorne	NI	86	A2
Llanbradach	WR	28	C1	Maghull	LM	54	C2
Llandaf	WR	28	C1	Magilligan*	NI	86	A1
Llandanwg	LM	43	C2	Maida Vale	LT	21	B1
Llandecwyn	LM	44	C1	Maidenhead	WR	31	C1
Llandeilo	WR	27	A1	Maiden Newton	WR	4	A2
Llandovery	WR	27	A1	Maidstone Barracks	SO	13	A1
Llandrindod	LM	35	C2	Maidstone East	SO	13	A1
Llandudno	LM	44	A1	Maidstone West	SO	13	A1
Llandudno Junction	LM	44	A1	Malahide	CI	86	C2
Llandudno Victoria	GO	44	A1	Malden Manor	SO	16	B2
Llandybie	WR	27	B1	Mallaig	SC	77	A2
Llanelli	WR	26	B2	Mallow	CI	83	B2
Llanfair Caereinion	WL	35	A2	Malton	ER	63	C1
Llanfairfechan	LM	44	A1	Malvern Link	WR	37	C1
Llanfairpwll	LM	43	A2	Manchester Airport (Proposed)	LM	46	A1
Llangadog	WR	27	A1	Manchester Oxford Road	LM	52	B1
Llangammarch	WR	27	A2	Manchester Piccadilly	LM	52	B1
Llangelynin	LM	33	A2	Manchester Square	BF	54	B1
Llangennech	WR	26	B2	Manchester United Football Ground*	LM	51	B2
Llangower	BA	44	C2				
Llangynllo	WR	36	B1	Manchester Victoria	LM	52	B1
Llanishen	WR	28	C1	Manea	ER	40	B2
Llanuwchllyn	BA	44	C2	Manningtree	ER	33	A2
Llanrwst	LM	44	B1	Manorbier	WR	25	B2
Llanwrda	WR	27	A1	Manor House	LT	21	A2
Llanwrtyd	WR	27	A2	Manor Park	ER	22	A2
Llwyngwril	LM	34	A2	Manor Road	LM	45	A1
Llwynpia	WR	27	C2	Manors	ER/TW	69	B2
Lochailort	SC	77	A2	Mansion House	LT	21	B2
Locheilside	SC	78	A1	Marble Arch	LT	21	B1
Lochgelly	SC	79	C1	March	ER	40	B1
Lochluichart	SC	81	C2	Marden	SO	13	A1
Lochside	SC	71	B2	Margate	SO	14	A1
Lochty	LY	79	C2	Marino	NI	85	A1
Lockerbie	SC	66	B1	Market Bosworth	SH	38	A2
Lockwood	ER	55	C2	Market Harborough	LM	39	B1
London Bridge	SO/LT	21	B2	Market Rasen	ER	48	A2
Londonderry	NI	86	A1	Markinch	SC	79	C1
London Fields	ER	22	B1	Marks Tey	ER	33	A1
London Road (Brighton)	SO	12	C1	Marlow	WR	31	C1
London Road (Guildford)	SO	11	A2	Marple	LM	52	C2
Longbenton	TW	69	A2	Marsden	ER	55	C2
Longbridge	LM	37	B2	Marske	ER	62	A2
Long Buckby	LM	38	C2	Marston Green	LM	38	B1
Longcross	SO	11	A2	Martin Mill	SO	14	B1
Long Eaton	LM	47	C2	Marton	ER	62	B2
Longfield	SO	12	A2	Maryland	ER	22	A1
Longford	CI	86	C1	Marylebone	LM/LT	21	B1
Longniddry	SC	73	A2	Maryport	LM	59	A2
Longport	LM	46	B1	Matlock	LM	47	B1
Long Preston	LM	55	A1	Matlock Bath	LM	47	B1
Longsight Staff Halt*	LM	52	B1	Mauldeth Road	LM	52	C1
Longton	LM	46	C2	Maxwell Park	SC	75	B2
Looe	WR	2	B1	Maybole	SC	64	A1

NAME	RAILWAY CODE	PAGE NO.	PAGE REF.	NAME	RAILWAY CODE	PAGE NO.	PAGE REF.
Maynooth	CI	86	C2	Motspur Park	SO	16	B2
Maze Hill	SO	22	C1	Mottingham	SO	18	A2
Meldreth	ER	32	A1	Mottram Staff Halt*	LM	46	A2
Melton*	ER	57	B2	Mouldsworth	LM	45	B2
Melton Mowbray	LM	39	A1	Moulsecoomb	SO	12	C1
Menheniot	WR	2	B1	Mount Florida	SC	76	C1
Menston	ER	56	B1	Mountain Ash*	WR	27	B2
Meols	LM	45	A1	Muine Bheag	CI	84	A1
Meols Cop	LM	54	C1	Muirend	SC	76	C1
Meopham	SO	12	A2	Muir of Ord	SC	81	C2
Merstham	SO	12	A1	Mullingar	CI	86	C1
Merthyr Tydfil	WR	27	B2	Muncaster Mill	RE	59	B2
Merthyr Vale	WR	27	B2	Mytholmroyd	ER	55	B2
Merton Park	SO	17	A1	Nafferton	ER	57	A2
Metheringham	ER	48	B2	Nailsea and Backwell	WR	8	A2
Mexborough	ER	56	C2	Nairn	SC	82	C1
Micheldever	SO	10	B2	Nant Gwernol	TL	34	A2
Micklefield	ER	56	B2	Nantwich	LM	46	B2
Middlesbrough	ER	63	A1	Nantyronen	LM	34	B2
Middlewood	LM	46	A2	Narberth	WR	26	B1
Midgham	WR	10	A2	Narborough	LM	38	A2
Mile End	LT	22	B1	Navan*	CI	86	C1
Miles Platting	LM	52	B1	Navigation Road	LM	51	C2
Milford (Surrey)	SO	11	B2	Neasden	LT	20	A2
Milford Haven	WR	25	B2	Neath	WR	27	C1
Millbrook (Beds.)	LM	31	A2	Needham Market	ER	41	C2
Millbrook (Hants.)	SO	9	C2	Neilston	SC	75	C1
Mill Hill (Lancs.)	LM	55	B1	Nelson	LM	55	B1
Mill Hill Broadway	LM	31	C2	Nenagh	CI	83	A2
Mill Hill East	LT	23	C1	Neston	LM	45	A1
Millom	LM	60	C1	Netherfield	LM	47	C2
Mills Hill (Proposed)	LM	52	A1	Nethertown	LM	59	B2
Millstreet	CI	83	B1	Netley	SO	10	C2
Milngavie	SC	75	A2	Newark Castle	ER	48	B1
Milnrow	LM	55	C2	Newark North Gate	ER	48	B1
Milton Keynes Central	LM	31	A1	New Barnet	ER	23	B1
Minehead	WS	7	B2	New Beckenham	SO	18	A1
Minffordd	LM/FR	43	C2	New Brighton	LM	53	B1
Minorca	ME	59	C2	Newbury	WR	10	A2
Minster	SO	14	A1	Newbury Park	LT	22	A2
Mirfield	ER	56	C1	Newbury Racecourse*	WR	10	A2
Mistley	ER	33	A2	Newby Bridge	LH	60	C1
Mitcham	SO	17	B1	Newcastle	ER/TW	69	B2
Mitcham Junction	SO	17	B1	New Clee	ER	58	C1
Moate	CI	86	C1	New Cross	SO/LT	22	C1
Mobberley	LM	46	A1	New Cross Gate	SO/LT	22	C1
Moira	NI	86	B2	New Eltham	SO	18	A2
Monifieth	SC	79	B2	Newhaven Harbour	SO	12	C1
Monkseaton	TW	70	A1	Newhaven Marine	SO	12	C1
Monks Risborough	LM	31	B1	Newhaven Town	SO	12	C1
Monkstown & Seapoint	CI	84	C2	New Hey	LM	55	C2
Montpelier	WR	8	A2	New Holland	ER	57	B2
Montrose	SC	80	C1	New Hythe	SO	12	A2
Monument (London)	LT	21	B2	Newington	SO	13	A1
Monument (Newcastle)	TW	69	B2	New Lane	LM	54	C2
Moorgate	ER/LT	21	B2	New Maiden	SO	16	B2
Moor Park	LM/LT	31	C2	Newmarket	ER	40	C2
Moorside	LM	51	A1	New Mills Central	LM	46	A2
Moorthorpe	ER	56	C2	New Mills Newtown	LM	46	A2
Morar	SC	77	A2	New Milton	SO	6	A1
Morchard Road	WR	7	C1	Newport (Essex)	ER	32	A2
Morden	LT	17	B1	Newport (Gwent)	WR	28	A2
Morden Road	SO	17	B1	New Pudsey	ER	56	B1
Morden South	SO	17	B1	Newquay	WR	1	B2
Morecambe	LM	54	A2	New Romney	RH	13	B2
Moreton (Dorset)	SO	5	A1	New Ross*	CI	84	B1
Moreton (Merseyside)	LM	45	A1	Newry	NI	86	B2
Moreton-in-Marsh	WR	30	A1	New Southgate	ER	23	C1
Morfa Mawddach	LM	34	A2	Newton (Greater Glasgow)	SC	76	C2
Morley	ER	56	B1	Newton-for-Hyde	LM	52	B2
Mornington Crescent	LT	21	B1	Newton Abbot	WR	3	B2
Morpeth	ER	68	B1	Newton Aycliffe	ER	62	A1
Mortimer	SO	10	A2	Newtondale Halt	NY	63	C1
Mortlake	SO	20	C2	Newton-le-Willows	LM	45	A2
Moses Gate	LM	51	A1	Newtonmore	SC	78	A2
Mosney	CI	86	C2	Newton-on-Ayr	SC	71	C1
Mossley	LM	55	B1	Newton St. Cyres	WR	3	B1
Mossley Hill	LM	53	C2	Newtown	LM	35	B2
Moss Side	LM	54	B1	Ninian Park*	WR	28	A1
Moston	LM	52	B1	Nitshill	SC	75	C2
Mostrim	CI	86	C1	Norbiton	SO	16	B2
Motherwell	SC	72	B1	Norbury	SO	17	B2

100

NAME	RAILWAY CODE	PAGE NO.	PAGE REF.	NAME	RAILWAY CODE	PAGE NO.	PAGE REF.
Normanton	ER	56	B1	Paisley Gilmour Street	SC	75	B1
North Acton	LT	20	B2	Paisley St. James	SC	75	B1
Northallerton	ER	62	C1	Palmers Green	ER	23	C2
Northampton	LM	39	C1	Pangbourne	WR	30	C2
North Berwick	SC	73	A2	Pannal	ER	56	A1
North Camp	SO	11	A1	Pantyffynnon	WR	27	B1
North Dulwich	SO	17	A2	Par	WR	2	B1
North Ealing	LT	20	B2	Parbold	LM	54	C2
Northfield	LM	37	B2	Park	LM	52	B1
Northfields	LT	20	C1	Park Royal	LT	20	B2
North Filton Platform*	WR	28	C2	Parkstone	SO	5	A2
Northfleet	SO	32	C2	Park Street	LM	31	B2
North Harrow	LT	19	A2	Parsons Green	LT	21	C1
Northiam	KS	13	B1	Parson Street	WR	8	B2
Northolt	LT	19	B2	Partick	SC/GG	75	B2
Northolt Park	LM	20	A1	Parton	LM	59	B2
North Queensferry	SC	73	A1	Patchway	WR	28	C2
North Road	ER	62	B1	Patricroft	LM	51	B1
North Sheen	SO	20	C2	Patterton	SC	75	C2
North Shields	TW	70	A1	Peartree	LM	47	C1
Northumberland Park	ER	24	C1	Peckham Rye	SO	21	C2
North Walsham	ER	50	C2	Pegswood	ER	68	B1
North Weald	LT	32	B2	Pelaw	TW	70	B1
North Wembley	LM/LT	20	A1	Pemberton	LM	54	C2
Northwich	LM	46	A1	Pembrey & Burry Port	WR	26	B2
Northwick Park	LT	20	A1	Pembroke	WR	25	B2
Northwood (Greater London)	LT	31	C2	Pembroke Dock	WR	25	B2
Northwood (Worcs.)	SV	37	B1	Penally	WR	26	B1
Northwood Hills	LT	31	C2	Penarth	WR	28	B1
North Woolwich	ER	22	B2	Pendleton	LM	51	B1
Norton Bridge	LM	46	C1	Pengam	WR	28	C1
Norwich	ER	41	A2	Penge East	SO	18	A1
Norwood Junction	SO	17	B2	Penge West	SO	18	A1
Nottingham	LM	47	C2	Penhelig	LM	34	B2
Notting Hill Gate	LT	21	B1	Penistone	ER	56	C1
Nuneaton	LM	38	B1	Penkridge	LM	37	A2
Nunhead	SO	22	C1	Penmaenmawr	LM	44	A1
Nunthorpe	ER	62	B2	Penmere	WR	1	C1
Nutbourne	SO	11	C1	Penrhyn (Gwynedd)	FR	44	C1
Nutfield	SO	12	A1	Penrhyndeudraeth	LM	44	C1
Oakengates	LM	37	A1	Penrith	LM	60	A2
Oakham	LM	39	A1	Penryn (Cornwall)	WE	1	C1
Oakleigh Park	ER	23	B1	Pensarn (Gwynedd)	LM	43	C2
Oakwood	LT	23	B2	Penshurst	SO	12	B2
Oakworth	KW	55	B2	Pentre-bach	WR	27	B1
Oban	SC	77	B2	Pen-y-Bont	LM	35	C2
Ockendon	ER	32	C2	Penybont	GW	26	A2
Ockley	SO	11	B2	Penychain	LM	43	C2
Okehampton*	WR	3	A1	Penyffordd	LM	45	B1
Oldfield Park	WR	9	A1	Penzance	WR	1	A1
Oldham Mumps	LM	52	A2	Percy Main	TW	70	B1
Oldham Werneth	LM	52	A2	Perivale	LT	20	B1
Old Hill	LM	87	C1	Perranwell	WR	1	C1
Old Roan	LM	53	A2	Perry Barr	LM	88	B1
Old Street	ER/LT	21	B2	Pershore	WR	37	C2
Old Trafford	LM	51	B2	Perth	SC	79	B1
Olton	LM	37	B2	Petersborough	ER	39	A2
Onchan Head	ME	59	C1	Petersfield	SO	11	B1
Ongar	LT	32	B2	Petts Wood	SO	18	B2
Ore	SO	13	C1	Pevensey & Westham	SO	12	C2
Ormskirk	LM	54	C2	Pevensey Bay	SO	12	C2
Orpington	SO	12	A1	Pewsey	WR	9	A2
Orrell	LM	54	C2	Piccadilly Circus	LT	21	B2
Orrell Park	LM	53	A2	Pickering	NY	63	C1
Orton Mere	NV	39	A2	Pilning	WR	28	C2
Osterley	LT	20	C1	Pilot Halt	RH	13	C2
Otford	SO	12	A2	Pimlico	LT	21	C2
Oulton Broad North	ER	42	B2	Pinhoe	WR	3	A2
Oulton Broad South	ER	42	B2	Pinner	LT	19	A2
Oval	LT	21	C2	Pitlochry	SC	78	B2
Overton	SO	10	A2	Pitsea	ER	33	C1
Oxenholme	LM	60	C2	Plaistow	LT	22	B2
Oxenhope	KW	55	B2	Plas Halt	FR	44	C1
Oxford	WR	30	C2	Pleasington	LM	54	B2
Oxford Circus	LT	21	B1	Pleasure Beach	BF	54	B1
Oxshott	SO	16	C1	Plockton	SC	80	C1
Oxted	SO	12	A1	Pluckley	SO	13	B1
Paddington	WR/LT	21	B1	Plumley	LM	46	A1
Paddock Wood	SO	12	B2	Plumpton	SO	12	C1
Padgate	LM	45	A2	Plumstead	SO	22	C2
Paignton	WR	3	B2	Plymouth	WR	2	C1
Paignton (Queen's Park)	TD	3	B2	Pokesdown	SO	5	A2

NAME	RAILWAY CODE	PAGE NO.	PAGE REF.	NAME	RAILWAY CODE	PAGE NO.	PAGE REF.
Polegate	SO	12	C2	Ramsgate	SO	14	A1
Polesworth	LM	38	A1	Rannoch	SC	78	B1
Pollokshaws East	SC	75	C2	Rathdrum	CI	84	A2
Pollokshaws West	SC	75	C2	Rathluirc	CI	83	B2
Pollokshields East	SC	76	B1	Rathmore	CI	83	B1
Pollokshields West	SC	76	B1	Rauceby	ER	48	C2
Polmont	SC	72	A2	Ravenglass	LM/RE	59	C2
Polsloe Bridge	WR	3	A2	Ravensbourne	SO	18	A1
Ponders End	ER	24	B1	Ravenscourt Park	LT	20	C2
Pontarddulais	WR	26	B2	Ravensthorpe	ER	56	C1
Pontefract Baghill	ER	56	B2	Rawcliffe	ER	57	B1
Pontefract Monkhill	ER	56	B2	Rayleigh	ER	33	C1
Pontlottyn	WR	27	B2	Rayners Lane	LT	19	A2
Pont-y-Pant	LM	44	B1	Rayners Park	SO	16	B2
Pontypool	WR	28	B1	Reading	WR	31	C1
Pontypridd	WR	27	C2	Reading West	WR	31	C1
Poole	SO	5	A2	Rectory Road	ER	21	A2
Poppleton	ER	56	A2	Redbridge (Greater London)	LT	22	C2
Portadown	NI	86	B2	Redbridge (Hants.)	SO	9	C1
Portarlington	CI	84	A1	Redcar Central	ER	62	A2
Portchester	SO	10	C2	Redcar East	ER	62	A2
Port Erin	ME	59	C1	Reddish North	LM	52	B1
Port Glasgow	SC	71	A2	Reddish South	LM	52	C1
Porth	WR	27	C2	Redditch	LM	37	C2
Porthmadog	LM/FR	43	C2	Redhill	SO	12	A1
Portlaoise	CI	84	A1	Redland	WR	8	A2
Portmarnock	CI	86	C2	Redruth	WR	1	C1
Portrush	NI	86	A1	Reedham (Norfolk)	ER	42	A1
Portslade	SO	12	C1	Reedham (Greater London)	SO	17	C2
Portsmouth & Southsea	SO	10	C2	Regent Centre	TW	69	A2
Portsmouth Arms	WR	7	C1	Regent's Park	LT	21	B1
Portsmouth Harbour	SO	10	C2	Reigate	SO	12	A1
Port Soderick	ME	59	C1	Renton	SC	71	A2
Port St. Mary	ME	59	C1	Retford	ER	48	A1
Port Sunlight	LM	53	C1	Rheidol Falls	LM	34	B2
Port Talbot	WR	27	C1	Rhiwbina	WR	28	C1
Potters Bar	ER	23	A1	Rhiwfron	LM	34	B2
Poulton-le-Fylde	LM	54	B1	Rhosneigr	LM	43	A1
Poynton	LM	46	A2	Rhydyronen	TL	34	A2
Prees	LM	45	C2	Rhyl	LM	44	A2
Prescot	LM	45	A2	Rhymney	WR	27	B2
Prestatyn	LM	44	A2	Ribblehead*	LM	61	C2
Prestbury	LM	46	A2	Rice Lane	LM	53	A2
Preston	LM	54	B2	Richmond	SO/LT	20	C1
Prestonpans	SC	73	A2	Rickmansworth	LM/LT	31	C2
Preston Park	SO	12	C1	Riddlesdown	SO	17	C2
Preston Road (Greater London)	LT	20	A1	Ridgmont	LM	31	A2
Prestwich	LM	51	A2	Riding Mill	ER	67	C2
Prestwick	SC	71	C2	Rishton	LM	55	B1
Primrose Hill	LM	21	B1	Robertsbridge	SO	13	B1
Princes Risborough	LM	31	B1	Roby	LM	45	A2
Prittlewell	ER	33	C1	Rochdale	LM	55	C1
Prudhoe	ER	67	C2	Roche	WR	1	B2
Pulborough	SO	11	C2	Rochester	SO	13	A1
Purfleet	ER	32	C2	Rochford	ER	33	C1
Purley	SO	17	C2	Rock Ferry	LM	53	C1
Purley Oaks	SO	17	C2	Roding Valley	LT	24	C2
Putney	SO	20	C2	Rogart	SC	82	B1
Putney Bridge	LT	21	C1	Rolleston	LM	48	B1
Pwllheli	LM	43	C2	Rolvenden	KS	13	B1
Quainton Road*	LM	31	B1	Roman Bridge	LM	44	B1
Quaker's Yard	WR	27	C2	Romford	ER	32	C2
Queenborough	SO	33	C1	Romiley	LM	52	C2
Queen's Park (Glasgow)	SC	76	C1	Romney Sands	RH	13	C2
Queen's Park (London)	LM/LT	21	B1	Romsey	SO	10	C1
Queen's Road (Peckham)	SO	22	C1	Roose	LM	54	A1
Queenstown Rd. (Battersea)	SO	21	C1	Ropley	MH	10	B2
Queensbury	LT	31	C2	Roscommon	CI	85	C2
Queensway	LT	21	B1	Roscrea	CI	84	A1
Quintrel Downs	WR	1	B2	Rose Grove	LM	55	B1
Quorn & Woodhouse	ML	38	A2	Rose Hill (Marple)	LM	52	C2
Radcliffe (Greater Manchester)	LM	55	C1	Rossall	BF	54	B1
Radcliffe (Notts.)	LM	47	C2	Rosslare Harbour (Mainland)	CI	84	B2
Radlett	LM	31	B2	Rosslare Harbour Pier	CI	84	B2
Radley	WR	30	B2	Rosslare Strand	CI	84	B2
Radyr	WR	28	C1	Rosyth	SC	73	A1
Raheny	CI	84	B2	Rosyth Dockyard*	SC	73	A1
Rainford	LM	54	C2	Rotherham	ER	50	A2
Rainham (Essex)	ER	32	C2	Rotherham Central (Proj.)	ER	50	A2
Rainham (Kent)	SO	13	A1	Rotherhithe	LT	22	C1
Rainhill	LM	45	A2	Rothley	ML	38	A2
Ramsey	ME	59	B2	Rowland's Castle	SO	11	C1

102

NAME	RAILWAY CODE	PAGE NO.	PAGE REF.
Rowley Regis	LM	37	B2
Rowntree Halt*	ER	56	A2
Royal Oak	LT	21	B1
Roy Bridge	SC	78	A1
Roydon	ER	32	B1
Royston	ER	32	A1
Royton	LM	52	A2
Ruabon	LM	45	C1
Rufford	LM	54	C2
Rugby	LM	38	B2
Rugeley	LM	37	A2
Ruislip	LT	19	A2
Ruislip Gardens	LT	19	A2
Ruislip Manor	LT	19	A2
Runcorn	LM	45	A2
Runcorn East	LM	45	A2
Rush and Lusk	CI	86	C2
Rushbrooke	CI	83	C2
Ruskington	ER	48	B2
Russell Square	LT	21	B2
Ruswarp	ER	63	B1
Rutherglen	SC	76	C1
Ryde Esplanade	SO	6	A2
Ryde Pier Head	SO	6	A2
Ryde St. John's Road	SO	6	A2
Rye	SO	13	C1
Rye House	ER	32	B1
St. Albans Abbey	LM	31	B2
St. Albans City	LM	31	B2
St. Andrew's Road	WR	28	C2
St. Annes-on-the-Sea	LM	54	B1
St. Austell	WR	1	B2
St. Bees	LM	59	B2
St. Botolphs	ER	33	A2
St. Budeaux (Ferry Road)	WR	2	C1
St. Budeaux (Victoria Road)	WR	2	C1
St. Columb Road	WR	1	B2
St. Denys	SO	9	C2
St. Enoch	GG	76	B1
St. Erth	WR	1	A1
St. George's Cross	GG	76	B1
St. Germans	WR	2	B2
St. Helens Junction	LM	45	A2
St. Helens Shaw Street	LM	45	A2
St. Helier	SO	17	B1
St. Ives	WR	1	A1
St. James' Park (Exeter)	WR	3	A2
St. James' Park (London)	LT	21	C2
St. James' Park (Newcastle)	TW	69	B2
St. James' Street, Walthamstow	ER	22	A1
St. John's	SO	22	C1
St. John's Wood	LT	21	B1
St. Keyne	WR	2	B1
St. Leonards Warrior Square	SO	13	C1
St. Margaret's (Herts.)	ER	32	B1
St. Margaret's (Gr. London)	SO	16	A1
St. Mary Cray	SO	12	A1
St. Michaels	LM	53	C2
St. Neots	ER	39	C2
St. Pancras	LM	21	B2
St. Paul's	LT	21	B2
Sale	LM	51	C2
Salford	LM	51	B2
Salfords	SO	12	B1
Salhouse	ER	42	A1
Salisbury	SO	9	B2
Saltaire	ER	55	B2
Saltash	WR	2	C1
Saltburn	ER	62	A2
Saltcoats	SC	71	C1
Salthill	CI	84	C2
Saltmarshe	ER	57	B1
Salwick	LM	54	B2
Sandbach	LM	46	B1
Sanderstead	SO	17	C2
Sandhills	LM	53	B1
Sandhurst	SO	11	A1
Sandling	SO	13	B2
Sandown	SO	6	A2
Sandplace	WR	2	B1
Sandwell & Dudley	LM	87	B2
Sandwich	SO	14	A1

NAME	RAILWAY CODE	PAGE NO.	PAGE REF.
Sandy	ER	39	C2
Sandycove	CI	84	C2
Sandymount	CI	84	C2
Sankey for Penketh	LM	45	A2
Santon	ME	59	C2
Saundersfoot	WR	26	B1
Saunderton	LM	31	C1
Sawbridgeworth	ER	32	B2
Saxilby	ER	48	A1
Saxmundham	ER	42	C1
Scarborough	ER	63	C2
Scotscalder	SC	82	A1
Scotstounhill	SC	75	B2
Scunthorpe	ER	57	C1
Seaburn	ER	70	C2
Seaford	SO	12	C2
Seaforth & Litherland	LM	53	A1
Seaham	ER	68	C2
Seahill	NI	85	A1
Seamer	ER	63	C2
Sea Mills	WR	28	C2
Seascale	LM	59	B2
Seaton	ST	4	A1
Seaton Carew	ER	62	A2
Seer Green	LM	31	C2
Selby	ER	56	B2
Selhurst	SO	17	B2
Sellafield	LM	59	B2
Selling	SO	13	A2
Selly Oak	LM	37	B2
Settle	LM	55	A1
Seven Kings	ER	32	C1
Sevenoaks	SO	12	A2
Seven Sisters	ER/LT	21	A2
Severn Beach	WR	28	C2
Severn Tunnel Junction	WR	28	C2
Shackerstone	SH	38	A1
Shadwell	LT	22	B1
Shakespeare Staff Halt*	SO	14	B1
Shalford	SO	11	B2
Shankhill	CI	84	A2
Shanklin	SO	6	A2
Shaw	LM	55	C2
Shawford	SO	10	B2
Shawlands	SC	75	C2
Sheerness-on-Sea	SO	33	C1
Sheffield	ER	50	B1
Sheffield Park	BL	12	B1
Shelford	ER	40	C1
Shenfield	ER	32	C2
Shenstone	LM	37	A2
Shenton (proposed)	SH	38	A1
Shepherd's Bush	LT	20	B2
Shepherd's Well	SO	14	A1
Shenley	ER	56	C1
Shepperton	SO	15	B1
Shepreth	ER	40	C1
Sherborne	SO	8	C2
Sheringham	ER/NN	50	C1
Shettleston	SC	76	B2
Shields Road	GG	76	B1
Shifnal	LM	37	A1
Shildon	ER	62	A1
Shiplake	WR	31	C1
Shipley	ER	56	B1
Shippea Hill	ER	40	B2
Shipton	WR	30	B1
Shirehampton	WR	28	C2
Shiremoor	TW	70	A1
Shireoaks	ER	47	A2
Shirley	LM	37	B2
Shoeburyness	ER	33	C1
Sholing	SO	9	C2
Shoreditch	LT	21	B2
Shoreham (Kent)	SO	12	A2
Shoreham-by-Sea	SO	12	C1
Shortlands	SO	18	B1
Shotton	LM	45	B1
Shotts	SC	72	B2
Shrewsbury	LM	36	A2
Sidcup	SO	32	C1
Silecroft	LM	60	C1

NAME	RAILWAY CODE	PAGE NO.	PAGE REF.	NAME	RAILWAY CODE	PAGE NO.	PAGE REF.
Silverdale	LM	60	C2	Stamford	ER	39	A2
Silver Street	ER	23	C2	Stamford Brook	LT	20	C2
Silvertown	ER	22	B2	Stamford Hill	ER	21	A2
Sinfin Central	LM	47	C1	Stanford-le-Hope	ER	32	C2
Sinfin North	LM	47	C1	Stanlow & Thornton	LM	45	A2
Singer	SC	75	A1	Stanmore	LT	31	C2
Sittingbourne	SO/SK	13	A1	Stansted	ER	32	A2
Skegness	ER	49	B2	Staplehurst	SO	13	B1
Skerries	CI	86	C2	Stapleton Road	WR	8	A2
Skipton	LM	55	A2	Starbeck	ER	56	A1
Slade Green	SO	32	C2	Starcross	WR	3	A2
Slaithwaite	ER	55	C2	Starr Gate	BF	54	B1
Slateford	SC	73	C1	Staveley	LM	60	B2
Sleaford	ER	48	C2	Staverton Bridge	DV	3	B1
Sleights	ER	63	B1	Stechford	LM	88	C2
Sligo	CI	85	B2	Stepney East	ER	22	B1
Sloane Square	LT	21	C1	Stepney Green	LT	22	B1
Slough	WR	31	C2	Stevenage	ER	32	A1
Small Heath	LM	88	C2	Stevenston	SC	71	C1
Smethwick Rolfe Street	LM	87	C2	Stewartby	LM	31	A2
Smethwick West	LM	87	B2	Stewarton	SC	71	B2
Smitham	SO	12	A1	Stirling	SC	78	C2
Smith's Park	TW	70	A1	Stockport	LM	52	C1
Snaefell	ME	59	C1	Stocksfield	ER	67	C2
Snaith	ER	56	B2	Stocksmoor	ER	56	C1
Snaresbrook	LT	22	A2	Stockton	ER	62	B2
Snodland	SO	12	A2	Stockwell	LT	21	C2
Snowdon Summit	SM	43	B2	Stogumber	WS	7	B2
Snowdown	SO	13	A2	Stoke-on-Trent	LM	46	C1
Sole Street	SO	12	A2	Stoke Mandeville	LM	31	B1
Solihull	LM	37	B2	Stoke Newington	ER	21	A2
Somerleyton	ER	42	B1	Stone	LM	46	C1
South Acton	LM	20	C2	Stonebridge Park	LM/LT	20	B2
Southall	WR	19	C2	Stone Crossing	SO	32	C2
Southampton	SO	9	C2	Stonegate	SO	12	B2
Southampton Airport	SO	10	C2	Stonehaven	SC	80	B2
Southampton Ocean Terminal*	SO	9	C2	Stonehouse	WR	28	B1
South Bank	ER	63	A2	Stoneleigh	SO	16	C2
South Bermondsey	SO	22	C1	Stourbridge Junction	LM	87	C1
Southbourne	SO	11	C1	Stourbridge Town	LM	87	C1
Southbury	ER	24	B1	Stowmarket	ER	41	C2
South Cape	ME	59	C2	Stranraer Harbour	SC	64	C1
South Croydon	SO	17	C2	Stratford	ER/LT	22	B1
South Ealing	LT	20	C1	Stratford-upon-Avon	LM	38	C1
Southease	SO	12	C1	Strathcarron	SC	81	C1
South Elmsall	ER	56	C2	Strawberry Hill	SO	16	A1
Southend Central	ER	33	C1	Streatham	SO	17	A2
Southend East	ER	33	C1	Streatham Common	SO	17	A2
Southend Victoria	ER	33	C1	Streatham Hill	SO	17	A2
Southfields	LT	17	A1	Stretford	LM	51	C2
Southgate	LT	23	C2	Strines	LM	46	A2
South Gosforth	TW	69	A2	Stromeferry	SC	81	C1
South Greenford	WR	20	B1	Strood	SO	13	A1
South Hampstead	LM	21	B1	Stroud	WR	29	B1
South Harrow	LT	20	A1	Sturry	SO	13	A2
South Kensington	LT	21	C1	Styal	LM	46	A1
South Kenton	LM/LT	20	A1	Sudbury (Suffolk)	ER	33	A1
South Merton	SO	17	B1	Sudbury & Harrow Road	LM	20	A1
South Milford	ER	56	A2	Sudbury Hill	LT	20	A1
Southminster	ER	33	B1	Sudbury Hill, Harrow	LM	20	A1
Southport	LM	54	C1	Sudbury Town	LT	20	A1
South Ruislip	LM/LT	19	A2	Sunbury	SO	15	A2
South Shields	TW	70	B2	Sunderland	ER	20	C2
South Tottenham	ER	21	A2	Sundridge Park	SO	18	A2
Southwick	SO	12	C1	Sunningdale	SO	11	A1
South Wimbledon	LT	17	A1	Sunnymeads	SO	31	C2
South Woodford	LT	24	C2	Surbiton	SO	16	B1
Sowerby Bridge	ER	55	B2	Surrey Docks	LT	22	C1
Spalding	ER	49	C1	Sutton (Co. Dublin)	CI	84	B2
Spean Bridge	SC	78	A1	Sutton (Surrey)	SO	17	C1
Spital	LM	53	C1	Sutton Coldfield	LM	88	A2
Spondon	LM	47	C1	Sutton Common	SO	17	B1
Spooner Row	ER	41	B2	Swale	SO	13	A1
Springburn	SC	76	B1	Swanage	SW	5	A2
Springfield	SC	79	C2	Swanley	SO	12	A2
Spring Road	LM	37	B2	Swanscombe	SO	32	C2
Squires Gate	LM	54	B1	Swansea	WR	27	C1
Stafford	LM	46	C2	Swanwick	SO	10	C2
Staines	SO	15	A1	Sway	SO	10	C1
Stainforth & Hatfield	ER	58	A2	Swaythling	SO	10	C2
Stallingborough	ER	58	C1	Swinderby	ER	48	B1
Stalybridge	LM	52	B2	Swindon	WR	29	C2

NAME	RAILWAY CODE	PAGE NO.	PAGE REF.
Swineshead	ER	49	C1
Swinton	LM	51	A2
Swiss Cottage	LT	21	B1
Sydenham (Belfast)	NI	85	B1
Sydenham (Greater London)	SO	18	A1
Sydenham Hill	SO	17	A2
Sydney Parade	CI	84	C2
Sylfaen	WL	36	A1
Syon Lane	SO	20	C1
Tackley	WR	30	B2
Tadworth	SO	12	A1
Taffs Well	WR	28	C1
Tain	SC	82	B1
Talbot Square	BF	54	B1
Talsarnau	LM	43	C2
Talybont	LM	33	A2
Tal-y-Cafn	LM	44	A1
Tamworth	LM	37	A1
Tany-y-Bwlch	FR	44	C1
Tan-y-Grisiau	FR	44	C1
Taplow	WR	31	C1
Tara St. (Dublin)	CI	84	C1
Tattenham Corner	SO	12	A1
Taunton	WR	8	B1
Taynuilt	SC	77	B2
Teddington	SO	16	A1
Tees-side Airport	ER	62	B1
Teignmouth	WR	3	B2
Temple	LT	21	B2
Tenby	WR	26	B1
Tenterden Town	KS	13	B1
Teynham	SO	13	A1
Thames Ditton	SO	16	B1
Thatcham	WR	10	A2
Thatto Heath	LM	45	A2
Theale	WR	10	A2
The Dell (Falmouth)	WR	1	C1
The Green	RE	60	B1
The Lakes	LM	37	B2
Theobalds Grove	ER	24	A1
The Rake (proposed)	LM	53	C1
Thetford	ER	41	B1
Theydon Bois	LT	32	B1
Thirsk	ER	62	C2
Thomastown	CI	84	B1
Thornaby	ER	63	A1
Thorne North	ER	57	C1
Thorne South	ER	57	C1
Thornford	WR	8	C2
Thornliebank	SC	75	C2
Thornton Abbey	ER	57	C2
Thornton Gate	BF	54	B1
Thorntonhall	SC	72	B1
Thornton Heath	SO	17	B2
Thorpe Bay	ER	33	C1
Thorpe Culvert	ER	49	B2
Thorpe-le-Soken	ER	33	B2
Three Bridges	SO	12	B1
Three Oaks	SO	13	C1
Thurgarton	LM	48	B1
Thurles	CI	83	A2
Thurso	SC	82	A1
Thurston	ER	41	C1
Tilbury Riverside	ER	32	C2
Tilbury Town	ER	32	C2
Tile Hill	LM	38	B1
Tilehurst	WR	30	C2
Timperley	LM	51	C2
Tipperary	CI	83	B2
Tipton	LM	87	B1
Tir-phil	WR	28	B1
Tisbury	SO	9	B2
Tiverton Junction	WR	7	C2
Todmorden	LM	55	B2
Tolworth	SO	16	B2
Tonbridge	SO	12	B2
Tonfanau	LM	33	A2
Tonypandy	WR	27	C2
Tooting	SO	17	A1
Tooting Bec	LT	17	A1
Tooting Broadway	LT	17	A1
Topsham	WR	3	A2
Torquay	WR	3	B2
Torre	WR	3	B2
Totnes	WR	3	B1
Totnes Riverside	DV	3	B1
Tottenham Court Road	LT	21	B2
Tottenham Hale	ER/LT	21	A2
Totteridge & Whetstone	LT	23	C1
Totton	SO	9	C1
Tower	BF	54	B1
Tower Hill	LT	21	B2
Town Green	LM	54	C2
Trafford Park	LM	51	B2
Tralee	CI	83	B1
Trefforest	WR	27	C2
Trefforest Estate	WR	27	C2
Trehafod	WR	27	C2
Treherbert	WR	27	B2
Treorchy	WR	27	C2
Trimley	ER	34	A1
Tring	LM	31	B1
Troed-y-Rhiw	WR	27	B2
Troon	SC	71	C2
Trooperslane	NI	85	A1
Trowbridge	WR	9	A1
Truro	WR	1	C2
Tufnell Park	LT	21	A1
Tullamore	CI	86	C1
Tulloch	SC	78	A1
Tulse Hill	SO	17	A2
Tunbridge Wells Central	SO	12	B2
Tunbridge Wells West	SO	12	B2
Turkey Street	ER	24	B1
Turnham Green	LT	20	C2
Turnpike Lane	LT	23	C2
Twickenham	SO	16	A1
Twyford	WR	31	C1
Ty Croes	LM	43	A1
Tygwyn	LM	43	C2
Tyndrum Lower	SC	78	B1
Tyndrum Upper	SC	78	B1
Tyne Dock	TW	70	B2
Tynemouth	TW	88	C2
Tyseley	LM	37	B2
Tywyn	LM	34	A2
Tywyn Pendre	TL	34	A2
Tywyn Wharf	TL	34	A2
Uckfield	SO	12	C2
Uddingston	SC	76	C2
Ulceby	ER	57	C2
Ulleskelf	ER	56	B2
Ulverston	LM	60	C1
Umberleigh	WR	7	C1
University (Birmingham)	LM	88	C1
University (Coleraine)	NI	86	A1
Upholland	LM	54	C2
Upminster	ER/LT	32	C2
Upminster Bridge	LT	32	C2
Upney	LT	32	C1
Upper Halliford	SO	15	B2
Upper Holloway	LM	21	A2
Upper Warlingham	SO	12	A1
Upton	LM	45	A1
Upton Park	LT	22	B2
Upwey	SO	5	A1
Urmston	LM	51	C1
Uttoxeter	LM	46	C2
Uxbridge	LT	19	B1
Valley	LM	43	A1
Vauxhall	SO/LT	21	C2
Victoria	SO/LT	21	C1
Victoria Park	NI	85	B1
Virginia Water	SO	11	A2
Waddon	SO	17	C2
Waddon Marsh	SO	17	B2
Wadhurst	SO	12	B2
Wadsley Bridge*	ER	47	A1
Wainfleet	ER	49	B2
Wakefield Kirkgate	ER	56	C1
Wakefield Westgate	ER	56	C1
Walkden	LM	51	A1
Walkergate	TW	69	B2
Wallasey Grove Road	LM	53	B1

NAME	RAILWAY CODE	PAGE NO.	PAGE REF.
Wallasey Village	LM	53	B1
Wallington	SO	17	C1
Wallsend	TW	70	B1
Walmer	SO	14	A1
Walsall	LM	87	A2
Walsingham	WW	50	C1
Waltham Cross	ER	24	A1
Walthamstow Central	ER/LT	22	A1
Walthamstow Queens Road	ER	22	A1
Walton (Merseyside)	LM	53	A2
Walton-on-Naze	ER	33	B2
Walton-on-Thames	SO	15	C2
Wanborough	SO	11	A1
Wandsworth Common	SO	17	A1
Wandsworth Road	SO	21	C2
Wandsworth Town	SO	21	C1
Wansbeck Road	TW	69	A2
Wansford	NV	39	A2
Wanstead	LT	22	A2
Wanstead Park	ER	22	A2
Wapping	LT	22	B1
Warblington	SO	11	C1
Ware	ER	32	B1
Wareham	SO	5	A2
Wargrave	WR	31	C1
Warham Halt	WW	50	C1
Warminster	WR	9	B1
Warnham	SO	11	B2
Warren Street	LT	21	B2
Warrington Bank Quay	LM	45	A2
Warrington Central	LM	45	A2
Warwick	LM	38	C1
Warwick Avenue	LT	21	B1
Warwick Road	LM	51	B2
Washford	WS	7	B2
Watchet	WS	7	B2
Waterbeach	ER	40	C2
Waterford	CI	84	B1
Wateringbury	SO	12	A2
Waterloo (London)	SO/LT	21	B2
Waterloo (Merseyside)	LM	53	A1
Water Orton	LM	38	B1
Watford	LT	31	C2
Watford High Street	LM	31	C2
Watford Junction	LM	31	C2
Watford North	LM	31	B2
Watford Stadium*	LM	31	C2
Watford West	LM	31	C2
Watton-at-Stone	ER	32	B1
Wedgwood	LM	46	C1
Weeley	ER	33	B2
Weeton	ER	56	A1
Welling	SO	32	C1
Wellingborough	LM	39	C1
Wellington	LM	37	A1
Wellington Bridge	CI	84	B1
Wells-on-Sea	WW	50	C1
Welshpool	LM	36	A1
Welshpool Raven Square	WL	36	A1
Welwyn Garden City	ER	32	B1
Welwyn North	ER	32	B1
Wem	LM	45	C2
Wembley Central	LM/LT	20	A1
Wembley Complex	LM	20	A2
Wembley Park	LT	20	A2
Wemyss Bay	SC	71	A1
Wendover	LM	31	B1
Wennington	LM	54	A2
West Acton	LT	20	B2
West Allerton	LM	53	C2
Westbourne Park	WR/LT	21	B1
West Brompton	LT	21	B1
Westbury	WR	9	A1
West Byfleet	SO	15	C1
West Calder	SC	72	B2
Westcliff	ER	33	C1
Westcombe Park	SO	22	C2
West Croydon	SO	17	B2
West Drayton	WR	19	B1
West Dulwich	SO	17	A2
West Ealing	WR	20	B1
Westenhanger	SO	13	B2
Westerfield	ER	33	A2
Westerton	SC	75	A2
West Finchley	LT	23	C1
Westgate-on-Sea	SO	14	A1
West Ham	ER/LT	22	B1
West Hampstead	LM/LT	21	A1
West Hampstead Midland	LM	21	A1
West Harrow	LT	20	A1
West Horndon	ER	32	C2
Westhoughton	LM	55	C1
West Jesmond	TW	69	B2
West Kensington	LT	21	C1
West Kilbride	SC	71	B1
West Kirby	LM	45	A1
West Malling	SO	12	A2
Westminster	LT	21	B2
West Monkseaton	TW	70	A1
West Norwood	SO	17	A2
Weston Milton	WR	8	A1
Weston-super-Mare	WR	8	A1
Westport	LT	85	C1
West Ruislip	LM/LT	19	A2
West Runton	ER	50	C1
West St. Leonards	SO	13	C1
West Street	GG	76	B1
West Sutton	SO	17	C1
West Wickham	SO	18	B1
West Worthing	SO	11	C2
Wetheral	ER	66	C2
Wexford	CI	84	B2
Weybourne	NN	50	C1
Weybridge	SO	15	C1
Weymouth	SO	5	A1
Weymouth Quay	SO	5	A1
Whaley Bridge	LM	46	A2
Whatstandwell	LM	47	B1
Whimple	WR	3	A2
Whitby	ER	63	B1
Whitchurch (Hants.)	SO	10	A2
Whitchurch (Salop)	LM	45	C2
Whitchurch (South Glam.)	WR	28	C1
Whiteabbey	NI	85	A1
Whitechapel	LT	22	B1
White City	LT	20	B2
Whitecraigs	SC	75	C2
Whitefield	LM	51	A2
White Hart Lane	ER	23	C2
Whitehaven	LM	59	B2
Whitehead	NI	86	A2
Whitehead RPSI Stn.*	NI	86	A2
White Notley	ER	33	B1
Whitland	WR	26	B1
Whitley Bay	TW	70	A2
Whitley Bridge	ER	56	B2
Whitlock's End	LM	37	B2
Whitstable	SO	13	A2
Whittlesea	ER	40	B1
Whittlesford	ER	32	A2
Whitton	SO	16	A1
Whyteleafe	SO	12	A1
Whyteleafe South	SO	12	A1
Wick	SC	82	A2
Wickford	ER	33	C1
Wickham Market	ER	42	C1
Wicklow	CI	84	A2
Widdrington	ER	68	B1
Widnes	LM	45	A2
Widney Manor	LM	37	B2
Wigan North Western	LM	54	C2
Wigan Wallgate	LM	54	C2
Wighton Halt	WW	50	C1
Wigton	LM	66	C1
Willesden Green	LT	20	A2
Willesden Junction	LM/LT	20	B2
Williamwood	SC	75	C2
Williton	WS	7	B2
Wilmcote	LM	38	C1
Wilmslow	LM	46	A1
Wilnecote	LM	38	A1
Wimbledon	SO/LT	17	A1
Wimbledon Chase	SO	17	B1
Wimbledon Park	LT	17	A1

NAME	RAILWAY CODE	PAGE NO.	PAGE REF.	NAME	RAILWAY CODE	PAGE NO.	PAGE REF.
Wimbledon Staff Halt*	SO	17	A1	Wood Street Walthamstow	ER	22	A1
Winchelsea	SO	13	C1	Wool	SO	5	A1
Winchester	SO	10	B2	Woolston	SO	9	C2
Winchfield	SO	11	A1	Woolwich Arsenal	SO	22	C2
Winchmore Hill	ER	23	C2	Woolwich Dockyard	SO	22	C2
Windermere	LM	60	B2	Wootton	IW	6	A2
Windsor & Eton Central	WR	31	C2	Wootton Wawen	LM	37	C2
Windsor & Eton Riverside	SO	31	C2	Worcester Foregate Street	WR	37	C1
Winnersh	SO	11	A1	Worcester Park	SO	16	B2
Winsford	LM	46	B1	Worcester Shrub Hill	WR	37	C1
Wisbech*	ER	40	A1	Workington	LM	59	A2
Wishaw	SC	72	B1	Worksop	ER	47	A2
Wistaston Road (Crewe Wks.)*	LM	46	C1	Worplesdon	SO	11	A2
Witham	ER	33	B1	Worstead	ER	50	C2
Witley	SO	11	B2	Worthing	SO	11	C2
Wittersham Road	KS	13	B1	Wrabness	ER	33	A2
Witton	LM	88	B1	Wraysbury	SO	31	C2
Wivelsfield	SO	12	C1	Wrenbury	LM	45	B2
Wivenhoe	ER	33	B2	Wressle	ER	57	B1
Woburn Sands	LM	31	A1	Wrexham Central	LM	45	B1
Woking	SO	11	A2	Wrexham General	LM	45	B1
Wokingham	SO	11	A1	Wroxham	ER	42	A1
Woldingham	SO	12	A1	Wye	SO	13	A2
Wolverhampton	LM	87	A1	Wylam	ER	67	C2
Wolverton	LM	31	A1	Wylde Green	LM	88	B2
Wombwell	ER	56	C1	Wymondham	ER	41	A2
Woodbridge	ER	42	C1	Wythall	LM	37	B2
Wood End	LM	37	C2	Yalding	SO	12	A2
Woodford	LT	24	C2	Yardley Wood	LM	37	B2
Woodgrange Park	ER	22	A2	Yarmouth	ER	42	A2
Wood Green	LT	23	C2	Yatton	WR	8	A2
Woodhall	SC	71	A2	Yeoford	WR	3	A1
Woodham Ferrers	ER	33	B1	Yeovil Junction	WR	8	C2
Woodhouse	ER	50	B2	Yeovil Pen Mill	WR	8	C2
Woodlands Road	LM	52	A1	Yetminster	WR	8	C2
Woodlawn	CI	85	C2	Yoker	SC	75	A2
Woodlesford	FR	56	B1	York	ER	56	A2
Woodley	LM	52	C2	Yorton	LM	45	C2
Woodmansterne	SO	12	A1	Youghal*	CI	83	B2
Woodside	SO	18	B1	Ystrad Mynach	WR	28	C1
Woodside Park	LT	23	C1	Ystrad Rhondda	WR	27	C2

INDEX TO MINOR RAILWAYS

NAME	PAGE NO.	PAGE REF.	NAME	PAGE NO.	PAGE REF.
Beamish Museum & Tramway	68	C1	Middleton Railway	57	B1
Bo'ness & Kinneil Railway	72	A2	Midland Railway Company	47	B1
Bowes Railway	69	C2	Mull & West Highland Railway	77	B2
Brecon Mountain Railway	27	B2	South Tynedale Railway	67	C1
Chasewater Railway	37	A2	Tanfield Railway	69	C1
Foxfield Railway	46	C2	Tramway Museum Society (Crich)	47	B1
Leighton Buzzard Narrow Gauge Rlv	32	A1	Welsh Highland Railway	43	C2
Lincolnshire Coast Light Railway	58	C1	Whipsnade & Umfolozi Railway	31	B2
Llangollen Railway Society	45	C1	Yorkshire Dales Railway	55	A2

KEY TO RAILWAY CODES

BA	Bala Lake Railway	LH	Lakeside & Haverthwaite Railway	SH	Shackerstone Railway
BF	Blackpool & Fleetwood Tramway	LL	Llanberis Lake Railway	SK	Sittingbourne and Kemsley Railway
BL	Bluebell Railway	LM	British Rail–London Midland	SM	Snowdon Mountain Railway
BM	Birmingham Airport	LT	London Transport	SO	British Rail–Southern
CI	Coras Iompair Eireann	LY	Lochty Railway	ST	Seaton Tramway
DV	Dart Valley Railway	ME	Isle of Man Railway	SV	Severn Valley Railway
ER	British Rail–Eastern	MH	Mid-Hants Railway	SW	Swanage Railway Company
FB	Fairbourne Railway	ML	Main Line Steam Trust	SY	Strathspey Railway
FR	Festiniog Railway	NI	Northern Ireland Railways	TD	Torbay and Dartmouth Railway
GG	Greater Glasgow P.T.E.	NN	North Norfolk Railway	TL	Talyllyn Railway
GO	Great Orme Tramway	NV	Nene Valley Railway	TW	Tyne & Wear Metro
GW	Gwili Railway	NY	North Yorkshire Moors Railway	WL	Welshpool & Llanfair Railway
IW	Isle of Wight Railway	RE	Ravenglass & Eskdale Railway	WR	British Rail–Western
KW	Keighley & Worth Valley Railway	RH	Romney, Hythe & Dymchurch Railway	WS	West Somerset Railway
KS	Kent & East Sussex Railway	SC	British Rail–Scottish	WW	Wells & Walsingham Railway

INDEX TO BRITISH RAIL ENGINEERING LTD. WORKS

NAME	PAGE NO.	PAGE REF.	NAME	PAGE NO.	PAGE REF.
Crewe	46	C1	Horwich	54	C2
Derby Litchurch Lane	47	C1	Shildon	62	A1
Derby Locomotive Works	47	C1	Swindon	29	C2
Doncaster	56	C2	Temple Mills	22	A1
Eastleigh	10	C2	Wolverton	31	A1
Glasgow	76	B1	York	56	A2

INDEX TO BRITISH RAIL LOCOMOTIVE STABLING
POINTS & CARRIAGE DEPOTS

CODE	NAME	PAGE NO.	MAP REF.	CODE	NAME	PAGE NO.	MAP REF.
AB	Aberdeen (Ferryhill)	80	B1	KY	Knottingley	56	B2
AC	Aberdeen Clayhills	80	B1	LA	Laira	2	C2
AF	Ashford (Chart Leacon)	13	B2	LE	Landore, Swansea	27	C1
AN	Allerton, Liverpool	53	C2	LG	Longsight Electric Depot	52	B1
AY	Ayr	71	C1	LJ	Llandudno Junction	44	A1
BC	Birkenhead Mollington Street	53	C1	LL	Liverpool Edge Hill	53	B2
BD	Birkenhead North	53	B1	LN	Lincoln	48	B2
BG	Botanic Gardens, Hull	57	B2	LO	Longsight Diesel Depot	52	B1
BH	Barrow Hill	47	A1	LR	Leicester	38	A2
BI	Brighton	12	C1	LV	Liverpool Street	21	B2
BJ	Bristol Malago Vale	8	B2	MA	Manchester Longsight	52	B1
BL	Blyth	68	B1	ME	Marylebone	21	B1
BM	Bournemouth	5	A2	MG	Margam	27	C1
BN	Bounds Green (HST)	23	C2	MH	Millerhill	73	C2
BP	Blackpool (Carriage)	54	B1	ML	Motherwell	72	B1
BQ	Bury	55	C1	MN	Machynlleth	34	A2
BR	Bristol Bath Road	8	B2	MR	March	40	A1
BS	Bescot	87	A2	NC	Norwich Crown Point	41	A2
BU	Burton	47	C1	NH	Newton Heath	52	A1
BW	Barrow	54	A1	NL	Neville Hill	57	A2
BX	Buxton	46	A2	NM	Nottingham (Carr. Sidings)	47	C2
BY	Bletchley	31	A1	NR	Norwich	41	A2
BZ	St. Blazey	1	B2	NW	Northwich	46	A1
CA	Cambridge	40	C1	OC	Old Oak Common (Loco.)	20	B2
CC	Clacton	33	B2	OM	Old Oak Common (Carriage)	20	B2
CD	Crewe Diesel Depot	46	C1	ON	Orpington	12	A1
CE	Crewe Electric Depot	46	C1	OO	Old Oak Common (HST)	20	B2
CF	Cardiff (Canton)	28	A1	OX	Oxford	30	B2
CG	Croxley Green	31	C2	OY	Oxley	87	A1
CH	Chester	45	B2	PA	St. Pancras	21	B2
CJ	Clapham Junction	21	C1	PB	Peterborough	39	A2
CK	Corkerhill	75	B2	PC	Polmadie (Carriage)	76	B1
CL	Carlisle Upperby	65	C1	PH	Perth Station	79	B1
CP	Crewe Carriage Shed	46	C1	PM	Bristol St. Philip's Marsh (HST)	8	B2
CR	Colchester	33	A1	PO	Polmadie	76	B1
CW	Cricklewood	20	A2	PZ	Penzance	1	A1
DN	Darlington	62	B1	RE	Ramsgate	14	A1
DR	Doncaster	58	B1	RG	Reading	31	C1
DT	Dunfermline (Townhill)	73	A1	RL	Ripple Lane	32	C2
DY	Derby Etches Park	47	C1	RR	Radyr	28	C1
EC	Edinburgh Craigentinny (HST)	73	C2	RY	Ryde	6	A2
ED	Eastfield	76	B1	SB	Shirebrook	47	B2
EH	Eastleigh	10	C2	SE	St. Leonards	13	C1
EM	East Ham	22	A2	SF	Stratford	22	A1
EN	Euston Carriage Shed	22	B2	SG	Slade Green	32	C2
EU	Euston Station	21	B2	SI	Soho	88	C1
EX	Exeter St. Davids	3	A1	SL	Stewarts Lane	21	C1
FH	Frodingham, Scunthorpe	57	C1	SP	Wigan (Springs Branch)	54	C2
FR	Fratton, Portsmouth	10	C2	SR	Stratford Repair Depot	22	A1
FW	Fort William	78	B1	ST	Severn Tunnel Junction	28	C2
GC	Glasgow Cowlairs	76	B1	SU	Selhurst	17	B2
GD	Gateshead	69	B2	SW	Swindon	29	C2
GI	Gillingham	13	A1	SY	Saltley	88	C1
GL	Gloucester	29	B1	SZ	Southall	19	B2
GM	Grangemouth	72	A2	TE	Thornaby	63	A1
GU	Guide Bridge	52	B2	TF	Thornton Field	22	B1
GW	Glasgow (Shields Road)	75	B2	TI	Tinsley	50	B2
HA	Haymarket	73	C1	TJ	Thornton Junction	79	C1
HD	Holyhead	43	A1	TO	Toton	47	C2
HE	Hornsey	21	A2	TS	Tyseley	88	C2
HF	Hereford	28	A2	TW	Tunbridge Wells West	12	B2
HG	Hither Green	18	A1	TY	Tyne Yard	69	C2
HI	Hitchin	31	A2	VR	Vale of Rheidol Railway	34	B2
HM	Healey Mills	56	C1	WB	Willesden Brent	20	B2
HO	Holbeck	57	A1	WC	Waterloo & City	21	B2
HR	Hall Road	53	A1	WD	East Wimbledon	17	A1
HS	Hammerton Street, Bradford	56	B1	WH	Wath	56	C2
HT	Heaton (HST)	69	B2	WJ	Watford Junction	31	B2
HY	Hyndland	75	B2	WK	Workington	59	A2
IL	Ilford	22	B2	WN	Willesden	20	B2
IM	Immingham	58	C2	WS	Worcester	37	C1
IP	Ipswich Station	33	A2	WT	Westhouses	47	B2
IS	Inverness	82	C2	WY	Westbury	9	A1
KD	Carlisle (Kingmoor)	65	C1	YC	York Clifton	56	A2
KM	Carlisle Yard	65	C1	YK	York	56	A2

INDEX TO FREIGHT TERMINALS AND YARDS

NAME	PAGE NO.	PAGE REF.	NAME	PAGE NO.	PAGE REF.
Abbey — BSC	27	C1	Bedworth	38	B1
Abbey (Shrewsbury)	36	A2	Beechgrove	9	B1
Abbey Foregate C.S.	36	A2	Beeston	47	C2
Abercwmboi Phurnacite	27	B2	Beighton P.W. Depot	50	B2
Aberdare	27	B2	Belford Quarry	74	C2
Abernant Colliery	27	B1	Belmont Yard (Doncaster)	58	B1
Aberpergwm Colliery	27	B2	Bennerley Colliery	47	C2
Aberthaw P.S.	7	B2	Bennettsbridge	84	A1
Abingdon	30	C2	Bentinck Colliery	47	B2
Abram Sidings	54	C2	Bentley Colliery	58	A1
Ackton Hall Colliery	56	C2	Berkeley Nuclear P.S.	29	B1
Acton Yard	20	B2	Bersham Colliery	45	B1
Aintree Containerbase	53	A2	Bescot Yard	87	A2
Akeman St.	31	B1	Bestwood Park Sidings	47	B2
Albert Opencast	54	C2	Beswick	52	B1
Albion	87	B2	Betteshanger Colliery	14	A1
Aldwarke — BSC	50	A2	Betws Drift Mine	27	B1
Alexandra Dock (Liverpool)	53	B1	Bevercotes Colliery	48	A1
Alexandra Dock Junc. (Newport)	28	B2	Bevois Park (Southampton)	9	C2
Allerton Bywater Colliery	56	B2	Bicester	30	B2
Allington	13	A1	Bickershaw Colliery	54	C2
Alloa	78	C2	Bidston Dock	53	B1
Alsager CCE Tip	46	B1	Bilsthorpe Colliery	47	B2
Amlwch	43	A2	Bilston	87	A1
Anchor — BSC (Scunthorpe)	57	C2	Bilston Glen Colliery	73	B1
Angerstein Wharf	22	C2	Birch Coppice Colliery	38	A1
Anglesea Sidings	37	A2	Birkenhead Docks	53	B1
Annat	78	B1	Birtley	69	C2
Appleby Frodingham — BSC	57	C1	Bishopbriggs	76	A1
Ardeer — ICI	71	C1	Blackwell Sidings	47	B2
Ardingly	12	B1	Blaenant Colliery	27	B1
Ardrahan	83	A2	Bletchington Cem. Wks.	30	B2
Ardrossan North	71	C1	Blidworth Colliery	47	B2
Ardwick West	52	B1	Blindwells Colliery	73	A2
Arkwright Colliery	47	B2	Blodwell Quarry	45	C1
Arncott	30	B2	Bloxwich	87	A2
Ashburys Yard	52	B1	Blyth P.S. & Docks	68	B1
Ashington Colliery	68	B1	Bold Colliery	45	A2
Ashton Gate	8	B2	Boldon	70	B1
Ashton-in-Makerfield	54	C2	Bolsover Coalite & Colliery	47	B2
Askern Colliery & Coalite	56	C2	Bordesley	88	C1
Attercliffe Goods	50	B1	Boulby	63	B1
Auchincruive	71	C2	Bow Creek	22	B1
Auchinleck	71	C2	Bow Goods	22	B1
Auchmuty	79	C1	Bowers Row Colliery	56	B1
Avenue Carbonisation	47	B1	Bowes Staithes	70	B1
Avenue (Leamington Spa)	38	C1	Bowhill Colliery	79	C1
Avonside Wharf	8	B2	Bradwell Nuclear P.S.	33	B1
Ayr Harbour	71	C1	Braunstone Gate	38	A2
Baddesley Colliery	38	A1	Bredbury	52	C2
Baglan Bay	27	C1	Bremmell Siding (Swindon)	29	C2
Baileyfield	73	C2	Brent	20	A2
Bagworth Colliery	38	A2	Brentford Goods	20	C1
Ballygeary	84	B2	Bridge Sidings (South Bank)	63	A2
Bamber Bridge CCE Depot	54	B2	Bridge Street (Northampton)	39	C1
Banbury Road (Oxford)	30	B2	Bridgeton Central Carr. Depot	76	B1
Bardon Hill	38	A2	Brierley Hill Steel Terminal	87	C1
Barham	41	C2	Briggs Sidings	46	B2
Barleith	71	C2	Brindle Heath	51	B2
Barlow Tip	56	B2	Bristol East Depot	8	B2
Barnburgh Colliery	56	C2	Bristol West Depot	8	B2
Barnwell	40	C1	British Oak Colliery	56	C1
Barnwood (Gloucester)	29	B1	Briton Ferry	27	C1
Barony Colliery	71	C2	Brodsworth Colliery	58	A1
Barrack St. (Dundalk)	86	B2	Bromford Bridge	88	B2
Barrington Cem. Wks.	40	C1	Brookhouse Colliery	50	B2
Barrow — BSC	54	A1	Brooklands Avenue (Cambridge)	40	C1
Barrow Colliery	56	C1	Broomloan GGPTE Depot	75	B2
Barrow Hill Yard	47	A1	Brotton Coal Depot	63	B1
Barrow Yard	54	A1	Broughton Lane	50	B1
Barton Hill (Bristol)	8	A2	Broughton Moor	59	A2
Barton Mill C.S.	10	A2	Brownhills	37	A2
Basford Hall Yard	46	C1	Brunthill	65	B1
Bates Colliery	68	B1	Brynlliw Colliery	26	B2
Bathgate	72	A2	BSC Abbey	27	C1
Bayston Hill Quarry	36	A2	BSC Aldwarke	50	A2
Becket St. (Oxford)	30	B2	BSC Anchor	57	C2
Bedenham	10	C2	BSC Appleby — Frodingham	57	C1
Bedwas Colliery	28	C1	BSC Barrow	54	A1
			BSC Bromford	88	B2

NAME	PAGE NO.	PAGE REF.
BSC Calder	72	C1
BSC Cargo Fleet	63	A1
BSC Clydebridge	76	C1
BSC Clydesdale	72	B1
BSC Corby	39	B1
BSC Dalzell	72	B1
BSC Ebbw Vale	28	B1
BSC Frodingham	57	C1
BSC Fullwood Foundry	72	B1
BSC Gartcosh	72	C1
BSC Glengarnock	71	B2
BSC Hardendale Quarry	60	A2
BSC Hartlepool South	62	A2
BSC Hunterston	71	B1
BSC Ickles	50	A2
BSC Imperial	72	C1
BSC Lackenby	63	A2
BSC Llanwern	28	C2
BSC Margam	27	C1
BSC Meadowhall	50	A1
BSC Monkshall	45	B1
BSC Panteg	28	B1
BSC Ravenscraig	72	B1
BSC Redcar	62	A2
BSC Roundwood	50	A2
BSC Shelton	46	B1
BSC Shepcote Lane	50	B1
BSC Shotton	45	B1
BSC South Bank	63	A2
BSC Skinningrove	63	B1
BSC Stanton	47	C2
BSC Stocksbridge	56	C1
BSC Templeborough	50	A2
BSC Thrybergh	50	A2
BSC Tinsley Park	50	B1
BSC Trafford Park	51	B2
BSC Trostre	26	B2
BSC Velindre	27	B1
BSC Walkergate	69	B2
BSC Whitehead	28	A2
BSC Wolverhampton	87	A1
BSC Workington	59	C1
Bull Point	2	C1
Bulmer's Works (Hereford)	28	A2
Bulwark St. (Dover)	14	B1
Burghead	82	C2
Burn Naze — ICI	54	B1
Burngullow	1	B2
Burrows Sidings (Swansea)	27	C1
Burtonwood	45	B1
Bush-on-Esk (Longtown)	66	C2
Butterwell Opencast	68	B1
Buttevant	83	B2
Buxton South Goods	46	A2
Cabra (Dublin)	84	C1
Cadder	76	A2
Cadeby Colliery	56	C2
Cadley Hill Colliery	38	A1
Caerwent	28	C2
Calder — BSC	72	C1
Calder Yard	72	C1
Caldon Low Quarry	46	B2
Callerton — ICI	69	A1
Calvert	31	A1
Calvert Lane (Hull)	57	B2
Calverton Colliery	47	B2
Cambois (Blyth)	68	B1
Cambus	78	C2
Camden C.S.	22	C2
Cameron Bridge	79	C1
Camlachie	76	B1
Canton	28	A1
Carbis Wharf	1	B2
Cargo Fleet — BSC	63	A2
Carne Point	2	B1
Carrington P.S. (Partington)	51	C1
Cart Coal Depot	54	A1
Carville	70	B1
Castle Donington P.S.	47	C2
Castle Foregate (Shrewsbury)	36	A2

NAME	PAGE NO.	PAGE REF.
Castlemungret	83	A2
Castle Works (Cardiff)	28	A1
Castleton P.W. Depot	55	C1
Cattewater	2	C2
Cavendish Sidings	53	B1
Celynen South Colliery	28	C1
Chacewater	1	C1
Chadderton	52	A1
Chaddesden	47	C1
Cheadle	46	C2
Cheetham Hill C.S.	52	B1
Chesterton P.W. Depot	40	C1
Chettisham	40	B2
Chilmark	9	B2
Chinnor Cem. Wks.	31	B1
City Basin (Exeter)	3	A2
Clatchard Craig Quarry	79	C1
Claydon Cem. Wks.	41	C2
Clayhills C.S. (Aberdeen)	80	B1
Cliffe	32	C2
Cliffe Hill	38	A2
Cliffe Vale	46	C1
Clifton Carr. Dep. (York)	56	A2
Clipstone Colliery	47	B2
Clydach-on-Tawe	27	B1
Clydebridge — BSC	76	C1
Clydeport FLT	71	A1
Clydesdale — BSC	72	B1
Coalfield Farm Opencast	38	A2
Coalfields Goods (Cambridge)	40	C1
Coalville	38	A1
Coatbridge FLT (Gartsherrie)	72	C1
Cockenzie P.S.	73	A2
Cockshute Sidings	46	C1
Codnor Park Sidings	47	B2
Coed Bach Washery	26	B2
Cofton Hackett — BL	37	B2
Coldham Lane (Cambridge)	40	C1
Coleham (Shrewsbury)	36	A2
Coleshill	38	B1
Colnbrook	19	C1
Colthrop	10	A2
Coltness	72	B1
Colwick Industrial Estate	47	C2
Comrie Colliery (Saline)	72	A2
Connington South CCE Tip	39	B2
Contentibus Bing	72	B2
Corby	39	B1
Coryton Oil Refinery	33	C1
Cotgrave Colliery	47	C2
Coton Hill Yard	36	A2
Cottam P.S.	48	A1
Coventry Colliery & Homefire	38	B1
Cowlairs	76	B1
Cowley Hill (St. Helens)	54	C2
Coxlodge	69	A2
Crag Hall	63	B1
Craigentinny C.S.	73	C2
Craiginches Yard (Aberdeen)	80	B1
Cranmore	9	B1
Crawley New Yard	12	B1
Crescent Wharf (Peterborough)	39	A2
Creswell Colliery	47	A2
Crianlarich Lower	78	C1
Cricklewood Recess Sidings	20	A2
Croft Quarry	38	A2
Crofton P.W. Depot	56	C1
Crombie	72	A2
Cronton Colliery	45	A2
Crossgate Sorting Sidings	70	B2
Crown Point (Norwich)	41	A2
Culloden Moor	82	C1
Currock C. & W. Shops	65	C1
Curzon Street Parcels	88	C1
Cuxton	12	A2
Cwm Bargoed	27	B2
Cwm Colliery	27	C2
Cwmmawr Colliery	26	B2
Cwmparc	27	C2
Cynheidre Colliery	26	B2

NAME	PAGE NO.	PAGE REF.	NAME	PAGE NO.	PAGE REF.
Dairycoates (Hull)	57	B2	Exeter Riverside Yard	3	A2
Dalmuir Riverside	75	A1	Exmouth Junction	3	A2
Dalzell — BSC & Dalzell New Yard	72	B1	Fairview Depot (Dublin)	84	C2
Danygraig FLT	27	C1	Fairwater CCE Depot	8	B1
Darfield Main Colliery	56	C2	Falkland Yard (Ayr)	71	C1
Daw Mill Colliery (Whiteacre)	38	B1	Far Cotton	39	A1
Dawdon Colliery	68	C2	Farnley	57	B1
Dean Hill	10	B1	Fawcett Street (Sunderland)	70	C2
Dean Lane	52	A1	Fawley Oil Refinery	10	C2
Dean Road	70	B2	Fazakerley P.W. Depot	53	A2
Dearne Valley Colliery	56	C2	Felin Fran	27	B1
Decoy Yard (Doncaster)	58	B1	Felixstowe Docks & FLT	34	A1
Dee Marsh Sidings	45	B1	Fen Drayton	40	C1
Deep Navigation Colliery	27	B2	Ferrybridge P.S.	56	B2
Deepdale Coal Depot	54	B2	Ferryhill	62	A1
Denby Colliery	47	B1	Ferryhill (Aberdeen)	80	B1
Denton Holme	65	C1	Ferry Road (Grangetown)	28	B1
Deptford	70	C2	Fiddlers Ferry P.S.	45	A2
Dereham	41	A1	Fishburn Coking Plant	62	A1
Derwenthaugh Coking Plant	69	B1	Fleetwood (Wyre P.S.)	54	B1
Devonport Dockyard	2	C1	Fletton	39	A2
Dewsbury Railway Street	56	C1	Flixborough Stather	57	C1
Dibles Wharf	9	C2	Follingsby FLT	70	C1
Didcot Distribution Centre	30	C2	Folly Lane	45	A2
Didcot P.S.	30	C2	Forders Sidings	31	A2
Dinnington Colliery	47	A2	Forth Sidings (Newcastle)	69	B2
Dinsdale P.W. Depot	62	B1	Foss Island Goods (York)	56	A2
Dinting Railway Centre	46	A2	Four Ashes	37	A2
Dinton	9	B2	Fowey	2	B1
Dock Street (Newport)	28	A2	Foynes	83	A1
Dodworth Colliery	56	C1	Friary Goods (Plymouth)	2	C1
Doe Hill	47	B2	Frickley Colliery	56	C2
Donnington	37	A1	Frodingham — BSC	57	C1
Dowlow	46	B2	Fryston Colliery	56	B2
Downhill C.S. (Edge Hill)	53	B2	Fulbourne	40	C2
Dragonby Sidings	57	C1	Fullwood Foundry — BSC	72	B1
Drakelow P.S.	38	A1	Furzebrook	5	A2
Drax P.S.	56	B2	Gabalfa Coal Depot (Cardiff)	28	A1
Draycott	47	C2	Galley Hill	13	C1
Drayton	11	C1	Gallows Close	63	C2
Dringhouses Yard (York)	56	A2	Garston Docks & FLT	53	C2
Drinnick Mill	1	B2	Gartcosh	76	B2
Dudley FLT	87	B1	Gartcosh — BSC	72	C1
Dufftown	82	C2	Gartsherrie Cem. Wks.	72	C1
Dundee West	79	B2	Garw Colliery	27	C2
Dunfermline Upper Goods	73	A1	Gatewen Coal Stocking Site	45	B1
Dungeness Nuclear P.S.	13	C2	Gedling Colliery	47	C2
Dunstable	31	A2	General Terminus (Glasgow)	76	B1
Dunston	69	B1	Giffen	71	B2
Duxford	32	A2	Glascoed	28	B1
Earles Sidings (Hope)	47	A1	Glasgow Salkeld St.	76	B1
Earley P.S.	31	C1	Glasshoughton Colliery	56	B2
Easington Colliery	62	A2	Glazebrook	51	C1
East Depot (Bristol)	8	B2	Glen Douglas	78	C1
Eastern Docks (Southampton)	9	C2	Glengarnock — BSC	71	B2
East Grimstead	10	B1	Godfrey Road (Newport)	28	A2
East Hecla Steelworks	50	A1	Goldthorpe Colliery	56	C2
East Usk Yard	28	A2	Goodrington C.S.	3	B2
Eastleigh East Yard	10	B2	Goonbarrow	1	B2
Eastgate	61	A2	Gorseinon	26	B2
Eastriggs	66	C1	Grain	33	C1
Ebbw Vale — BSC	28	B1	Grand Canal St. (Dublin)	84	C1
Ecclesfield East	50	A1	Grangemouth	72	A2
Edwalton	47	C2	Granton	73	B2
Eggborough P.S.	56	B2	Green Market (Low Fell)	69	C2
Elderslie	75	B1	Greetland	55	B2
Eling Wharf	9	C1	Gresty Lane (Crewe)	46	C1
Elland P.S.	55	B2	Gresty Road (Crewe)	46	C1
Ellington Colliery	68	B1	Griffin Wharf — FLT	33	A2
Elsecar CCE Tip	56	C2	Grimethorpe Colliery	56	C2
Elstow	31	A2	Grosvenor EMU Depot	21	C1
Elswick	69	B1	Guild Street (Aberdeen)	80	B1
Ernesettle	2	B2	Gunness	57	C1
Eskmeals	59	C2	Gunnie	72	C1
Essington Wood Colliery	37	A2	Gushetfaulds FLT	76	B1
Etherley CCE Tip	62	A1	Gwaun-cae-Gurwen Colliery	27	B1
Euxton	54	C2	Haig Colliery	59	B2
Evanton	82	C1	Halewood	45	A2
Exeter City Basin	3	A2	Halling Cem. Wks.	12	A2
			Hamble Oil Ref.	10	C2

NAME	PAGE NO.	PAGE REF.	NAME	PAGE NO.	PAGE REF.
Hams Hall P.S.	38	B1	ICI Tunstead	46	A2
Hamworthy Goods & FLT	5	A2	ICI Weston	45	A2
Handsworth & Smethwick	88	C1	ICI Wilton	63	A2
Harbury Cem. Wks.	38	C1	ICI Winnington	46	A1
Hardendale Quarry	60	B2	Ickles Yard (Rotherham)	50	A2
Harrison's Siding (Shap)	60	B2	Immingham	58	C2
Harton Low Staithes	70	B2	Ince Marshes — Shellstar	45	A2
Hartshill Quarry	38	B1	Ince Moss CCE Tip	54	C2
Harworth Colliery	47	A2	Inchicore	84	C1
Harworth Glassworks	47	A2	Inshaw Works	72	B1
Hartlepool South — BSC	62	A2	Inveralmond	79	B1
Hatfield Colliery	56	C2	Inverhouse	72	B1
Haverton Hill — ICI	63	A1	Ironbridge P.S.	37	A1
Hawkesbury Lane	38	B1	Islip	30	B2
Hawkhead	75	B1	James Watt Dock (Bogston)	71	A1
Hawthorn Coll & Coking Plant	68	C2	Jarrow	70	B1
Haydock	54	C2	Jersey Marine	27	C1
Healey Mills Yard	56	C1	Kellingley Colliery	56	B2
Heathfield	3	B1	Kennett	40	C2
Heaton	69	B2	Keresley	38	B1
Hele & Bradninch	7	C2	Ketton Cem. Wks.	39	A2
Hem Heath Colliery	46	C1	Kilbarry Sidings (Cork)	83	C2
Hendon	70	C2	Killingholme Oil Terms.	57	C2
Herbrandston Oil Ref.	25	B2	Killoch Colliery	71	C2
Herrington Colliery	68	C1	Kilmastulla	83	A2
Hessay	56	A2	Kineton	38	C1
Hethersett	41	A2	King George Dock (Hull)	57	B2
Hexthorpe Sidings	58	B1	Kingmoor Yard	65	B1
Heysham Moss	54	A2	Kingsbury	38	B1
Heysham Nuclear P.S.	54	A2	Kingscourt	86	C1
Heywood	55	C1	Kingsland Road Goods (Bristol)	8	B2
Hickleton Colliery	56	C2	Kings Meadow	47	C2
High Marnham P.S.	48	B1	Kingsnorth	33	C1
Highgate L.T. Depot	21	A1	King Street (Blackburn)	55	B1
Highgate Wood L.T. Sidings	21	A1	Kinsley Drift Mine	56	C2
Hillhouse Goods (Huddersfield)	55	C2	Kirk Sandall	58	A2
Hillhouse ICI Works	54	B1	Kirkcaldy Harbour	73	A1
Hillhouse Quarry	71	C2	Kirkdale EMU Depot	53	B1
Hillside Distillery	80	C1	Kirton	57	C2
Hillwood Quarry	73	A1	Kittybrewster Coal Depot	80	A1
Hilton	47	C1	Kiveton Park Colliery	47	A2
Hindlow	46	B2	Knighton CCE Sidings	38	A2
Hinksey Yard (Oxford)	30	B2	Knockshinnoch Colliery	65	A1
Hither Green Yard	18	A1	Kyle St. (Ayr)	72	C1
Holborough Cem. Wks.	12	A2	Lackenby — BSC	63	A2
Holditch Colliery	46	B1	Lady Windsor Colliery	27	C2
Holles Street (Grimsby)	58	C1	Laira C.S.	2	C2
Holmes Yard (Lincoln)	48	B2	Laisterdyke	56	B1
Holmethorpe	12	A1	Lakeland Colliery	59	A2
Holywell Junction	45	A1	Lambton Coking Plant	68	C1
Hookagate P.W. Depot	36	A2	Landor Street Inland Port	88	C1
Hope (Earles Sidings) Cem. Wks.	47	A1	Laurencekirk	80	C1
Hope Street (Manchester)	51	B2	Lavant	11	C1
Hopetown	62	B1	Law Junction	72	B1
Horbury — Procor Works	56	C1	Lawley St. — FLT & NCL	88	C1
Horden Colliery	62	A2	Layerthorpe	56	A2
Horrocksford Cem. Works	55	B1	Lea Hall Colliery	37	A2
Hotchley Hill	47	C2	Lecarrow	85	C2
Hothfield	13	B1	Leith South & Docks	73	B2
Houghton Main Colliery	56	C2	Lenton P.W. Depot	47	C2
Hucknall Colliery	47	C2	Letchworth P.S.	32	A1
Hull New Yard	57	B2	Leven Dock Coal Depot	79	C2
Humber Oil Ref.	58	C2	Leyton P.W. Yard	22	A1
Humberstone Road (Leicester)	38	A2	Lidlington CCE Tip	31	A2
Hunslet East	57	B1	Lillie Bridge LT P.W. Depot	21	C1
Hunslet Engine Co.	57	B1	Limbury Road (Luton)	31	A2
Hunslet Yard	57	B1	Linby Colliery	47	B2
Hunterston	71	B1	Lindsey Oil Ref.	58	C2
Huntspill	8	C1	Linwood — Talbot	75	B1
ICI Ardeer	71	C1	Lisduff	84	A1
ICI Castner — Kellner	45	A2	Littlemore	30	B2
ICI Haverton Hill	63	A1	Littleton Colliery	37	A2
ICI Hillhouse	54	B1	Liverpool Rd. (Manchester)	51	B2
ICI Lostock	46	A1	Liversedge	56	B1
ICI Over & Wharton	46	B1	Livingston	72	A2
ICI Powfoot	66	C1	Llandarcy Oil Ref.	27	C1
ICI Rocksavage	45	A2	Llandeilo Junction Yard	26	B2
ICI Severnside	28	C2	Llanharan Colliery	27	C2
ICI Snodgrass	71	C1	Llanstephan	26	B2
ICI Thornton	54	B1	Llanthony (Gloucester)	29	B1

NAME	PAGE NO.	PAGE REF.	NAME	PAGE NO.	PAGE REF.
Llantrisant	27	C2	Monkton Coking Plant	70	B1
Llanwern — BSC	28	B1	Monktonhall Colliery	73	C2
Lochaber Aluminium Works	78	B1	Monkwearmouth	70	C2
Lochrin Works	72	C1	Monmore Green	87	A1
London Int. Ft. Term. (LIFT)	22	A1	Moor Green Colliery	47	B2
London Road (Carlisle)	65	C2	Moorfield P.S.	28	A2
London Road (Glasgow)	76	B1	Moorswater	2	B1
London Road LT Depot	21	C2	Moreton-on-Lugg	36	C2
Long Eaton	47	C2	Morris Cowley	30	B2
Long Marston	29	A2	Mossend Yard	72	B1
Longannet P.S.	72	A2	Mostyn	45	A1
Longbridge — BL	37	B2	Mountain Ash NCB Workshops	27	B2
Longsight FLT & C.S.	52	B1	Mountfield	12	C2
Longtown	66	C2	Mountsorrel Quarry	38	A2
Lostock — ICI	46	A1	Muirhouse CCE Workshops	76	B1
Lostock Hall	54	B2	Nandern Wharf	2	B2
Low Fell CCE Sidings	69	C2	Nantgarw Colliery	27	C2
Low Gates	62	C1	Neath Abbey Wharf	27	C1
Ludgershall	10	A1	Nene C.S. (Peterborough)	39	A2
Lugton	71	B2	New Bilton Cem. Wks.	38	B2
Lynemouth Colliery	68	B1	New Ross	84	B1
Machen Quarry	28	C1	New Yard (Hull)	57	B2
Maerdy Colliery	27	B2	Newbiggin	60	A2
Maesglas CCE Tip	28	A2	Newbridge	28	C1
Maesteg Washery	27	C1	Newburn Yard (Hartlepool)	62	A2
Maindee CCE Depot	28	A2	Newcourt	3	A2
Maindy	28	A1	Newtonhead Coal Depot	71	C1
Malago Vale C.S.	8	B2	Newton Noyes	25	B1
Mallaig Junction Yard	78	B1	Normanby Park	57	C1
Maltby Colliery	47	A2	North Elmham	41	A1
Manchester Int. Ft. Term. (MIFT)	51	B2	North Gawber Colliery	56	C1
Mansfield Colliery	47	B2	North Tees P.S.	62	A2
Mansfield Concentration Sidings	47	B2	North Wall (Dublin)	84	C2
Mantle Lane (Coalville)	38	A1	Northam Yard (Southampton)	9	C2
Manton Wood Colliery	47	A2	Northenden Cem. Term.	51	C2
Manvers Colliery & Washery	56	C2	Northenden — GMC Waste Term.	52	C1
Marchon Chem. Wks.	59	B2	Northfleet Cem. Wks.	32	C2
Marchwood	9	C1	Northwich Yard	46	A1
Margam Yard	27	C1	Norwich P.S.	41	A2
Marine Colliery	28	B1	Norwich Victoria	41	A1
Marino Point	83	C2	Norwood Yard	17	B2
Maritime FLT (Southampton)	9	C1	Nostell Colliery	56	C1
Markham Colliery	47	B2	Nunnery C.S.	50	B1
Markham Main Colliery	58	A2	Oakamoor	46	C2
Marsh Lane (Leeds)	57	A1	Oakdale Colliery	28	B1
Marsh Mills	2	C2	Oakley	72	A2
Marsh Pond	8	B2	Offord	40	C1
Marshgate (Doncaster)	58	B1	Ogmore Vale Washery	27	C2
Marshmoor	32	B1	Old Dalby	47	C2
Maxwelltown	65	B2	Old Kilpatrick	75	A1
Mayfield Parcels (Manchester)	52	B1	Ollerton Colliery	47	B2
Meadowhall — BSC	50	A1	Onllwyn Colliery	27	B1
Meaford P.S.	46	C1	Orchardhall	72	A2
Meldon	2	A2	Ordsall Lane	51	B2
Melksham	9	A1	Orgreave	50	B2
Melton	42	C1	Over & Wharton — ICI	46	B1
Menstrie	78	C2	Overseal Sidings	38	A1
Merehead Quarry	9	B1	Oxcroft Colliery	47	C2
Merthyr Vale Colliery	27	B2	Oxley C.S.	87	A1
Methil Dock & P.S.	79	C2	Oxwellmains Cem. Wks.	74	A1
Metro-Cammell (Birmingham)	88	C2	Padiham P.S.	55	B1
Mickleover Test Centre	47	C1	Padworth	10	A2
Mid Cannock Opencast	37	A2	Paisley Underwood	75	B1
Middlesbrough Goods	63	A1	Palace Gates Coal Depot	23	C2
Middleton Towers	40	A2	Pallion	70	C2
Middlewich	46	B1	Panteg — BSC	28	B1
Mile End Stone Term.	22	B1	Par Harbour	2	B1
Milford Sidings	56	B2	Park Royal	20	B2
Mill Pit Colliery	27	C1	Parkandillack	1	B2
Millbrook FLT	9	C1	Parkeston Quay (Harwich)	33	A2
Millerhill Yard	73	C2	Parkneuk Works	72	B1
Millfield Coal Depot	70	C2	Parkside Colliery	45	A2
Millfield (Stockton)	62	A2	Parkway Market	50	B1
Misterton	48	A1	Partington Oil Ref. & Chem. Wks.	51	C1
Mode Wheel	51	B2	Peak Forest	46	A2
Mold	45	B1	Penallta Colliery	28	C1
Mold Junction Sdgs. & CCE Tip	45	B1	Penallta Junction Tip	27	C2
Monckton Coking Plant	56	C1	Penderyn Quarry	27	B2
Monk Bretton	56	C1	Pengam FLT	28	A1
Monkshall — BSC	45	B1	Penrhiwceiber Colliery	27	B2

NAME	PAGE NO.	PAGE REF.	NAME	PAGE NO.	PAGE REF.
Pensnett (Shut End)	87	B1	St. Blazey Yard	1	B2
Penyffordd Cem. Wks.	45	B1	St. Dennis CCE Tip	1	B2
Pesspool	68	C1	St. James Sidings (New Cross)	22	C1
Peterborough East	39	A2	St. Johns Colliery	27	C2
Petteril Bridge	65	C2	St. Marnocks (Kilmarnock)	71	C2
Philadelphia	68	C1	St. Mary's Yard (Derby)	47	C1
Pig's Bay	33	C1	St. Nicholas (Carlisle)	65	C1
Pitstone Cem. Wks.	31	B1	Salkeld Street (Glasgow)	76	B1
Plaistow & West Ham	22	B1	Sallins	86	C1
Platin Cem. Wks.	86	C2	Salt End	57	B2
Plean	72	A2	Santon Foreign Ore Terminal	57	C2
Plymstock	2	C2	Sculcoates	57	B2
Point of Ayr Colliery	44	A2	Scunthorpe Coal Terminal	57	C2
Polkemmet Colliery (Whitburn)	72	B2	Scunthorpe West Yard	57	C1
Polmaise Colliery	72	A2	Seafield Colliery	73	A1
Ponsandane C.S. & HST Depot	1	A1	Seaforth FLT	53	A1
Pontarddulais Stocking Site	26	B2	Seaham Colliery	68	C1
Pontsmill	1	B2	Seal Sands	63	A2
Port Clarence	63	A1	Seaton-on-Tees	62	A2
Port Elphinstone	80	A1	Selby Drift Mine	56	B2
Port Sunlight	53	C1	Selsdon	17	C2
Port Tennant	27	C1	Severn Tunnel Junction Yard	28	C2
Portfield	11	C1	Severnside — ICI	28	C2
Portobello FLT & CCE Depot	73	C2	Seymour Yard & Stocking Site	47	A2
Portwood	52	C1	Shap	60	B2
Powfoot — ICI	66	C1	Sharlston Colliery	56	C1
Preston Street (Whitehaven)	59	B2	Sharpness	29	B1
Prince of Wales Colliery	56	B2	Sheepbridge	47	A1
Purfleet Wharf	32	C2	Sheerness Steelworks	33	C1
Puriton	8	B1	Sheffield Freight Terminal	50	B1
Pye Hill Colliery	47	B2	Shellhaven Oil Ref.	33	C1
Pylle Hill	8	B2	Shelton Abbey	84	A2
Quedgeley	29	B1	Shelton — BSC	46	B1
Queen Alexandra Dock	28	A1	Shepcote Lane — BSC	50	B1
Quidhampton	9	B2	Sherwood Colliery	47	B2
Radstock	9	A1	Shewalton Tip	71	C2
Radway Green	46	B1	Shieldhall	75	B2
Radyr Yard	28	C1	Shirebrook Colliery	47	B2
Railway Street (Dewsbury)	56	C1	Shireoaks Colliery	47	A2
Railway Street (Newcastle)	69	B2	Shore Road (Birkenhead)	53	B1
Railway Technical Centre	47	C1	Shotton — BSC	45	B1
Raisby Hill Quarry	62	A1	Shut End Coal Depot	87	B1
Ramsden Dock (Barrow)	54	B1	Silverdale Colliery	46	B1
Ratcliffe-on-Soar P.S.	47	C2	Silverhill Colliery	47	B2
Rathbone Road Coal Depot	53	B2	Silverwood Colliery	50	A2
Ravenhead	45	A2	Simonside Wagon Works	70	B1
Ravenscraig	38	A1	Sinclairtown	79	C1
Rawdon Colliery	38	A1	Sizewell Nuclear P.S.	42	C1
Rectory Junction	47	C2	Skellow	58	A1
Red Bank C.S.	52	B1	Skinningrove — BSC	63	B1
Redbridge CCE Depot	9	C1	Slateford CCE Depot	73	C1
Redcar — BSC	62	A2	Small Heath Coal Depot	88	C1
Redcar Ore & Mineral Terms.	62	A2	Smalmstown	66	C2
Redmire	61	C2	Smithy Lye C.S.	76	B1
Renishaw Park Colliery	47	A2	Smithywood Coking Plant	50	A1
Rewley Road (Oxford)	30	B2	Snailwell	40	C2
Rhoose Cem. Wks.	7	A2	Snodgrass — ICI	71	C1
Rhosgoch	43	A2	South Bank	63	A2
Riccarton	71	C2	South Hetton Colliery	68	C1
Richborough P.S.	14	A1	South Kirkby Colliery	56	C2
Ridham Dock	13	A1	South Lynn	40	A2
Ripple Lane Yard	32	C2	Southam Cem. Wks.	38	C1
Roath Goods	28	A1	Southwark EMU Depot	21	B2
Roath Dock	28	A1	Southwick	70	C2
Robeston Oil Ref.	25	B2	Speke Yard	53	C2
Rochester Docks	13	A1	Spekeland Road Goods (Liverpool)	53	B2
Roosecote P.S.	54	A1	Springfield Goods (Falkirk)	72	A2
Rose Heyworth Colliery	28	B1	Springmill Street (Bradford)	56	B1
Roseisle	82	C2	Staines West	15	A1
Roskear	1	C1	Stainton CCE Tip	65	B1
Ross Junction Tip	72	B1	Stairfoot	56	C2
Rossington Colliery	58	B2	Standard Gauge Steam Trust	88	C2
Roundwood — BSC	50	A2	Stanlow Oil Ref.	45	A2
Royston Drift Mine	56	C1	Stanton — BSC	47	C2
Ruddington	47	C2	Stanton Gate	47	C2
Rufford Colliery	47	B2	Stanway	33	A1
Rugeley P.S.	37	A2	Starryshaws Siding	72	B2
Ryburgh	50	C1	Staythorpe P.S.	48	B1
Rylstone	55	A2	Steamport (Southport)	54	C1
Saffron Lane P.S.	38	A2	Steamtown (Carnforth)	60	C2

NAME	PAGE NO.	PAGE REF.	NAME	PAGE NO.	PAGE REF.
Stella North P.S.	69	B1	Tytherington Quarry	29	C1
Stella South P.S.	69	B1	Valley	43	A1
Stewarts Lane	21	C1	Valley Goods (Bradford)	56	B1
Stocksbridge — BSC	56	C1	Vane Tempest Colliery	68	C2
Stockton FLT	63	A1	Velindre — BSC	27	B1
Stockton North Shore	62	B2	Victoria Coal Depot (Norwich)	41	A2
Stockton South	62	B2	Virgil St. Coal Depot	28	A1
Storrs Hill	56	C1	Upperby Carriage Depot	65	C1
Stourton FLT	57	B1	Upton Park Coal Depot	22	B2
Strand Road (Preston)	54	B2	Uskmouth P.S.	28	B2
Stranraer Town	64	C1	Wakefield C. & W. Shops	56	C1
Stratford FLT	22	A1	Walker	70	B1
Stratford Market	22	B1	Walkergate — BSC	69	B2
Sudbrook	28	C2	Wallerscote — ICI	46	A1
Sunderland South Dock	70	C2	Walton Old Junction	45	B1
Sutton Colliery	47	B2	Wandsworth Road	21	C1
Sutton-in-Ashfield	47	B2	Wapping Wharf	8	B2
Sutton Manor Colliery	45	A2	Warcop	61	B1
Sutton Park	88	A2	Wardley	70	B1
Swains Park Colliery	37	A1	Warrington Yard	45	B1
Swalwell Colliery	69	B1	Warsop	47	B2
Swanscombe Cem. Wks.	32	C2	Warsop Main Colliery	47	B2
Swansea East & Docks	27	C1	Washbeck (Scarborough)	63	C2
Sweet Dews	57	B2	Washwood Heath Yard	88	B2
Syston	38	A2	Waterloo Goods (Aberdeen)	80	B1
Taff Merthyr Colliery	27	B2	Waterside Colliery	64	A2
Tallington	39	A2	Waterston Oil Ref.	25	B2
Tanhouse Lane	45	A2	Watford Cardiff Road P.S.	31	C2
Tara Mines	86	C1	Wath Sidings	56	C2
Tavistock Junction	2	C2	Wearmouth Colliery	70	C2
Taylors Lane P.S.	20	B2	Weaste	51	B2
Tees Dock	63	A2	Wednesbury	87	B2
Tees Yard	63	A1	Welbeck Colliery	47	B2
Teesport	63	A2	Wensum (Norwich)	41	A2
Teignbridge	3	B1	Wernos Washery	27	B1
Temple Mills Yard	22	A1	West Burton P.S.	48	A1
Thame	31	B1	Westburn Works	76	C2
Thames Haven	33	C1	Westbury Yard	9	C2
Thames Wharf	22	B1	West Depot (Bristol)	8	B2
Thoresby Colliery	47	B2	Western Docks (Southampton)	9	C2
Thorney Mill	19	C1	West Hallam Opencast	47	C2
Thornton — ICI	54	B1	West Somerset Quarry	9	B1
Thornton Fields C.S.	22	B1	Westerleigh	29	C1
Thornton Yard	79	C1	Westfield Colliery	79	C1
Thorpe Marsh P.S.	58	A2	Westoe Colliery	70	B2
Three Bridges P.W. Depot	12	B1	Westthorpe Colliery	47	A2
Thrislington	62	A1	Whatley Quarry	9	B1
Thrybergh — BSC	50	A2	Wheldale Colliery	56	B2
Thurcroft Colliery	47	A2	Whifflet	72	C1
Tibshelf Sidings	47	B2	Whiteacre (Daw Mill Colliery)	38	B1
Tidal Yard (Cardiff)	28	A1	Whitehall Road Goods (Leeds)	57	A1
Tidenham Quarry	28	C2	Whitehead — BSC	28	A2
Tilmanstone Colliery	14	A1	Whitemoor Yard	40	A1
Tinsley Park — BSC	50	B1	Whitlingham	42	A1
Tinsley Yard	50	B1	Whittington	45	C1
Tivoli (Cork)	83	C2	Whitwell Colliery & Quarry	47	A2
Topley Pike Quarry	46	A2	Whitwick Sidings	38	A1
Torksey	48	A1	Widdrington Colliery	68	A1
Toton Yard	47	C2	Willesden Yards & FLT	20	B2
Tower Colliery	27	B2	Willington P.S.	47	C1
Townhead Coal Depot	71	C1	Wilton — ICI	62	A2
Townhill Yard	73	A1	Winfrith	5	A1
Trafford Park Sidings & FLT	51	B2	Winnington — ICI	46	A1
Trawsfynydd Nuclear P.S.	44	C1	Wirksworth Quarry	47	B1
Trecwn	25	A2	Wisbech	40	A1
Trelewis Drift Mine	27	B2	Wolstanton Colliery	46	B1
Tremorfa Steelworks	28	A1	Wolverhampton Steel Terminal	87	A1
Trentham Sidings	46	C1	Woodburn CCE Shops	50	B1
Trostre — BSC	26	B2	Woodston	39	A2
Trowse (Norwich)	41	A2	Woodville (Swains Park Coll.)	38	A1
Tuebrook (Edge Hill)	53	B2	Wood Yard CCE Sdgs. (Doncaster)	58	B1
Tunstead Quarry — ICI	46	A2	Woolley Colliery	56	C1
Tuxford	48	B1	Wootton Bassett	29	C2
Tweedmouth	74	B2	Worksop Yard	47	A2
Tyne Dock	70	B1	Yoker Yard	75	B2
Tyne Yard	69	C2	Yorkshire Main Colliery	56	C2
Tyneside Central Freight Depot	69	B2	Youghal	83	B2

(If a freight terminal cannot be located in this index, refer to the passenger index for the reference of the adjoining station.)